AS ABOVE
SO BELOW

"As above, so below."

AS ABOVE
SO BELOW

Paths to Spiritual Renewal in Daily Life

RONALD S. MILLER AND
THE EDITORS OF NEW AGE JOURNAL

JEREMY P. TARCHER, INC.
Los Angeles

Library of Congress Cataloging-in-Publication Data

Miller, Ronald S.
  As above, so below : paths to spiritual renewal in daily life /
  Ronald S. Miller and the editors of New Age journal.
    p. cm.
  Includes biographical references.
  ISBN 0-87477-659-7 : $13.95
  1. Spiritual life. 2. New Age movement. I. Title.
BL624.M497 1992
291.4–dc20   91-38673
                                                        CIP

Jeremy P. Tarcher, Inc.
5858 Wilshire Blvd., Suite 200
Los Angeles, CA 90036

FRONTISPIECE

Calligraphy by Chungliang Al Huang, courtesy of Living Tao Foundation.

PHOTO CREDITS

Mark Antman/The Image Works, page 34; Archivi Alinari/Art Resources, page 119;
Association for Humanistic Psychology, page 95; Beringer/Dratch/The Image
Works, page 241; Bildarchiv Foto Marburg/Art Resource, page 296; Fariba
Bogzaran, page 134; Karen Bussolini/Positive Images, page 234; Alan Carey/The
Image Works, pages 156, 281; Elizabeth Crews/The Image Works, pages 108, 182;
Culver Pictures, pages 113, 119, 137; Bob Daemmrich/The Image Works, pages 37,
207; Eastcott/Nomatiuk/The Image Works, page 177; Mauna Eichner, page 217;
Rohn Engh/The Image Works, pages 85, 203, 248; Harriet Gans/The Image
Works, page 212; George Gardner/The Image Works, page 276; Shelley Gazin/The
Image Works, page 26; Giraudon/Art Resource, page 149; John Griffin/The Image
Works, page 196; Cary Herz, page 67; Jerry Howard/Positive Images, pages xvi, 4,
14, 22, 47, 70, 90, 142, 260, 263, 272, 279, 288; The Image Works Archives, page 6;
Kathleen Kokolias, page 57; Larry Kolvoord/The Image Works, page 171; Roger
Kose, page 164; Martin Miller/Positive Images, page 190; Vicki Noble, page 146;
Ogust/The Image Works, page 225; Karen Preuss/The Image Works, page 221;
Dorothy Rossi, page 127; Spiritual Life Institute, page 51; Jack Spratt/The Image
Works, page 44; Ben Swets, page 254; Topham/The Image Works, page 73; Miles A.
Vich, page 98; M. Wojnarowicz/The Image Works, page 238.

Distributed by St. Martin's Press, New York

Design by Susan Shankin

Printed on recycled paper.
Manufactured in the United States of America
10 9 8 7 6 5 4 3 2 1

First Edition

For my father and mother,
Charles and Marie Miller,
who are no longer here;
and for my wife and son,
Karen and Jason,
who carry on a legacy of love.

CONTENTS

ACKNOWLEDGMENTS

I have carried this book within the secret sanctuary of my imagination for many years, and now that it has safely made the passage from the world of conception to the world of ink on paper, I would like to thank those who facilitated and eased the birth process.

I am deeply indebted to Phillip Whitten, former editor of *New Age Journal,* a man of integrity and compassion, who saw my potential and who selected me for this project. While the entire staff of *New Age Journal* deserves thanks, I would like to single out Peggy Taylor for her wise and experienced guidance; Lisa Yane for editorial assistance rendered under the duress of publication deadlines; and Karen Monti Lindo for her enthusiastic support from beginning to end.

I am grateful to my visionary publisher, Jeremy Tarcher, whose passion for truth inspired me to contact and write from my creative depths; to my editor, Connie Zweig, whose wide-ranging knowledge, consummate skills, and tireless effort have contributed to the book's clarity and impact; to Paul Murphy for his tireless work in overseeing production and to Susan Shankin for her superb book design; to the staff at Jeremy P. Tarcher, Inc., whose support went beyond the call of professional duty; and to the numerous people whom I interviewed, whose insights and spirit pervade the book.

For nurturing the dreams of my youth, my heartfelt appreciation goes to Eric and Michele Horsefield. Among the many faithful friends who helped and encouraged me along the way, I thank Allan and Eleanore Buchanan, Tim and Carol Johnson, Stephen Borow, and Ron Stein. If a person's fortune is measured in terms of friendship, I am a wealthy man indeed.

Most of all, I thank my lovely wife, Karen, for her generosity of spirit, her constant love, and her critical support as my principal reader during the book's long and intense birthing. I also send special thanks to my son, Jason, that bright, cheerful boy who inspired me to write as perhaps no muse or exalted teacher ever could. If in this book I have soared into the heavens, it is because my loving family provided the home base I could return to from my explorations.

INTRODUCTION

Thousands of years ago in ancient Egypt, the great master alchemist Hermes Trismegistus, believed to be a contemporary of the Hebrew prophet Abraham, proclaimed this fundamental truth about the universe: "As above, so below; as below, so above." This maxim implies that the transcendent God beyond the physical universe and the immanent God within ourselves are one. Heaven and Earth, spirit and matter, the invisible and the visible worlds form a unity to which we are intimately linked.

Explaining this idea further in *Steps to Freedom,* Sufi scholar Reshad Field writes: " 'As above, so below' means that the two worlds are instantaneously seen to be one when we realize our essential unity with God. . . . The One and the many, time and eternity, are all One."

When we live this simple but profound truth in our everyday lives, we discover spiritual renewal even when paying bills, shopping for groceries, and helping our children with their homework. Our most mundane activities carry a sense of the sacred because we do not partition life into segregated areas designated *spiritual* and *worldly.* Following the dictum "As above, so below," we unite the sacred and the profane, extending our spiritual practice beyond traditional inner-directed exercises to include loving our families, making a living, serving our communities, and caring for the Earth.

As is the human body,
so is the cosmic body.
As is the human mind,
so is the cosmic mind.
As is the microcosm,
so is the macrocosm.
As is the atom,
so is the universe.

THE UPANISHADS

Today, many people from all walks of life are attempting to live in this manner. Dissatisfied with the approach of mainstream religions, we are searching for new forms of spirituality to make our daily lives more meaningful and socially relevant.

We find little support in the old forms of spirituality, which separate the above and the below into antagonists. In this traditional approach, as evidenced by most religions East and West, God is separate from the Earth; spirit and matter coexist as partners with irreconcilable differences; and people devalue the body, sexuality, the emotions, and the natural world. Because it separates the divine from nature, this world view unknowingly sanctions the exploitation of nature, which it considers to exist only to serve humankind, and contributes to our current ecological dilemmas.

The emerging spirituality, by contrast, encourages us to experience a more relaxed, trusting, and loving relationship between the above and the below. Drawn from diverse sources—spiritual renewal in Judaism and Christianity, shamanism, feminine spirituality and Goddess religion, and ecology—it acknowledges the sacredness of the body, sexuality, the emotions, and the natural world. Rather than focusing on salvation in some disembodied realm, it sees the world of matter as divine and as worthy of love as the immaterial spiritual realm. And because *fallen* nature is redeemed and divinized, the emerging spirituality gives rise to an ecological vision that honors the planet and its multitude of species as a single living entity with whom we can learn to live in greater harmony and reverence. Indeed, if humankind is to heal its alienation from nature and protect the world from ecological destruction, we may need to embrace this new orientation with all due speed or face the consequences of our current dysfunctional value systems.

While the emergence of a new spirituality has been predicted by numerous religious scholars and visionaries throughout most of this century, its shape and features have been coming more clearly into focus since the flowering of the consciousness movement in the 1960s, '70s, and '80s. During this period, the esoteric (or hidden, mystical) teachings of the world's great spiritual traditions made their way into mainstream Western culture. Yoga and Zen intermingled with rediscovered forms of Western mysticism; psychology expanded its field of inquiry to include the spiritual or transpersonal dimension; mythology and dreamwork gained many thousands of serious students; and with the addictive nature of contemporary life coming to light, many took up Twelve Step spirituality to recover from alcohol and drug addiction, eating disorders, and child abuse. While all these diverse spiritual forces were shaping the culture, the older spiritual traditions, having encountered the twin forces of feminism and ecology, began embracing *green* values that address the current ecological crisis.

In sum, from this great eclecticism currently under way, our culture is giving birth to new forms of spirituality that offer practices, values, and a world view appropriate to our age. This book chronicles the journeys of contemporary men and women as they uncover this emerging spirituality in the laboratory of their own lives. With its practical advice, exercises, anecdotes, and quotations, *As Above, So Below* also serves as a guidebook for uniting the sacred and the profane in our everyday lives.

The first two chapters, which present an overview of the emerging spirituality and guidelines for practicing spirituality in everyday life, provide the general context for the book. Chapter 3 looks at renewal in the Judeo-Christian tradition, focusing on the rediscovery of mystical, meditative practices that many people have been searching for in Eastern religions. Chapter 4 investigates shamanism, the ancient path practiced by tribal medicine men and women that gives us direct contact with the hidden dimensions of the universe and that promotes reverence for nature.

The next three chapters deal with transpersonal psychology, which explores the interface between spirituality and psychology; mythology, which connects us to the archetypal foundations of the human psyche; and dreams, which depict the ongoing drama of our personal mythology in pictorial form. Together, they offer insights and practices to gain increasing familiarity with what psychologist Abraham Maslow called the "farther reaches of human nature." They are three distinct paths that tie the worlds above to the worlds below.

The next three chapters look at spiritual innovation in popular self-help movements. Chapter 8, Feminine Spirituality, explores the grassroots movement that is restoring the feminine principle as a divine force in our culture through Goddess religion and women's psychology. The next chapter focuses on the men's movement, which helps men escape from destructive, "macho" masculinity to connect with a more mature, earth-cherishing form of male spirituality. Chapter 10 looks at how Twelve Step spirituality, inspired by Alcoholics Anonymous' famous approach, is helping people recover from various forms of addiction and co-dependence.

Chapter 11, which covers new developments in mind/body approaches to medicine, explores how a healthy spirit and positive emotions contribute to physical health. Chapter 12 considers the creative life as a genuine spiritual path that can lead to breakthroughs in art, science, and the business world. The next chapter focuses on ecology, which emphasizes the interconnectedness between humankind and the natural world and gives practical suggestions for living with greater awareness of our links to all of life. Chapter 14, Compassionate Action, looks at how spirituality and social activism are merging into engaged forms of spiritual practice aimed at alleviating suffering in the world. The last chapter deals with the shadow, the dark, unwanted parts of the personality that are typically repressed in traditional spiritual approaches. Practitioners of the emerging spirituality work on integrating the shadow, so that instead of struggling for perfection as in the older approach, they strive for wholeness based on an acceptance of their full humanity.

The breadth of this exploration suggests that we are living in an age of spiritual reinvention, a transitional age that leaves the safety and security of the known to seek out the new, the untested, the possible. What could be more exciting, yet more filled with uncertainty and apprehension? To keep our balance, we need to temper our adventurous spirits with the wisdom of the past; exercise discrimination in assessing the true and valuable from the merely momentary and sensational; and develop the courage to stand on our own two feet in spiritual maturity, trusting in the authority and reliability of our own inner natures to guide and inspire us. On this quest, we also need to:

- Nurture an openness for change, rather than ensconcing ourselves in the deadening security of what we have been taught is the one true way. We can live the beauty of our questions, without forcing a premature conclusion to our investigations.
- Honor all spiritual traditions not as finished products, but as evolutionary experiments that are capable of further growth and transformation.
- Cultivate an ecology of cultures, taking from each the wisdom, skills, and practices necessary to help forge a spirituality capable of addressing our planetary crisis.
- Extend compassion to ourselves as aspirants who yearn for the glorious heights but who are required to traverse the lower depths in the pursuit of greater consciousness. This realization gives us the humility to grow without rejecting ourselves for our human limitations.

Armed with this understanding, like Odysseus we can set sail into the unknown not with fear and despair, but with faith in ourselves and the human spirit to meet the challenges that beset our planet with skillful and compassionate action. As warriors of the spirit, we journey not for conquest or self-gain, but to acquire the wisdom and practical skills to make us stewards of our ailing, but remarkably beautiful and resourceful, planet. When we return, seasoned from our adventures in the spirit, we can transmit the gift of life to our descendants and to countless generations who will inherit a fertile and hospitable planet Earth.

Ronald S. Miller

CHAPTER 1

THE EMERGING SPIRITUALITY

Falling in Love with Our World

Most of us begin the spiritual journey suffering from a case of mistaken identity. The following teaching tale about Jesus and Moses on the golf course throws light on our predicament.

The two great teachers have teed up for a long hole when Jesus unexpectedly pulls out a seven iron.

"Jesus, it's a long hole," says Moses. "You'll never make it with a seven iron. Better use a driver."

Jesus smiles and replies, "Arnold Palmer does it."

When the ball sails into a water hazard, Moses generously volunteers to shag it. Approaching the lake, he parts the waters, picks out the ball, then returns it to Jesus, who immediately tees up again and takes out the seven iron.

"Jesus, you've already tried that iron," Moses admonishes. "Trust me, the hole is too long. Use the driver."

"Arnold Palmer does it," says Jesus, who hits the ball once again into the same water hazard. This time, however, Jesus decides to shag the ball himself. The next foursome of players, who have caught up from behind, look on in astonishment as he approaches the hazard, walks across the water, and picks out the ball.

"Who does he thinks he is," says one man, "Jesus Christ?"

"No," answers Moses sadly. "Unfortunately, he thinks he's Arnold Palmer."

As is the inner, so is the outer; as is the great, so is the small; as it is above, so it is below; there is but One Life and Law: and he that worketh it is ONE. *Nothing is inner, nothing is outer; nothing is great, nothing is small; nothing is high, nothing is low, in the Divine Economy.*

HERMETIC AXIOM

1

"Like the Jesus of this story," writes psychologist Joan Borysenko in *Guilt Is the Teacher, Love Is the Lesson,* "many of us lose touch with our own indwelling Divine nature—the unlimited creative potential of love the real Jesus assured us could literally move mountains." The reason, she reminds us with disarming simplicity, is that we have forgotten who we really are.

In the normal process of growing up, most of us gradually lose touch with our creative essence through an unconscious conditioning process enforced by parents, educators, religious teachers, and the media. We cling to impoverished and limited self-images, a condition called sleep or dreaming by the spiritual traditions.

I sought my soul—but my soul I could not see. I sought my God—but my God eluded me; I sought my brother—and found all three.

ANONYMOUS

"Each of us is in a profound trance, consensus consciousness, a state of partly suspended animation, of stupor, of inability to function at our maximum level," writes psychologist Charles Tart in *Waking Up: Overcoming the Obstacles to Human Potential.* "Automatized and conditioned patterns of perception, thinking, feeling, and behaving dominate our lives. . . . We appear to be intelligent and conscious, but it is all automatized programs."

We need a wake-up call to rouse us from our culturally induced, trance-like state. That call comes in many forms: as mystical prayer in Christianity and Judaism; Earth-cherishing Native American practices; transpersonal therapy; guidance from mythology and dreams; new forms of feminine and masculine spirituality; and Twelve Step programs that fight addictive behavior using prayer and meditative practices. Many of the higher practices and liberating insights in these approaches come from a common source known as the Perennial Philosophy, the esoteric core of all the world's spiritual traditions.

THE UNIFYING FACTOR

In his landmark book *The Perennial Philosophy,* Aldous Huxley reveals that a "highest common factor" links the world's religious traditions. He calls this unifying factor the Perennial Philosophy, "the metaphysic that recognizes a divine reality substantial to the world of things and lives and minds; the psychology that finds in the soul something similar to, or even identical with divine Reality; the ethic that places man's final end in the knowledge of the immanent and transcendent Ground of being. . . ."

Proponents of the perennial wisdom point out that each religion has an *exoteric,* or public, form, whose theological beliefs, rituals, and liturgy separate it from other religions, as well as an *esoteric,* or private, form, in which they demonstrate a remarkable unanimity in principle and practice, providing meditative disciplines that help us overcome our trancelike condition and experience our rootedness in the divine. "The spiritual dimension of culture is not an array of dogmatic world views bristling with contradictions," writes philosopher Lex Hixon in *Coming Home,* "but a spectrum of contemplative practices, equivalent in essence, which lead toward experience rather than toward doctrinal assertion."

In whatever form it appears, writes Huxley, the Perennial Philosophy has four fundamental doctrines at its core:

- The everyday world and our personal consciousness are manifestations of an underlying divine reality. Hindus call it Brahman, Buddhists call it the One Mind, while Christian mystics such as Meister Eckhart refer to it as the Godhead.
- Human beings can realize the existence of the Divine Ground "by a direct intuition, superior to discursive reasoning." According to Buddha, if our realization remains strictly intellectual, without firsthand experience, we are like shepherds of other people's cows. Mohammed calls the person fitting this description an ass bearing a load of books.
- We possess a hidden higher self, the spark of divinity within the soul, which reflects this transcendental reality in our lives. By fulfilling certain necessary conditions, such as making ourselves more loving and compassionate, we can clear away the mental and emotional static that separates us from this inner reality, enabling the higher self to assume a central, guiding role in our lives.
- This awakening—called enlightenment, deliverance, or salvation in the various traditions—is the goal or purpose of human life. When we achieve this complete transformation of consciousness, we awaken from our limited, often painful condition and reconnect with our true nature.

What lies behind us and what lies before us are tiny matters compared to what lies within us.

RALPH WALDO EMERSON

INNER AWAKENING

Each of the world's sacred traditions teaches that the potential for this realization depends on awakening an inner source of transcendental love and wisdom. Christianity proclaims that the Kingdom of Heaven lies within. Hinduism proposes that Atman (the immanent, eternal self) is one with Brahman (the universal ground of being). The Buddhist tradition declares, "Look within, thou art the Buddha"; Sufis say that "he who knows himself knows his Lord."

While the prophets, saints, and sages of all traditions have subscribed to the Perennial Philosophy, its basic tenets do not conflict with the fundamental doctrines of the world's great religions. Thus we can remain practicing Christians, Jews, Moslems, Hindus, Buddhists, transpersonal psychologists, shamans, or feminists without violating the spirit or intention of the perennial wisdom. Our journey starts from the place in consciousness where we find ourselves.

This quest, with its exaltations, obstacles, allurements, and triumphs, has been described by philosopher Paul Brunton as a homeward journey, a nostalgic yearning for self-knowledge and fulfillment. "There is only one Duty," he writes. "It is to realize the divinity within." Brunton calls the spiritual quest our "most sacred life purpose, the most honored ground of [our] existence, and everything else must be made to subserve it."

Today, many people worldwide are responding to this sacred quest by exploring the hidden depths within their own and other spiritual traditions. As the perennial wisdom is rediscovered and adapted to the challenges of the modern world, its messages of cross-cultural unity and the harmony of humanity and nature may provide the visionary guidance we need to help heal our alienation from the Earth, our neighbors, and the sustaining source of our lives.

Q.
What does a Zen monk say at a hot dog stand?

A.
"Make me one with everything."

An American Tradition

The perennial wisdom forms an intermittently visible stream that has profoundly affected Western civilization, says futurist Willis Harman, author of *Global Mind Change.* It appeared in the Greek and Egyptian mystery schools, then later as the underground traditions of Kabbalism, Sufism, and Rosicrucianism that influenced the Middle East and Europe. It also appeared in the Transcendentalism of early Americans such as Ralph Waldo Emerson and Henry David Thoreau, in the prophetic writings of Teilhard de Chardin, and most recently in the consciousness movement in the United States and Western Europe.

Most people are unaware that Freemasonry, a particular embodiment of the perennial wisdom, played a leading role in the emergence of democratic government in the United States, Harman points out. Freemasons believed that the institution of representative democracy rests on a belief in spiritually free citizens in touch with divine guidance. At once esoteric and political, they envisioned an enlightened society founded on the radical principles of liberty, equality, and fraternity. Many of the Founding Fathers, such as Benjamin Franklin and George Washington, belonged to

Masonic lodges. In fact, of the fifty-six signers of the Declaration of Independence, approximately fifty were Masons. In launching the American experiment, the Founding Fathers believed that a higher wisdom would establish a new world order, based on democracy, the freedom of science from ecclesiastical authority, and global unity.

In the nineteenth century, the Transcendentalists fanned the flame of perennial wisdom in America. Philosophers such as Emerson wrote and preached that humanity had a direct channel to higher wisdom through the faculty of intuition. Arching over everyone "like a temple," said Emerson, was the invisible Oversoul, an indwelling source of truth, goodness, and beauty independent of any outside authority or institution. We realize our divine possibilities by awakening to the soul, which discloses its revelations to the mind directly through intuition.

Writing of the soul's influx into the mind, Emerson proclaims in "The Over-Soul": "When it breathes through his intellect, it is genius; when it breathes through his will, it is virtue; when it flows through his affection, it is love." Such a radical reliance on inner guidance aims at bridging the two worlds, the transcendental and the everyday—surely one of the chief tenets of the Perennial Philosophy.

Later, Pierre Teilhard de Chardin, a Jesuit paleontologist, envisioned

The eye by which I see God is the same as the eye by which God sees me. My eye and God's eye are one and the same—one in seeing, one in knowing, and one in loving.

MEISTER ECKHART

a species-wide evolution culminating in Omega Point, a collective enlightenment toward which all of creation is laboring. The planetization of humanity inspires its vision-holders with the joy of action and the zest for life. "If each of us can believe," writes Teilhard in *The Future of Man*, "that he is working so that the Universe may be raised, in him and through him, to a higher level, then a new spring of energy will well forth in the heart of Earth's workers. The whole organism, overcoming a momentary hesitation, will draw its breath and press on with strength renewed."

The Perennial Philosophy also found a willing and persevering disciple in Mohandas Gandhi, whose nonviolent *satyagraha* (or "soul force") movement led to Indian independence. Most recently, the perennial wisdom has taken form as the consciousness movement in the United States. This unique brand of American spirituality, rooted in the West's metaphysical tradition, flowered in the 1960s, '70s, and '80s as people revolted against the spiritual void created by an overweening materialism and began embracing inner-directed values.

During this period, the once-secret teachings of the Perennial Philosophy came out of the closet, flooding our culture with books, tapes, and seminars about Yoga, Zen Buddhism, shamanism, Kabbalah, and many other of the world's wisdom traditions. As Eastern spiritual teachers popularized their traditions in the West, a democratization of esoteric knowledge took place, based on an eager eclecticism among spiritual seekers. This same period also gave birth to humanistic psychology (with its call for an expanded human potential) and transpersonal psychology (with its use of meditative disciplines as a therapeutic tool). For the first time in history, millions of people had the knowledge, techniques, and cultural support to make everyday spirituality a significant force for social change in the world.

In previous ages people attracted to the perennial wisdom would withdraw from the world, seeking the cloistered silence of monasteries and ashrams to transcend the world's suffering through personal liberation. But as modern exponents of the Perennial Philosophy point out, this inward turning is only one-half of the story. The modern age requires that we use our newly gained wisdom to transform the world, rather than to transcend it.

Following in the footsteps of America's Transcendentalists, Marilyn Ferguson, author of the ground-breaking best-seller *The Aquarian Conspiracy*, argues that social transformation must rest on personal, inner change. Her vision of an emergent culture, rooted in a marriage of break-

The notion that man has a body distinct from his soul is to be expunged; this I shall do by . . . melting apparent surfaces away, and displaying the infinite which was hid.

WILLIAM BLAKE

7

through science and the perennial wisdom, calls for a society with more humane institutions, governed by spiritual values and having the self-actualization of its members uppermost in mind.

Those who pursue the path of transformation, observes Ferguson, typically go through four stages of development:

- an entry point;
- an exploration phase, in which we seek teachers and practices to bring forth our inner knowledge;
- an integration stage, in which we unite our spiritual and everyday identities; and
- a conspiracy stage, in which we join with like-minded explorers to heal and transform society.

"So many people have undergone personal transformation that their effect on society is having geometric—not arithmetic—impact," she says. "Society is beginning to adapt itself to these new values, and we've created an atmosphere of doing the vision in the everyday world."

THE GREAT SEAL OF THE UNITED STATES

Can the Perennial Philosophy inspire political action in the modern world? As evidence that it can, Willis Harman points to the Founding Fathers of the United States, visionary yet intensely practical men who subscribed to Freemasonry, an esoteric bearer of the ancient wisdom.

Masons, who believe that transcendental forces play a crucial role in shaping human events, listen to their deep, intuitive center, then act guided by the divine plan. Harman sees a direct connection between the New World's great democratic experiment and the superconscious wisdom that brought it into being. The symbolism of the Great Seal on the reverse side of the dollar bill, he explains, portrays the Founding Fathers' vision of the nation sustained and guided by higher wisdom.

Dominating the obverse of the seal is an eagle, which in earlier versions was the phoenix, an ancient symbol of rebirth through enlightenment. The olive branch and arrows in the bird's talons represent the new order's commitment to peace, along with its willingness to protect itself against all detractors. The banner held by the eagle reads *E pluribus unum*, or "unity from many," referring both to political unity and the higher unity described by the world's mystics and philosophers. The phrase *novus ordo seclorum*, or "a new order of the ages is born," announces that the nation's democratic experiment would initiate a new spiritually based

Truth is a river that is always splitting up into arms that reunite. Islanded between the arms, the inhabitants argue for a lifetime as to which is the main river.

CYRIL CONNOLLY

REASSESSING THE AQUARIAN CONSPIRACY

One reason that our economic, political, and educational institutions have resisted change despite the best efforts of visionary Aquarian conspirators has to do with unresolved conflicts within the conspirators themselves, said Marilyn Ferguson in a recent interview.

"In our initial naivete in the 1970s and '80s, we believed ourselves to have a monolithic, uni-directional self that was entirely committed to personal and social transformation," she observes. "But subpersonality work of the past decade has revealed that we are composed of numerous, often warring subselves that have competing agendas that make action in the world anything but straightforward. Thus one part of us says, 'I want to work for a better world,' while another part, deaf to this idealistic voice, says, 'Pardon me, but I'm interested only in securing my own private happiness and having fun.'"

Most people in the consciousness movement overestimated their degree of spiritual development and were blind to their hidden selves and conflicting motivations, Ferguson points out. When they joined peace organizations or worked to transform social institutions, parts of themselves acted in enlightened ways, while the unacknowledged parts muddied their relationships with others and sabotaged their social effectiveness. Now older and wiser, having suffered a number of often painful, disillusioning, and humbling revelations, we are realizing that inner change is a slower, more demanding project than we at first realized.

"Given the external focus of our culture, it's natural that we rushed out to reform society before completing the preliminary work of putting our internal houses in order," Ferguson says. "But we need not apologize for our zeal and impatience in calling attention to the economic injustice and ecological destruction threatening our world. We have achieved much, and now, if we have the humility to complete our spiritual education, integrate our subselves, and live our professed values with integrity in our personal relationships and in the marketplace, we can enter a new phase of spiritual social activism that promises to be more effective than our first attempt."

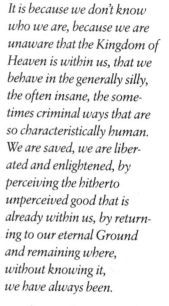

It is because we don't know who we are, because we are unaware that the Kingdom of Heaven is within us, that we behave in the generally silly, the often insane, the sometimes criminal ways that are so characteristically human. We are saved, we are liberated and enlightened, by perceiving the hitherto unperceived good that is already within us, by returning to our eternal Ground and remaining where, without knowing it, we have always been.

ALDOUS HUXLEY

The heart that breaks open can contain the whole universe.

JOANNA MACY

order for the world. The experiment is inaugurated with confidence because *annuit coeptis,* or "He [God] favors our undertaking."

The most conspicuous symbol, the unfinished pyramid with the all-seeing eye in the capstone position, suggests that only when divine intuition is in such a position will the structure be complete. This suggests that the works of the nation remain incomplete unless they incorporate divine insight; the nation will flourish when its leaders are guided by super-conscious intuition.

"Industrialized society faces a maze of problems, involving energy, the environment, population and world poverty," says Harman. "Rather than yield to despair, we could turn to the root symbols and traditions of our nation, which point to a knowable, transcendental realm of experience from which national choices can be made. If someone proposed an enlightened society based on an Eastern belief system, such a notion would fail. But if someone suggests that we now make operative the vision shared by the Founding Fathers at this country's inception, the notion might arouse public consensus."

HARBINGERS OF CHANGE

Because of a number of conditions worldwide—including the ecological crisis, the failure of technology to solve our problems, and the need for spiritual renewal—some social observers believe that now is the first time in human history that the Perennial Philosophy can serve as a catalyst for planetary healing. Consider, for example, how the following broad trends are converging in our times:

An unrestrained materialism. The world's exponential growth in population and the demand for greater amounts of material goods, along with a drain on our energy sources, all make our way of life maladaptive, says George Leonard, author of *The Transformation.* For a voluntary, non-catastrophic transformation of society, we need to value gentleness rather than aggression, cooperation rather than competition, and stewardship rather than acquisitiveness. To grow beyond our addiction to materialism and to help ensure our survival as a species, we need to embrace a lifestyle of greater inner satisfaction as taught by the Perennial Philosophy.

The need for spiritual renewal. In recent years we have witnessed a decline in religious involvement and a simultaneous increase in the number of people having mystical experiences. A Gallup poll indicates that 78 million Americans either don't belong to a church or temple or attend only

I want to know how God created this world. I am not interested in this or that phenomenon, in the spectrum of this or that element; I want to know his thoughts; the rest are details.

ALBERT EINSTEIN

infrequently—a figure up from 61 million in 1978. Yet surveys conducted in 1973 and the mid-1980s by priest/sociologist Andrew Greeley show increases in the incidence of paranormal experiences, such as ESP and visions. In one survey, for example, 35 percent of people reported having mystical experiences "that seemed to lift them outside themselves," while 5 percent said they were "bathed in light" like the apostle Paul.

For religions to satisfy our deep craving for inner experience, they must let go of themselves as *religions*—belief systems focusing on dogma and ritual—and recover themselves as *spiritualities*—ways of life that promote direct, inner connection with the divine. According to theologian Matthew Fox and physicist Brian Swimme in *Manifesto! For a Global Civilization,* religious renewal requires that we return to our mystical roots and appreciate the West's spiritual geniuses, such as St. Francis of Assisi and Meister Eckhart. This renewal promises "the return of cosmic consciousness; of the dark; of silence; of mystery; of depth; of the non-verbal."

The rebalancing of our scientific culture. Many cultural analysts believe that the unbalanced growth of science over the last several centuries has eroded the spiritual values that sustained our civilization over the millennia. Our scientific culture, with its mechanistic bias, exploits nature and suppresses intuitive knowledge. The recent reemergence of the Perennial Philosophy, with its emphasis on inner awareness and the embeddedness of humankind in nature, may help rebalance our culture's one-sided pursuit of technological knowledge. After being exiled for several centuries, our spiritual traditions may be staging a comeback at a time when the reconciliation of science and spirit is desperately needed.

A changing concept of the divine. "The one-sided emphasis on deity as a loving father simply can't hold any longer," says Peter Caddy, co-founder of Findhorn, a spiritual community in northern Scotland. "As our God-concept becomes more androgynous, we'll relate to the source of life as both God and Goddess." The mystical marriage of God the Father, with his emphasis on law and reason, and God the Mother, with her emphasis on love, compassion, and intuition, will give birth to an ecological spirituality that sees the Earth and all its life forms as sacred and beautiful.

Globalization. As we become planetary citizens, allegiance to the Earth supersedes loyalties to regional or national identities. We become planetary stewards, says Jean Houston, author of *The Search for the Beloved,* entrusted with the task of governing and managing the living Earth.

I'm astounded by people who want to "know" the universe when it's hard enough to find your way around Chinatown.

WOODY ALLEN

11

Like substances percolating in a test tube, these forces may require a catalyst to bring the reaction to completion. Might the Perennial Philosophy serve as that catalyst? Willis Harman answers in the affirmative:

> The Perennial Philosophy is the only viewpoint broad enough to address our personal and planetary concerns. Its insistence that the inner and outer form one unified whole helps account for environmentally sound action based on the perception of our shared interdependence. If the basic assumptions of the perennial wisdom become the dominant vision of modern society, life a few generations from now will be as different from modern industrial society as our current lifestyle is from the Middle Ages.

INTIMATIONS OF A NEW SPIRITUALITY

In the last decade of the twentieth century, perhaps in response to the magnitude of our global crisis, spirituality has been coming down to Earth, bringing the above and the below into greater harmony with each other. Rather than seeking personal salvation in an immaterial realm, practitioners of the emerging spirituality attempt to "body forth" their spiritual realization in the world of matter. By viewing the Earth as sacred, we can bring the Divine into everyday life. By yoking the mystical with the practical, the transcendent with the commonplace, we can test out our spiritual realization not just in monasteries and ashrams, but in the marketplace, in schools and universities, and in the healing professions. Believing that spiritual realization and political expression mirror each other, we can manifest our wisdom in compassionate action aimed at healing the Earth.

"During the '60s, '70s and '80s, our spiritual quests usually focused on developing personhood through growth and therapy; on exploring the transpersonal through drugs, meditation and mysticism; and on seeking extraordinary phenomena of a psychic or mystical nature," says David Spangler, former co-director of the Findhorn community in Scotland and author of *Emergence: The Rebirth of the Sacred*. "Now we need to take whatever gains we've made and redress the balance by practicing an *everyday spirituality* that nourishes interpersonal relationships, the environment, and the ordinary."

In the earlier phases of our spiritual quest, people separated everyday life, with its cooking, cleaning, home finances, and child-rearing, from sacramental activities, such as meditation, prayer, and worship. This form of cultural dualism is gradually giving way to what Spangler calls an "incarnational spirituality" that celebrates the sacredness of the ordinary. Spiritual qualities developed through inner work—such as mindfulness,

Three kinds of souls, three prayers:

1. I am a bow in your hands, Lord. Draw me, lest I rot.

2. Do not overdraw me, Lord. I shall break.

3. Overdraw me, Lord, and what cares if I break!

NIKOS KAZANTZAKIS

discrimination, gratitude, and a sense of wonder—can open up new dimensions to activities typically regarded as mundane.

Besides redressing the split between the sacred and the ordinary, the emerging spirituality aims at relating the individual to the collective, Spangler says. People in the '70s and '80s emphasized personal empowerment as a reaction against feelings of powerlessness and conformity. The new challenge involves using personal growth and transpersonal awareness to work for the well-being of the community and the larger environment.

THE HEALING OF MIND/BODY DUALISM

The resacralization of everyday life liberates us from many of the other-worldly aspects of traditional patriarchal spirituality, according to Buddhist scholar Joanna Macy. For more than 3,000 years, Eastern and Western practitioners of mainstream spirituality have subscribed to the dualism of spirit and matter, mind and body. This fundamental rupture between the sacred and the everyday places our hopes for salvation in a transcendent realm, free from ordinary physical embodiment.

In the patriarchal mindset, the physical world, the body, and sexuality are viewed as enemies whose downward pull chain the spirit to an inferior dimension of existence. Most spiritual practices aim, therefore, at separating the spirit from this fallen, desacralized world, called *maya* in the Hindu tradition—the world of illusion. Striving to follow codes of moral perfection, practitioners of these paths disown what Carl Jung called the shadow, the dark, unwanted parts of the personality containing emotional and instinctual impulses that are at odds with an ideal image of detachment and self-control.

In patriarchal religion people relate to God as a transcendent male power removed from the Earth, a monarch who rules with Divine authority. The social order reflects this masculine bias in hierarchies that invest men with power over women, the downtrodden in society, and nature. Instead of emphasizing a vertical escape path, says Macy, the new spirituality redirects its focus by moving more deeply into matter, in effect "falling in love with our world." Drawing on both patriarchal and Earth-centered traditions, such as Native American and Goddess religions, this erotic spirituality recognizes the sacredness of the senses, the body, sexuality, and the natural world. Only such a full-bodied approach, she argues, can end our alienation from the Earth and enable us to save our world from ecological destruction.

The emerging spirituality proclaims that the Divine expresses itself

Sometimes I go about pitying myself, and all the time I am being carried on great winds across the sky.

OJIBWAY SAYING

13

The touch of Earth is always reinvigorating to the son of Earth, even when he seeks a supraphysical Knowledge. It may even be said that the supraphysical can only be really mastered in its fullness . . . when we keep our feet firmly on the physical. "Earth is His footing," says the Upanishad, whenever it images the Self that manifests in the universe.

SRI AUROBINDO

both as God and Goddess, transcendent to and immanent in the world. The nonhierarchical social order that derives from this new orientation distributes power to men and women based on partnership, rather than on the dominance of one group over another. Practitioners of the new spirituality strive for wholeness rather than perfection, consciously working with their shadow qualities instead of repressing them.

The old approach, essentially contemplative and ascetic, shunned political involvement in the world, while the new approach, with its active, outgoing emphasis, insists on yoking the spiritual with the political. As the new attitude takes roots in our culture, engaged forms of spirituality are surfacing everywhere, manifesting the wisdom gained through inner work in acts of compassionate service.

"A major task for Buddhism in the West . . . is to ally itself with religious and other concerned organizations to forestall the potential catastrophes facing the human race: nuclear holocaust, irreversible pollution of the world's environment, and the continuing large-scale destruction of non-renewable resources," writes Zen teacher Philip Kapleau in *A Pilgrimage to the Buddhist Temples and Caves of China*. "We also need to lend our physical and moral support to those who are fighting hunger, poverty, and oppression everywhere in the world."

In the same vein, Vietnamese meditation teacher Thich Nhat Hanh asserts that meditation prepares us for a return to society. "Our daily lives, the way we drink, what we eat, has to do with the world's political situation," he writes in *Being Peace.* "Meditation is to see deeply into things, to see how we can change, how we can transform our situation."

SOMETHING OLD, SOMETHING NEW

As patriarchal spirituality gives way to an approach that celebrates what was previously devalued and maligned by theologians—the Earth, the feminine, the body, and sexuality—we need to revise our understanding of what *spiritual* means. To focus and clarify our thinking, Connie Zweig, editor of *To Be A Woman* and *Meeting the Shadow,* has come up with the following chart:

The Old Spirituality	*The New Spirituality*
Transcendent God	Transcendent and immanent God/Goddess
Otherworldly	In the here and now
Anti-world	Engaged with the world
Hierarchical	Nonhierarchical
Patriarchal	Partnership
Introverted	Introverted/extroverted
Solitary	Solitary/communal
Isolationist	Ecological
Apolitical	Politically and socially conscious
Anti-body	Embodied
Anti-shadow	Includes shadow
Dualistic (separates the spiritual from the mundane)	Unified

For us to regard the Bomb (or the dying seas, the poisoned air) as a monstrous injustice to us would suggest that we never took seriously the injunction to love. Perhaps we thought all along that Gautama and Jesus were kidding, or their teachings were meant only for saints. But now we see, as an awful revelation, that we are all called to be saints—not good necessarily, or pious or devout—but saints in the sense of just loving each other.

JOANNA MACY

INTEGRAL SPIRITUALITY

The emerging spirituality, says Michael Murphy, co-founder of the Esalen Institute, represents a course correction of the traditional ascetic programs developed in the world's ashrams and monasteries. Murphy believes the modern age requires integral practices that address the physical, emotional, mental, and spiritual needs of today's practitioners. By drawing on the time-tested practices of the past, such as Yoga, Zen, Judeo-Christian and Islamic mysticism, transpersonal psychologies such as psychosynthesis, and martial arts and modern sports research, we are giving birth to the spiritual practices appropriate to our age.

Most spiritual traditions regard the body only as an instrument of salvation, rarely as a co-equal partner worthy of illumination in its own right, Murphy argues. However, like Indian philosopher Sri Aurobindo, he believes the universe is in "the body-building business" within an evolutionary framework unknown to our religious forebears. Rather than escape the body, therefore, we ascend through spiritual practice to unitive consciousness, then bring those transformative energies back into the human body, evolving it into a progressively divinized form.

The body is capable of "a remarkable range of exceptional and metanormal functioning [that] might herald a new dimension of human evolution," writes Murphy in *The Future of the Body*. Examples include telepathy, clairvoyance, precognition, and distant spiritual healing. Ascetic, otherworldly religious traditions view these *siddhis* (or "powers") as obstacles and temptations in our path, while integral spirituality views them as precursors of our full humanhood. Here are some of Murphy's guidelines for integral practices:

- They must be suited to our individual makeup. There are no single or right practices that apply to everyone.
- They require a strong and developing autonomy. "Only by assuming responsibility for our own development can we learn from our mistakes, sharpen our discrimination, and establish an identity strong enough to sustain the difficulties of high-level change," writes Murphy. "If, on the other hand, we give that authority to a guru or group, we may limit our disciplines and overlook our particular strengths and shortcomings."
- They educate the whole person, including body, emotions, mind, volition, and spirit.
- They require multiple mentors, rather than single gurus. To engage our various capacities, we study with meditation masters, psychologists, bodywork specialists, and athletic trainers.
- They develop a witnessing consciousness that transcends physical, emotional, and mental functioning.
- They depend on creative improvisation. "Though they draw on the experiences of many fields," he writes, "[integral practices] do not have detailed maps for all their activities, and few clearly established lines of progression, and for that reason they depend on a certain amount of trial and error, the love of adventure and improvisation."

Murphy concludes: "We live in an age of great religious reinvention, and we're synthesizing the best of the old and the new to forge our own particular brand of modern yoga. In this transitional age, we need to realize that the final word has not been delivered on any front."

Matter is less material and the mind less spiritual than is generally supposed. The habitual separation of physics and psychology, mind and matter, is metaphysically indefensible.

BERTRAND RUSSELL

AN ECO-YOGA FOR THE WEST

As traditions converge, we are witnessing the development of a "green Buddhism" and what has been termed an eco-yoga. Georg Feuerstein, author of *Yoga: Technology of Ecstasy* and *Sacred Sexuality,* argues that any tradition that ignores the Earth, the body, and sexuality will find very few adherents in the upcoming years. "We can no longer pursue exclusively quietistic goals. How can we practice yogic breathing exercises when the air itself is polluted? How can we find ourselves (let alone God) when we obstruct our view by piling up mountains of garbage?"

Feuerstein offers the following guidelines for practicing eco-yoga, the union of yogic spirituality with an ecologically based social activism:

1. Adopt a simpler, more ecologically sensitive lifestyle. Take stock of your consumption patterns and decide how you can help reduce energy consumption and pollution in your immediate environment. Accept that you are co-responsible for the current crisis.
2. Rethink the ethical injunctions of your spiritual path in ecological terms. For example, the moral restraint of nonviolence in yoga implies that our lifestyle should not rob other species of their habitats. The yogic injunction against stealing cautions us against conspicuous consumption, including the needless wasting of food. Surplus food destined to become garbage can be used to feed our less fortunate fellow humans.
3. Stay in touch with your natural environment. Living in cities seduces people into having a merely abstract relationship with the Earth. It is important to touch the soil, tend flowers or trees, taste clean spring water, and enjoy the exuberance of wildlife. Inwardness without such grounding often amounts to little more than neurotic escape.
4. Join forces with a local ecology group and become politically active. Do not be exclusively concerned with your own salvation while ignoring the larger context in which you live. At the very least, generously support activist groups like Greenpeace, Friends of the Earth, Sierra Club, or the National Wildlife Federation. As part of your spiritual discipline, help preserve and restore the balance of our natural environment so that future generations can enjoy and benefit from it.
5. Daily remind yourself that life is a precious gift that must not be squandered. If your heart is open, gratitude and praise will flow easily from your lips.

God is so omnipresent . . . That God is an angel in an angel, and a stone in a stone, and a straw in a straw.

JOHN DONNE

AWAKENING TO THE NEW SPIRITUALITY

Physician/healer W. Brugh Joy describes how awakening to the emerging spirituality struck him with the unpredictability of an earthquake. It brought with it the instantaneous collapse of the spiritual values and certainties that had sustained him during the earlier years of his quest.

In 1981 Joy, author of *Avalanche: Heretical Reflections on the Dark and the Light,* ascended to the summit of the Great Pyramid of Cheops in Egypt for a sunrise meditation. He describes his rebirth this way:

> In the glow of the early morning sun, without warning my body was seized by powerful convulsions, which for me often forecast the collapse of spiritual values. 'Oh God, not again!' I cried. Within four minutes everything I held as sacred collapsed into a heap. Gone were Christ's inspiration, the Buddha's compassion, and the sense of spiritual upliftment I experience when contemplating Tibetan Buddhism, Native American beliefs, Zen, or Judaism. The pain of my losses was so great that I cried out involuntarily.
>
> Instinctively, I clutched at something, anything to fill this painful void, but an inner voice counseled me, 'Don't fill this painful place with anything. Let life teach you what spirit is.'
>
> Shocked yet ecstatic, I realized that many of my spiritual beliefs were filters that shielded me from a direct encounter with the mystery of matter, the Earth, sexuality, and emotion. I later came to understand that religion erects huge, almost impenetrable defenses against the so-called "lower" forces of physicality, sexuality, and emotion because their spontaneity threatens the mind's need for detached control. Because the traditional spiritual path had served as an escape from these fundamental mysteries, I had to re-apprentice myself to Life and embrace everything in its totality, the light and the dark, mind and body, matter and form.
>
> As I've learned to penetrate more deeply into matter and to honor its mystery, I feel more intimately connected to all of life. No longer do I conceive of myself as a divine spark that has to liberate itself from the downward pull of matter. Awakened into matter, I'm so overwhelmed and inspired by it that I've experienced a profound renovation of my viewpoint.

EMBRACING OUR HUMANITY

Is spiritual realization for everyone? Brugh Joy thinks so—not by following the traditional ascetic path leading to a predetermined summit of realization, but by embracing our full humanhood.

"By conforming to spiritual ideals imposed from the outside through the force of tradition, people often channel themselves into models of behavior that violate their inner essence," he says. "We all are guaranteed realization when we strip away our pre-conceived notions about spiritual perfection, give up striving for some idealized end-point called 'enlightenment,' and discover the magnificence of what we already are and live that fully."

. . . thou canst not stir a flower
Without troubling of a star.

FRANCIS THOMPSON

THE GOLDEN RULE

A version of the Golden Rule—"Do unto others as you would have them do unto you"—exists in each of the world's major religions, demonstrating the universal importance of right conduct to the Perennial Philosophy. The following examples are excerpted from *The World's Living Religions* (Charles Scribner's Sons, 1936) by Robert Ernest Hume.

Hinduism. Do naught to others which, if done to thee, would cause thee pain: this is the sum of duty.

Buddhism. A clansman [should] minister to his friends and familiars . . . by treating them as he treats himself.

Confucianism. The Master replied: ". . . What you do not want done to yourself, do not do unto others."

Taoism. To those who are good to me, I am good; and to those who are not good to me, I am also good. And thus all get to be good. To those who are sincere with me, I am sincere; and to those who are not sincere with me, I am also sincere. And thus all get to be sincere.

Zorastrianism. Whatever thou dost not approve for thyself, do not approve for anyone else. When thou hast acted in this manner, thou art righteous.

Judaism. Take heed to thyself, my child, in all thy works; and be discreet in all thy behavior. And what thou thyself hatest, do to no man.

Christianity. All things therefore whatsoever ye would that men should do unto you, even so do ye also unto them.

Greek philosophy. Do not do to others what you would not wish to suffer yourself. Treat your friends as you would want them to treat you.

This prescription does not mean abandoning spiritual disciplines, but it does mean honoring the unique requirements of our own individuation process, Joy asserts. By imitating behavior we think is spiritual, we set ourselves up for grief and disillusionment, especially when we invariably fail

Awe enables us to perceive in the world intimations of the divine, to sense in small things the beginning of infinite significance, to sense the ultimate in the common and the simple; to feel in the rush of the passing the stillness of the eternal.

ABRAHAM JOSHUA HESCHEL

to reach the goal touted by all the traditions. We berate ourselves for having failed; we magnify our shortcomings by comparing ourselves to others we think have succeeded; or in a fit of anguish, we give up the spiritual endeavor entirely, because it appears to demand a godlike perfection beyond our frail means of achievement. We may even grow cynical when we compare the end state described in all the traditions with the varying degree of human imperfection we see in our fellow travelers.

Joy recommends dropping hierarchical notions of spiritual growth, giving up the self-contradictory notion of spiritualizing ourselves, and valuing the powerful mystery already perfected at our core. "Over the ages we've lacerated our bodies, rigidly disciplined our minds and oftentimes broken our spirits in an obsessive pursuit to make ourselves better than we are," he observes. "Our task now is to discover what we are, not what we should be. This complete acceptance of our nature, the 'high' and the 'low,' the 'acceptable' and the 'unacceptable,' the mind and the body, will give birth to a spirituality that embraces and ennobles the entirety of our being."

RESOURCES

Recommended Reading

The Perennial Philosophy, Aldous Huxley (Harper & Row, 1944). The classic anthology on the Perennial Philosophy, with numerous quotations from Eastern and Western sources. Beautifully written.

Coming Home: The Experience of Enlightenment in Sacred Traditions, Lex Hixon (Jeremy P. Tarcher, 1989). Explores the essence of many spiritual paths, including Tantric, Zen, Christian, Jewish, Sufi, and Taoist approaches.

What Is Enlightenment?, John White, editor (Jeremy P. Tarcher, 1985). An anthology of essays on the theme of self-realization.

America's Secret Destiny, Robert Hieronimus (Destiny Books, 1989). An intriguing exposition of how the Perennial Philosophy, as expressed in Freemasonry and Rosicrucianism, influenced the Founding Fathers of our nation.

Global Mind Change, Willis Harman (Knowledge Systems, 1988). Discusses how the Perennial Philosophy can provide the guiding vision to deal with our current ecological, political, and social problems.

No Boundary, Ken Wilber (Shambhala Publications, 1981). A transpersonal view of human development by the foremost contemporary exponent of the Perennial Philosophy.

Be Here Now, Ram Dass (Crown Publishers, 1971). This modern classic, which describes a Western psychologist's encounter with Eastern mysticism, gives practical guidelines for living a spiritual life.

Professional Organizations and Publications

The Foundation for Traditional Studies (1633 Q Street, NW, Washington, DC, 20009; 202–667–1194). Disseminates information on the world's spiritual and cultural traditions through its twice-yearly newsletter, *Sophia,* which includes listings of related books, concerts, publications, videotapes, and conferences.

The Institute for Perennial Studies (P.O. Box 1128, Lake Ozark, MO 65049; 314–365–0186). Seeks the "re-evaluation of culture based on a perennial wisdom which emphasizes harmony and integration with Nature and views humanity as a spiritual entity within Creation." Send a self-addressed stamped envelope to receive a copy of the institute's recommended reading list on the Perennial Philosophy.

Gnosis: A Journal of the Western Inner Traditions. Published by the Lumen Foundation (P.O. Box 14217, San Francisco, CA 94114–0217; 415–255–0400, $15/year, quarterly). This highly readable publication accents Western forms of the Perennial Philosophy.

The Quest: A Quarterly Journal of Philosophy, Science, Religion and the Arts. Published by the Theosophical Society (P.O. Box 270, Wheaton, IL 60189; 708–668–1571, $14/year). Draws on the wisdom found in all religious traditions.

Avaloka: A Journal of Traditional Religion and Culture (249 Maynard NW, Grand Rapids, MI 49504; $12/year). Published each fall, this journal has essays and articles by representatives of traditional cultures, such as the Dalai Lama and Robert Aitken.

EVERYDAY SPIRITUALITY

Finding the Extraordinary in the Ordinary

One day Krishnamurti, the world-famous spiritual teacher, was traveling by car to Ranikhet, a hill station in the Himalayas. Krishnamurti was sitting in the front seat, next to the driver. In the back seat, Pupul Jayakar, a student and biographer of the venerable teacher, and her friend were discussing lofty topics, such as self-knowledge and awareness, as the car climbed steadily past waterfalls, steep gorges, and hills covered with flowers.

Suddenly the back-seat philosophers felt a jolt, but they paid it no attention and returned to their conversation. A few seconds later, Krishnamurti asked them what they were discussing. "Awareness," they answered.

"Did you notice what happened just now?" he asked quizzically.

"No."

"We knocked down a goat," he said. "Did you not see it?"

"No."

"And you were discussing awareness," he said pointedly.

His terse observation etched itself indelibly in Jayakar's memory: "No more words were necessary. It was devastating."

This incident, described by Jayakar in *Krishnamurti: A Biography,* underscores one of the major predicaments of the spiritual path. Like Krishnamurti's students, we often prefer discussing metaphysical abstractions

Eighty percent of success is showing up.

WOODY ALLEN

to dealing with the chores, responsibilities, and sometimes upsetting events of daily life. In fact, many people enter spiritual life with the unconscious hope that practices such as meditation will help them transcend problems with money, sexuality, power, and the unfinished pain of childhood.

No matter how idealistic our hopes, however, we eventually learn that spirituality is not about leaving life's problems behind, but about continually confronting them with honesty and courage. It is about ending our feeling of separation from others by healing our relationships with parents, co-workers, and friends. It is about bringing heightened awareness and compassion to our family life, careers, and community service.

BEFRIENDING OUR HUMANITY

"At the beginning of the spiritual journey, many of us pushed away our humanity in an attempt to embrace our divinity," observes the popular spiritual teacher Ram Dass. "We tried to live up to images of 'holiness' based on monastic models imported from the East. We practiced meditation, devotional chanting, and other sophisticated yogic techniques, but these strategies often kept us from dealing with our hidden desires, emotional vulnerabilities, and family entanglements—issues associated with being human. Over the past several decades, we've been learning to accept rather than reject our human qualities, creating a new partnership between the mundane and transcendent parts of ourselves."

Besides disowning essential aspects of our humanity, many people applied a Western goal orientation, competitive spirit, and not-so-subtle egotism to their Eastern disciplines. Using practices such as meditation to strengthen rather than discipline their egos, they collected unusual transcendental experiences in the same way consumers acquire cars and TV sets to enhance their self-image. This process, dubbed spiritual materialism by Chogyam Trungpa, Rinpoche, the late Tibetan Buddhist teacher, feeds the ego's constant desire for self-aggrandizement through higher forms of knowledge and virtue. Since blissful meditation experiences and psychic phenomena can seduce us into exaggerating our progress, Trungpa recommends giving up attachment to them and settling down to the more mature task of undoing "our neurotic games, our self-deceptions, our hidden hopes and fear."

"We expect the teachings to solve all our problems," he writes in *The Myth of Freedom*. "We expect to be provided with magical means to deal with our depressions, our aggressions, our sexual hangups. But to our sur-

Fear less, hope more; eat less, chew more; whine less, breathe more; talk less, say more; hate less, love more; and all good things are yours.

SWEDISH PROVERB

Why put on the robe of the monk, and live aloof from the world in lonely pride? Behold! My heart dances in the delight of a hundred arts; and the Creator is well pleased.

KABIR

prise we realize that this is not going to happen. It is very disappointing to realize that we must work on ourselves and our suffering rather than depend upon a savior or the magical power of yogic techniques."

This dashing of expectations occurs again and again on the spiritual quest as we continually unmask our pretensions and self-serving motives. Eventually, says Trungpa, we give up our achievement orientation, and "we fall down and down and down, until we touch the ground, until we relate with the basic sanity of earth. When we are grounded, there is no room for dreaming or frivolous impulse, so our practice at last becomes workable. We begin to learn how to make a proper cup of tea, how to walk straight without tripping. Our whole approach to life becomes more simple and direct."

SPIRITUALITY ROMANTICIZED

Jack Kornfield, a teacher of Buddhist vipassana meditation, shares a similar perspective about the naive and simplistic hopes of Western spiritual seekers. In the '60s and '70s such seekers embraced Eastern practices with a zeal that he calls idealistic and romantic. They believed that by following "perfect" gurus and by practicing certain "complete and wonderful" teachings, they could leave the messy business of life behind and enter the Pure Land of Enlightenment.

As the '80s unfolded, however, some people faced their broken expectations and began to realize that developing consciousness requires more practice and discipline than they initially imagined. They found that psychotherapy helped heal deep personal woundedness, loneliness, fear, and grief, which remained untouched by meditation practice. And they began to extend the notion of practice beyond prayer, chanting, and meditation to include interpersonal communication, sexuality, work, family life, community involvement, and ecological values—all of which were completely ignored in the first heady rush of spiritual idealism that led up, up, and away from the world.

"After three decades of experimentation, what's emerging now is a mature spirituality," says Kornfield. "It doesn't fragment life into 'spiritual' and 'mundane' fields of action, but rather sees it as a unitary whole requiring our full, heartfelt response wherever we find ourselves. Its arena of practice includes not only traditional disciplines, but raising children, paying bills, driving our cars, and relating to our neighbors. In a very real sense, the entirety of life becomes the field of growth and insight."

The shift we need to make is both a shift in consciousness and a major restructuring of all the institutions of society. We need to engage in active, nonviolent resistance to the destruction being mounted all around us. At the same time, we need to develop and make real our alternative visions; start the businesses; live in the households, grow the gardens that embody our ideals. In so doing, we can experiment with our ideals on a small scale and find out if they actually work in practice.

STARHAWK

Usually people interested in spiritual development think in terms of the importance of mind, that mysterious, high and deep thing that we have decided to learn about. But strangely enough, the profound and the transcendental are to be found in the factory. It may not fill you with bliss to look at it, it may not sound as good as the spiritual experiences that we have read about, but somehow reality is to be found there, in the way in which we relate with everyday problems. If we relate to them in a simple, earthy way, we will work in a more balanced manner, and things will be dealt with properly.

CHOGYAM TRUNGPA

Mature spirituality has little to do with altered states of consciousness, Kornfield adds. "Powerful meditation and visionary experiences often initiate people into spiritual life, waking them up to untapped potentials. But mental disciplines such as meditation cannot singlehandedly sustain us on our journeys. We also need to open our hearts, then embody our love in everyday acts of attentive living. This integration of wisdom, love, and embodied action, which requires years of inner and outer work, constitutes our spiritual curriculum in today's modern world."

MATURE SPIRITUALITY

All the way to heaven is heaven.

ST. CATHERINE OF SIENA

What distinguishes mature from naive spirituality? Kornfield, author of the forthcoming book *A Path with Heart,* offers the following guidelines:

In spiritual maturity, we have a more long-term, inclusive vision. We see that spiritual practice is not a quick fix; it has cycles of inward meditation, followed by outward acts of compassionate service to our communities and the environment. This vision unites yoga or contemplation and social action as complementary practices.

We integrate the personal with the universal. In the idealistic stage, we attempt to express universal compassion, aspiring to be like Bodhisattvas who work for the liberation of all sentient beings, or yogis who have transcended the need for sex or material possessions. In spiritual maturity, we love the universal in the particular, caring for our spouse, our children, our parents, our community, and the piece of Earth on which we live.

We work less on reaching enlightenment and more on developing the capacity to love. Blissful meditation experiences may tempt us away from the world, but as Zen master Dogen says, enlightenment means being intimate with the joys and sorrows of everyday life without compulsively grasping at or running away from anything. As we grow in maturity and bring more compassion, patience, and openness to all our encounters, we shift our focus away from asking "When will I reach enlightenment?" to "How can I love more effectively through daily acts of attentive living?"

Realizing that no simple formulas apply to everyone, we develop the courage to live a unique spiritual life, in our own idiosyncratic way. While archetypal patterns exist to guide seekers, in the West individuals can find their own way within these deeper patterns by honoring their unique backgrounds, temperaments, values, and creative capacities.

In the earlier stages, we may imitate spiritual models, such as Jesus, Buddha, Gandhi, or Mother Teresa. Later we realize that adopting outer forms of behavior, such as rigid models of disciplined living, can do harm to our inner nature. To remain true to ourselves, we can receive the support of communities, spiritual guides, and teachings, but we must learn to listen to our own hearts and to become our own teachers, using these resources only as aids to explore the unknown.

We give up splitting growth into spiritual and psychological components. We see it as a continuum of practice, which may include powerful meditation experiences, followed by a release of early-life trauma, followed by a deeper capacity for inner stillness, followed by the healing of more personal issues. On this spiral of growth, as we work courageously with whatever arises in the context of a spiritual practice, at certain points we may choose to enter psychotherapy or to pursue Twelve Step recovery programs. At other points, we might enter a monastery for a period of silent contemplation.

Early in the spiritual journey, in our zeal to achieve enlightenment, we tried skipping over our personal sorrows and limitations by simply transcending into higher awareness. But no matter how high we went, we were always dragged back to the level of unresolved personal issues from the past. Because meditation and spiritual practices can be used to suppress feelings or to escape from problems, we therefore may need the tools of Western psychology to deal with these blocks. Many areas of growth, such as sexuality and intimacy, career issues and early childhood wounds, are better served by Western therapy than by meditation. A number of emerging therapies, such as Psychosynthesis, Reichian or Grof breath work, and Jungian dreamwork, bring a spiritual perspective to the personal dimension of life.

We commit ourselves to passionate action in the world, without becoming overly attached to the success or failure of our endeavors. Spiritual traditions call this ability to remain centered despite the fluctuations of outer conditions "being in the world but not of it." In the earlier stages, people confused non-attachment with lack of commitment, saying, "I don't give a damn, I don't care, I'm not really attached to my marriage or my job." In spiritual maturity, recognizing that such an attitude of indifference stems from a fear of life, we commit to our spouses, professions, and social action, developing compassion and equanimity through a balanced engagement with life.

LAYING THE FOUNDATIONS

To build the edifice of a mature spiritual life, we need to construct a foundation based on an honest appraisal of our personal strengths and weaknesses, according to yoga scholar and practitioner Georg Feuerstein. Unwilling to face their neuroses, spiritual seekers sometimes escape into practices that prevent them from developing balanced personalities. Some

Rabbi Zusya of Hanipol used to say, "If they ask me in the next world, 'Why were you not Moses?' I will know the answer. But if they ask me, 'Why were you not Zusya?' I will have nothing to say."

MARTIN BUBER

people, for example, may choose solitary, introspective approaches to avoid interpersonal conflict and intimacy, while others may flee into communities to fulfill desperate needs for social belonging.

Before committing to a particular path, therefore, Feuerstein recommends that prospective spiritual seekers explore their psychological profiles with counselors trained in such matters. They also should do preliminary reading and research, which includes interviewing experienced practitioners, in much the same way that high school students go on interviews before choosing which universities to attend.

"Too many people use spiritual disciplines such as meditation to avoid facing problems with their careers, personal finances, or relationships," Feuerstein says. "At the very beginning, therefore, with great compassion and humility, we should inquire into our motivations for taking up certain practices."

Are we yearning for enlightenment because we don't feel equal to daily life and its responsibilities? Are we attracted to a certain spiritual path because unconsciously we know that we can avoid our neurotic entanglements with the opposite sex? Are we meditating to escape from financial problems that despite our best metaphysical efforts never disappear?

Familiarity with our assets and liabilities prepares us for the accelerated confrontations with self that await us when we commit to a spiritual path, Feuerstein counsels. "The path not only brings blissful meditation experiences, but tests and tears that make us more fully human as we confront our hidden shadow selves," he explains. "If we don't construct an honest, workable foundation brick by brick, years later the structure will collapse, and the process of becoming authentic will be more painful than at the beginning."

Doing work which has to be done over and over again helps us recognize the natural cycles of growth and decay, of birth and death, and thus become aware of the dynamic order of the universe. "Ordinary" work, as the root meaning of the term indicates, is work that is in harmony with the order we perceive in the natural environment.

FRITJOF CAPRA

HEALTHY SPIRITUALITY

Once launched on our path, we should learn to discriminate healthy spirituality from its unhealthy counterfeit, cautions transpersonal psychologist Frances Vaughan, author of *The Inward Arc.* Addictive spirituality creates dependence in the practitioner (frequently to authoritarian leaders and their communities), an avoidance of personal responsibility, and loss of individuality through social controls, such as fear, guilt, or greed for power or bliss. It also tends to suppress rational inquiry into the teachings.

Healthy spirituality, on the other hand, supports the practitioner's freedom, autonomy, self-esteem, and social responsibility. It is based on experience, rather than belief or dogma; it does not create idols out of spiritual teachers; and it empowers students by emphasizing democratic forms of learning and teaching, rather than the authoritarian model that has dominated spiritual life for millennia.

"When we're spiritually immature and we fear assuming responsibility for ourselves, we may choose authoritarian forms of instruction," says Vaughan. "We think, 'Somebody must be able to mediate the great mysteries of existence to me. Somebody must know what truth is.' Later, when we outgrow our dependence on external sources of wisdom, we may gravitate toward more democratic spiritual environments, in which there exists greater equality between teachers and students."

These democratic forms, she says, appear to be emerging in our culture in proliferating Twelve Step addiction recovery programs and in grass-roots spiritual movements that address people's inner needs in informal settings that lack the rigidity of traditional organizations.

"No matter what our level of spiritual development, we need teachers and supportive communities to motivate us and to provide corrective feedback on our journey toward wholeness," adds Vaughan. "Like children growing up in the family, we start in a state of dependence, go through adolescent struggles for independence, only to arrive at the mature state of interdependence, in which we balance the need for autonomy with the need for committed relationships with significant others. As we slowly grow in our practice, we shouldn't adopt the heroic posture that we can do everything alone. We really need each other in spiritual life just as we do in our more ordinary pursuits."

First I was dying to finish high school and start college.
And then I was dying to finish college and start working.
And then I was dying to marry and have children.
And then I was dying for my children to grow old enough for school so I could return to work.
And then I was dying to retire.
And now, I am dying. . . . And suddenly realize I forgot to live.

ANONYMOUS

COMMITMENT TO THE PATH

Spiritual life is a little like love and marriage, observes Stephan Bodian, editor of *Yoga Journal* and a longtime practitioner of Eastern meditative disciplines. In the early stages we fall passionately in love with the teachings, a teacher, the prospect of our growth—or all three. Once the initial euphoria of the honeymoon phase wears off, however, we settle down to a more mature, committed relationship to our path. The maturity of the marriage phase helps see us through the ups and downs, the exhilarating breakthroughs, and the moments of profound disillusionment that make up a lifetime practice. On that journey of discovery, Bodian offers the following advice:

Subject spiritual teachers and their communities to careful scrutiny before making a commitment. Find out to your own satisfaction whether the teacher's behavior accords with the teachings, whether open-minded discussions are encouraged, and whether the lifestyle promotes self-responsibility.

After sampling the wide variety of meditative practices available, build a strong foundation by following a single path or practice for five or ten years. Long-term practice reveals how the mind works, and the insight we gain helps us learn to live a more balanced, effective life. After five or ten years, we then can borrow from other teachings to suit our individual growth needs. But if we start becoming eclectic before having grounded ourselves in one tradition, we may fall prey to a dilletantism that only works against us.

Be aware of the tendency to transfer unresolved parental issues to spiritual teachers. Often, we project unmet needs for approval, love, and appreciation onto our guides. Withdrawing such projections keeps us from being unconsciously manipulated and wounded by our compelling needs.

Learn from the inevitable mistakes you make, but avoid becoming embittered and disillusioned in the process. Our stumblings and seeming errors—even the dead-ends that occasionally befall us—amount to learning experiences on the path, another form of teaching. Sometimes we learn that a cherished teacher or a path that we've invested with passionate energy doesn't accord with our highest interests. We shouldn't generalize from our limited experience, in effect casting the whole spiritual path out of our hearts. We should pick ourselves up and continue, older and a bit wiser, realizing that the path is authentic and that there are indeed mature teachers who can provide guidance on our journey.

Give up the notion that there is a final state to attain. Spiritual life consists of ongoing practice undertaken as a lifetime work. This realization breeds humility, especially when we realize that in our initial infatuation with enlightenment, we underestimate the amount of inner work necessary to free us from our addictive patterns of thought and behavior.

If you continue this simple practice every day, you will obtain a wonderful power. Before you attain it, it is something wonderful, but after you obtain it, it is nothing special.

SHUNRYU SUZUKI

DAILY LIFE AS SPIRITUAL EXERCISE

As we grow in spiritual understanding, our notion of practice undergoes an evolution. At first, we partition off specific times and places for our Yoga, prayer, or meditation. For example, we may set aside formal periods of meditation to quiet the mind's ceaseless agitation—called "monkey mind" in the yogic tradition—and then return to the nonpractice arena of daily life, frequently to lose our equilibrium in traffic, at work, or in upsetting relationships. Eventually, as meditative awareness deepens and per-

RITUALIZING THE FAMILY FIGHT

One of the most neglected ways of bringing the spirit into everyday life is through ritual, defined by Jungian lecturer Robert A. Johnson as symbolic behavior that carries the power of the inner world into visible and physical form. Rituals serve as natural human tools for awakening religious awe, connecting us to our inner selves and channeling the nourishing energy of the unconscious into work and relationships.

In *Ecstasy: Understanding the Psychology of Joy,* Johnson describes how a young couple routinely became embroiled in vicious fights every weekend that involved thrown dishes and the threat of physical violence. In mythological terms, the couple was expressing Dionysian energy—the instinctual, ecstatic, enlivening power of life—in destructive ways. To contain their conflict, they created a Dionysian ritual using the following basic rules:

1. Don't do anything that would hurt others, literally or on the unconscious level.
2. Have respect and courtesy for others and for yourself.
3. Don't provoke confrontation or be dramatic.
4. Affirm personal responsibility for the Dionysian quality.

One Saturday morning, writes Johnson, the combatants "stood in the center of the bedroom and bowed to each other, much as opponents in a judo match do. They exchanged their opinions under the strictest, most formal rules of courtesy and respect. They were free to say whatever they wished as long as they followed these rules. When each felt that there was no more to say, they again stood in the center of the room, bowed to each other, and formally closed the exchange. In this way the fight was symbolically confined within the circle of the ceremony and would not leak into everyday life."

When the husband later reported that ritual combat had made the weekend idyllic, Johnson replied, "You have discovered ritual. . . . You have taken the Dionysian element in its crudest, roughest, least intelligent form and discovered the stuff of miracle, its transformation into ecstasy and joy."

The time of business does not with me differ from the time of prayer, and in the noise and clatter of my kitchen, while several persons are at the same time calling for different things, I possess God in as great tranquility as if I were upon my knees at the blessed sacrament.

BROTHER LAWRENCE

meates all aspects of life, the inner and outer worlds merge as mirror reflections of each other. Practice, like clothing initially reserved only for
special occasions, becomes part of our daily wardrobe, worn with ease
wherever we find ourselves.

Practice need not be limited to conventionally spiritual disciplines,
but can include numerous forms of activity, including walking, washing
dishes, cooking dinner, and even changing the diapers. According to
Karlfried Graf von Dürckheim, author of the classic work *Daily Life as
Spiritual Exercise,* practice involves achieving technical mastery in some
activity, then repeating it endlessly. The constant repetition of simple activities frees consciousness from goal-orientation, enabling us to connect
with our innermost essence and to bring its illuminating presence into our
everyday affairs. Because all things and events potentially can trigger contact with our divine center, no special time need be set aside in living the
ordinary day as practice. Each moment serves as a "summons calling us to
recollect and prove ourselves."

"Whether in the kitchen or working at an assembly-belt, at the type-
writer or in the garden, talking, writing, sitting, walking or standing, dealing with some daily occurrence, or conversing with someone dear to us—
whatever it may be, we can approach it 'from within' and use it as an opportunity for the practice of becoming a true man [or woman]," writes
von Dürckheim.

"Daily tasks, by their very familiarity, serve to free us from the grip of
the ego and its quenchless thirst for success," he continues. "Even the practice and repeated effort to master something new can be put to the service
of the inner work. In everything one does it is possible to foster and maintain a state of being which reflects our true destiny. When this possibility
is actualized the ordinary day is no longer ordinary. It can even become an
adventure of the spirit."

*Do little things in an extraor-
dinary way; be the best one
in your line. You must not let
your life run in the ordinary
way; do something that
nobody else has done, something that will dazzle the
world. Show that God's creative principle works in you.
Never mind the past. Though
your errors be as deep as the
ocean, the soul itself cannot
be swallowed up by them.
Have the unflinching determination to move on your
path unhampered by limiting
thoughts of past errors.*

PARAMAHANSA YOGANANDA

ACHIEVING MASTERY

Like von Dürckheim, human-potential pioneer George Leonard, author
of *Mastery,* believes that practice can reveal the miracle of commonplace
life. Leonard views practice as positive activity pursued on a regular basis
not for any desired outcome, but for the sake of the activity itself. Involving body, mind, and spirit, it includes the traditional disciplines of Yoga,
Zen, and Aikido, along with such activities as gardening, jogging, pottery,
painting, and journal writing.

"When done with the right attitude, practice eliminates the tension, competitiveness, and fear of failure that contaminate much of our normal activity," says Leonard. "Gardening to win prizes or to impress our friends misses the point. But if we garden for the sheer joy of the activity, attending to each moment with full concentration and enthusiasm, we may in fact win prizes—but as a byproduct of our practice, never as the desired outcome. Because the benefits come to us effortlessly, we shortcircuit the anxiety that accompanies most activity."

True practice violates the canons of Western consumer culture, which encourages people to seek immediate gratification. According to television commercials, life at its best consists of an endless series of climactic moments. These acquisitive, ecstatic scenarios (when, for example, the boy gets the girl, or the new VCR, or the beer, or the foreign luxury car) subtly condition us to expect life's ideal rhythm to consist of moments of transport devoid of disciplined effort. We expect satisfaction to come from the outside, always as more—more pleasure, more possessions, more exciting relationships.

Such a distorted expectation, Leonard argues, goes against the built-in learning curve that leads to mastery. During the learning cycle we typically go up a little, down a little, then plateau for a while. If we diligently persist in learning, eventually we break through to a new level of competence. The process then repeats itself, but this time the plateau occurs at a higher level. Most learning consists of extended plateau periods in which we solidify progress through repetitive activity, followed by little spurts of improvement.

"To really grow, we must be willing to stay on the plateau without immediate gratification for quite some time before a new spurt of progress occurs," says Leonard. "Whether we feel elated or depressed, whether we're bored or inspired, whether we see rapid progress or none at all, if we just continue practicing without looking for results, the momentum of the practice eventually will take care of itself. The paradox is that if we give up our achievement orientation and competitive urge, the willingness not to make progress leads to progress."

To acquire mastery, Leonard recommends practicing with enough regularity and flexibility that "if we miss an occasional day, we won't feel damned for eternity." He also suggests practicing in a community, using the social environment to inspire committed, disciplined training.

Although our initial efforts may feel clumsy and unnatural, eventually practice picks up its own momentum and becomes a positive addiction. We begin to have more energy and improved health, along with increased mental clarity and self-esteem. If we are tempted to miss a day because of inertia or a self-pitying plea for rest, merely reflecting on the benefits of practice helps overcome the resistance of entrenched habit patterns.

With repeated practice, we give up our restless search for happiness in the next moment and learn that by inhabiting each moment with full awareness, we experience a deepening sensory aliveness and richness. Even such mundane activities as vacuuming or washing dishes can be elevated into practice by doing them with mindful precision, rather than with the disgruntled haste that normally attends troublesome chores.

"The best practice entices us with its endless possibilities," says Leonard. "It's like a journey in which as we advance one mile toward the destination, it recedes two miles toward the horizon. We're not discouraged by this, but in fact exhilarated, because a practice having infinite possibilities opens us to a life of constant learning. Every attainment serves as a platform for new and unceasing explorations in consciousness."

"How are you?"

"Perfect, thank you. I'm traveling incognito."

"Oh? As what are you disguised?"

"I am disguised as myself."

"Don't be silly. That's no disguise. That's what you are."

"On the contrary, it must be a very good disguise, for I see it has fooled you completely."

NASRUDIN

PAYING BILLS AND OTHER SPIRITUAL PRACTICES

To find the extraordinary in the ordinary, the sacred in the profane, sounds appealing in theory. But how do we realize it in practice? According to David Spangler, everyday spirituality requires mindfulness, an alert quality of mind that nonjudgmentally observes what happens in each moment. When mindfulness is present, a deep, penetrating awareness develops that gives insight into the world and ourselves. This penetrating quality of mind enables us to respond to the present with greater spontaneity and freedom.

Here are Spangler's tips on how domestic activities carried out with awareness can contribute to everyday spirituality:

Paying the bills. When confronting the monthly stack of bills, you may experience great amounts of worry, apprehension, and fear. You may think, "Where's the money coming from? How can I meet all my expenses?" The process also may bring up parental conditioning about money, to which you may react like an automaton.

Rather than react to them, observe these inner influences as they arise in your consciousness. Paying the bills then becomes a meditation that evokes your unresolved shadow issues about money. By observing your conditioned responses without judgment or condemnation, you develop a platform of awareness that helps weaken the automatic programs you've been running, enabling you to consciously choose more effective forms of behavior.

Grocery shopping. With our usual task-oriented mentality, a grocery store represents nothing more than a means to fulfill survival needs. But when experienced mindfully, the same store represents the end point of a huge distribution network that extends throughout the world, linking the productive activity of thousands of people to your neighborhood. From this point of view, the grocery store is really a purveyor of global consciousness.

When you shop without awareness, you fall prey to the tyranny of the everyday, caught in the deadening perception of mechanical routine and boredom. But when you shop consciously, you experience a sense of wonder and delight at the abundance of available foods. You also practice discrimination by selecting the healthiest foods, rather than those that are simply attractively packaged. Experiencing sensory aliveness and exercising discernment help convert a seemingly routine experience into a subtle, nonrepeatable exercise in wakefulness.

Parenting. All spiritual traditions encourage dropping personal preconceptions and expectations to see life as it is. No greater application of this spiritual practice exists than in raising children.

Don't worry; be happy.

MEHER BABA

The moment one gives close attention to anything, even a blade of grass, it becomes a mysterious, awesome, indescribably magnificent world in itself.

HENRY MILLER

The next message you need is right where you are.

RAM DASS

The next time you are tempted to say "You can't do that" or "You're a bad boy or girl," try dropping these limiting judgments and definitions, and let Zen mind—the beginner's mind of openness and limitless possibilities— take its place. Staying mindful requires a real effort, especially since familiarity tends to blunt perception. But by practicing a nonjudgmental, non-expectant perception with your children, you will watch with delight as they solve difficult homework problems you thought were beyond their ability or share their toys with friends without being told to do so.

37

MINDFULNESS FOR A HEALTHY WORLD

Mindfulness, the essential discipline of spiritual growth in Buddhism, has an important role to play in the health and survival of our world, according to Vietnamese meditation teacher Thich Nhat Hanh. Obsessed with acquiring possessions and filling up time with distracting activities, society makes it difficult for people to remain awake and mindful, he says. Forty thousand children die of hunger every day in the Third World, yet we continually ignore the immensity of this suffering. The purpose of meditation is to remember.

In *The Miracle of Mindfulness,* Nhat Hanh quotes a Buddhist scripture on how to cultivate mindfulness: "When walking, the practitioner must be conscious that he is walking. When sitting, the practitioner must be conscious that he is sitting. When lying down, the practitioner must be conscious that he is lying down. . . . No matter what position one's body is in, the practitioner must be conscious of that position. Practicing thus, the practitioner lives in direct and constant mindfulness of the body. . . ." He then adds: "The mindfulness of the positions of one's body is not enough, however. We must be conscious of each breath, each movement, every thought and feeling, everything which has any relation to ourselves."

Just a little practice of mindfulness can reveal how our habitual thoughts, attitudes, and actions contribute to suffering in the world or its alleviation. For example, when we pick up a Sunday newspaper, says Nhat Hanh in *Being Peace,* we can generate the awareness that printing such a heavy edition, weighing up to three or four pounds, may require cutting down an entire forest. Mindfulness reveals the causative link between a pleasurable habit normally taken for granted and the growing problem of deforestation. In this way, awareness doesn't take us *away* from the world as does the traditional spirituality; it moves us *toward* it, putting us squarely into the realm of ethical decision-making.

Similarly, before hopping into the car for a non-essential drive, we might remember that two million square miles of forest land have been destroyed by acid rain, caused in part by automobile emissions. With this awareness, we may decide to cancel our trip and to participate in other activities, such as meditative walking or work in the garden. And before eating a piece of meat, we can generate the awareness that large amounts of grain are required to produce one pound of beef. We may decide that eating a bowl of cereal does more to alleviate malnutrition than eating a meat dish. In fact, if Western countries would reduce consumption of meat and alcohol by 50 percent, says French economist François Peroux,

In order to be utterly happy the only thing necessary is to refrain from comparing this moment with other moments in the past, which I often did not fully enjoy because I was comparing them with other moments of the future.

ANDRÉ GIDE

this lifestyle change alone could prevent much of the suffering in Third World countries.

Besides abstaining from acts having harmful planetary consequences, Nhat Hanh believes we need to change our hurried, distracted personal habits, which do violence to our inner being. When we sip tea hurriedly and nervously with a friend in a café, thinking about upcoming business transactions, we not only do violence to our enjoyment of the tea but we destroy the living reality of the moment. On the other hand, drinking tea in a leisurely manner with a friend, savoring the beverage's subtle aroma and the unhurried give-and-take rhythm of conversation, creates a condition of inner calmness that in its own unobtrusive way may contribute to world peace.

"We seem to believe that our daily lives have nothing to do with the situation of the world," Nhat Hanh writes. "But if we do not change our daily lives, we cannot change the world. Drinking a cup of tea, picking up a newspaper, using toilet paper, all these things have to do with peace. Because nonviolence can be called awareness, we must be aware of what we are, of who we are, and of what we are doing."

I like reality. It tastes of bread.

JEAN ANOUILH

BREATHING THROUGH

In spite of all the information available about impending ecological catastrophe and the growing misery of one-half the world's population, we still tend to repress this awareness in our daily lives. In *Despair and Personal Power in the Nuclear Age,* Joanna Macy explains why: We are afraid that by opening up to the omnipresence of world suffering, we would be overwhelmed and shattered by feelings of dread, grief, anger, and powerlessness. Because the pain is so immense, we immunize ourselves against it by patterns of avoidance and psychic numbing.

Just as bereaved people need to release their numbed energies by grieving the loss of loved ones, Macy believes we need to release unacknowledged feelings about our threatened planet. Feelings of pain for the world are natural and healthy, she says, and unblocking them releases paralyzed energy, clears the mind for effective action, and reconnects us with the larger web of life. In feeling our distress on behalf of human life and fellow species, we unleash the power of compassion (which means "feeling with"), enabling us to act creatively for our common world.

Macy has developed exercises in what she terms "social mysticism" to help us break through to deeper levels of spiritual awareness. The following breathing-through exercise can help you deal with painful information without erecting defenses against it. It can help you remain alert while reading the bad news in newspapers, being present with people in pain, or preventing burnout if you are a social activist.

And this final story on awareness:

Buddhist meditation teacher Jack Kornfield was driving with his three-year-old daughter, Caroline, one night along some twisting roads in San Anselmo, California.

"Daddy," Caroline said, "the stars are moving."

"Oh, Caroline, that's probably an airplane," Kornfield responded. "Does it have red and green lights?"

"No, Daddy," she insisted, "the stars are moving."

I did not go to the "Maggid" of Mezeritch to learn Torah from him but to watch him tie his boot-laces.

A Hasidic Saint

Relax and center on your breathing. Visualize your breath as a stream flowing up through your nose, then down through your windpipe and lungs. As you breathe down through your lungs, picture a hole in the bottom of your heart. Now visualize the breath-stream passing through your heart and out through that hole to reconnect with the larger web of life around you.

As you continue breathing, drop all defenses and open your awareness to the suffering that is present in the world. Let it approach in the form of concrete images of your fellow beings in pain and need, in fear and isolation, in prisons, hospitals, tenements, or hunger camps. There is no need to strain for these images; they are present to you by virtue of our interexistence. Breathe in the vast and countless hardships not only of our fellow humans, but of our animal brothers and sisters as well, as they swim the seas and fly the air of this ailing planet.

Breathe in that pain like a dark stream, up through your nose, down through your trachea, lungs, and heart, and out again into the world net. Don't hang on to the pain, but let it pass through your heart and out again, surrendering it to the healing resources of life's vast web.

With Shantideva, the Buddhist saint, we can say, "Let all sorrows ripen in me." We help them ripen by passing them through our hearts, making good, rich compost out of all that grief, learning from it, enhancing our larger, collective knowing.

If you experience an ache in the chest, a pressure within the rib cage, that is all right. The heart that breaks open can contain the whole universe. Your heart is that large. Trust it, and keep breathing.

Exercises in Mindfulness

Mindfulness means being aware of what is happening in the present moment, according to Buddhist meditation instructor Joseph Goldstein. This alert, perceptive state, when combined with concentration, develops a mind that is balanced, poised, and focused. We need not limit the practice to formal periods of sitting meditation but can apply it to whatever we are doing, whether we are sitting, standing, walking, washing clothes, or eating dinner.

Here are several mindfulness exercises taken from *The Miracle of Mindfulness: A Manual on Meditation* by Thich Nhat Hanh:

Mindfulness while making tea. Prepare a pot of tea to serve a guest or to drink by yourself. Do each movement slowly, in mindfulness. Do not let one detail of your movements go by without being mindful of it. Know that your hand lifts the pot by its handle. Know that you are pouring the fragrant warm tea into the cup. Follow each step in mindfulness. Breathe gently and more deeply than usual. Take hold of your breath if your mind strays.

Washing the dishes. Wash the dishes relaxingly, as though each bowl is an object of contemplation. Consider each bowl as sacred. Follow your breath to prevent your mind from straying. Do not try to hurry to get the job over with. Consider washing the dishes the most important thing in life. Washing the dishes is meditation. If you cannot wash the dishes in mindfulness, neither can you meditate while sitting in silence.

Mindfulness of the positions of the body. This can be practiced in any time and place. Begin to focus your attention on your breath. Breathe quietly and more deeply than usual. Be mindful of the position of your body, whether you are walking, standing, lying, or sitting down. Know where you walk; where you stand; where you lie; where you sit. Be mindful of the purpose of your position. For example, you might be conscious that you are standing on a green hillside in order to refresh yourself, to practice breathing, or to stand. If there is no purpose, be mindful that there is no purpose.

Life is a school. Why not try taking the curriculum?

PROVERB

"Well, maybe you saw a falling star," Kornfield tendered. "They're so wonderful, and we get to see them once in a while."

"No, Daddy," she said adamantly, "the stars are moving."

Slightly annoyed, he answered, "Caroline, the stars do not move."

But because his daughter did not relent, Kornfield looked up and observed that each time the car rounded a bend, the stars behind the trees moved above them.

Reflecting on the situation, Kornfield said, "My commonsense intelligence told me that the stars are immobile, but when I actually put aside my expectations and looked without a predetermined conclusion, I realized that my daughter was right. In that humbling moment, I realized that Caroline sees with the eyes I try to teach people to use through meditation."

RESOURCES

Recommended Reading

Mastery, George Leonard (Dutton/New American Library, 1990). Explains how a regular practice or discipline—from Aikido to gardening to Yoga—can break our addiction to instant gratification and heighten the miracle of commonplace life.

Being Peace, Thich Nhat Hanh (Parallax Press, 1987). Sound advice on transforming spiritual practice into an engaged form of social activism to ease suffering in society.

The Experience of Insight: A Natural Unfolding, Joseph Goldstein (Shambhala Publications, 1987). A manual of insight meditation with practical guidelines for living.

Daily Life as Spiritual Exercise: The Way of Transformation, Karlfried, Graf von Dürckheim (Harper & Row, 1971). A spiritual classic about how to use everyday experience as a vehicle to express one's connection to transcendental reality.

Shambhala: The Sacred Path of the Warrior, Chogyam Trungpa, Rinpoche (Bantam Books, 1986). Gives instructions for living a sane, balanced life through developing meditative awareness.

Journey of Awakening: A Meditator's Guidebook, Ram Dass (Bantam Books, 1990). Offers a smorgasbord of meditation techniques, plus advice on avoiding the pitfalls of spiritual life.

Chop Wood, Carry Water, Rick Fields, Peggy Taylor, Rex Weyler, and Rick Ingrasci (Jeremy P. Tarcher, 1984). A down-to-earth guidebook for finding spiritual fulfillment in the modern world.

Inevitable Grace, Piero Ferrucci (Jeremy P. Tarcher, 1990). Explores spiritual and creative breakthroughs in the lives of great men and women.

Journal Writing

Many people have found journal-keeping to be a powerful way to start or deepen a spiritual practice. For insight and guidance, consider:

Progoff Intensive Journal Programs (Dialogue House, 80 East 11th Street, New York, NY 10003; 212-673-5880 or 800-221-5844). Developed by psychologist Ira Progoff, programs help participants integrate different aspects of their lives—relationships, work, social service, and spirituality—through a structured process of journal-keeping. Workshops are held nationwide at churches, retreat centers, mental-health centers, colleges, and other community institutions.

Spiritual Autobiography, a workshop taught by novelist Dan Wakefield, author of *Returning* (Doubleday, 1988) and *The Story of Your Life: Writing a Spiritual Autobiography* (Beacon Press, 1990), helps people explore their spiritual past and understand their present. Wakefield's approach includes drawings that stimulate childhood memories, timed writings about mentors and key experiences of connection and alienation, and reading aloud in an atmosphere of intimacy and trust. The workshop is available at holistic education centers nationwide.

Christina Baldwin (P.O. Box 27533, Minneapolis, MN 55427) also leads workshops on journal writing as a spiritual practice. If you can't make it to a workshop, her book *Life's Companion: Journal Writing as a Spiritual Quest* (Bantam/New Age, 1991) is an excellent guide.

For oral guidance in journal writing, try Kathleen Adams's sixty-minute audiotape *The Journal Tape: Techniques for Self-Discovery and Spiritual Growth Through Journal Writing.* The tape is available for $10.95 plus $3 shipping and handling from Sounds True Recordings, 1825 Pearl Street, Boulder, CO 80302; 303-449-6229.

LIVING OUR WESTERN SPIRITUAL TRADITIONS

Meeting the Challenge of Change

There is a famous Hasidic tale about Eisik, son of Yekel, an impoverished but devout man, who has a recurring dream about a glorious treasure that awaits him under a bridge in a distant city. To free himself from this strange obsession, Eisik travels to the foreign city and after much hardship discovers the bridge, which is guarded by soldiers. As he contemplates the treasure, the soldiers arrest him. In self-defense, Eisik relates his dream to the captain of the guard, who releases the simpleminded peasant on the condition that he never again believe in dreams.

To illustrate his point, the captain cites his own absurd experience: He dreams repeatedly of treasure located beneath the stove of a certain Eisik, son of Yekel, in a distant village. Bemused, the peasant returns home and, to his amazement, finds the treasure beneath his own stove.

NEGLECTED TRADITIONS

Like Eisik, the Judeo-Christian tradition has spiritual wealth so close to home that its discovery often comes as a revelation to those who have stormed Eastern temples in search of inner truth. That wealth takes the form of mystical, contemplative practices that for centuries have guided Western seekers on the path to union with God. Both contemplative

To Say Torah And Be Torah

This is what Rabbi Leib, son of Sarah, used to say about those rabbis who expounded the Torah: "What does it amount to—their expounding the Torah! A man should see to it that all his actions are a Torah and that he himself becomes so entirely a Torah that one can learn from his habits and his motions and his motionless clinging to God."

Christianity and the mystical branch of Judaism known as Kabbalah have developed uniquely Western forms of prayer and meditation. Largely neglected and obscured during the past several centuries, these practices have been resurfacing recently in response to a growing hunger for authentic spiritual experience among people dissatisfied wth mainstream religion.

"Every religion has a mystical core," writes Brother David Steindl-Rast, a Benedictine monk, in an article in *ReVision* magazine. "The challenge is to find access to it and to live in its power. In this sense, every generation of believers is challenged anew to make its religion truly religious."

In general, religion takes two forms: the *exoteric* and the *esoteric*. Followers of the exoteric approach subscribe to the doctrines, precepts, and rituals of their churches and synagogues, satisfied to relate to the transcendent without experiencing it directly. Followers of the esoteric approach, acknowledging that beliefs and rituals only point the way to an experiential goal, journey inward to merge with the transcendent ground of their being. For these people, labeled mystics by the religious establishment, the experience of higher states of awareness takes precedence over belief, meditative stillness over verbal prayer, and inner knowledge over reliance on external authority.

The number of people seeking mystical experience has been increasing recently in the West to fill a void created by mainstream religion, which frequently denies us access to own interiority. Sensing that their religious education is incomplete, many people are discovering the Christian mystical writings of St. John of the Cross, St. Theresa of Avila, and Meister Eckhart. Yearning to reignite the original fire stifled by religious formalism, they are exploring the profound forms of Western Yoga hidden in the Jewish mystical tradition of the Kabbalah, the Zohar, and Hasidism. In exploring the renaissance of interest in religion's deeper potential, we will first look at the Christian mystical tradition, then at its Jewish counterpart.

RETURN TO THE ROOT

Throughout the centuries, the mystical path in Christianity has been rooted in an unquenchable longing for divine love that prompts people to take up transformative disciplines. According to Evelyn Underhill in her classic study *Mysticism*, these practices lead to a purification of personal will, a process often compared to the self-immolation of a moth drawn to a flame.

As Underhill puts it: "[Mysticism] implies . . . the abolition of individuality; of that hard separateness, that 'I, Me, Mine' which makes of

My religion is very simple— my religion is kindness.

Dalai Lama

There is no room for God in him who is full of himself.

Hasidic Saying

THE POWER OF COMPASSION

Hasidism, the most popular form of Jewish mysticism, places great emphasis on the examples set by its *tzaddikim,* enlightened saints or masters known to have the same spiritual powers as described in classic Yoga texts. The following story about Rabbi Zusya, recounted by Martin Buber in *Tales of the Hasidim: The Early Masters,* illustrates the *tzaddik's* boundless compassion and ability to awaken people to spiritual life.

Once Rabbi Zusya came to an inn, and on the forehead of the innkeeper he saw long years of sin. For a while he neither spoke nor moved. But when he was alone in the room, which had been assigned to him, the shudder of vicarious experience overcame him in the midst of singing psalms and he cried aloud, "Zusya, Zusya, you wicked man! What have you done! There is no lie that failed to tempt you, and no crime you have not committed. Zusya, foolish, erring man, what will be the end of this?" Then he enumerated the sins of the innkeeper, giving the time and place of each as his own, and sobbed. The innkeeper had quietly followed this strange man. He stood at the door and heard him. First he was seized with dull dismay, but then penitence and grace were lit within him, and he woke to God.

I should like to call attention to the following facts. During the past thirty years, people from all civilized countries of the earth have consulted me. I have treated many hundreds of patients . . . Protestants . . . Jews [and a small number of Catholics]. Among all my patients . . . over thirty-five . . . there has not been one whose problem in the last resort was not that of finding a religious outlook on life. It is safe to say that every one of them fell ill because he had lost that which the living religions of every age have given to their followers, and none of them has really been healed who did not regain his religious outlook.

C. G. JUNG

man a finite isolated thing. It is essentially a movement of the heart, seeking to transcend the limitation of the individual standpoint and to surrender itself to ultimate Reality; for no personal gain, to satisfy no transcendental curiosity, to obtain no other-worldly joys, but purely from an instinct of love. . . . The mystic is 'in love with the Absolute' not in any idle or sentimental manner, but in that vital sense which presses at all costs and through all dangers toward union with the object beloved."

While people stereotypically think of mystics as world-denying introverts, Underhill sees them as humanity's "ambassadors to the absolute," whose contribution to civilization cannot be overestimated. She calls the fully blossomed mystic a "pioneer of humanity, a sharply intuitive and painfully practical person: an artist, a discoverer, a religious or social reformer, a national hero, a 'great active' amongst the saints."

Underhill distinguishes five stages in the classical Mystic Way. The first stage, *awakening*, sifts our center of gravity from the personal to the spiritual self and is often accompanied by intense feelings of joy and exaltation. The second stage, *purification of the self*, involves taking up ascetic practices aimed at detaching us from the tyranny of undisciplined sensory life and egotism.

Purgation results in the *illumination of the self*, also known as the first mystic life. The purified self enjoys a deep and satisfying intimacy with the absolute, yet the self remains separate from the source it contemplates in prayerful silence.

To annihilate this last remaining barrier, the mystic enters what St. John of the Cross calls the Dark Night of the Soul. This period of isolation, loneliness, and spiritual stagnation brings on the mystical death that totally purges self-will. It leads to what Underhill calls the *unitive life*, or second mystic life, in which we experience union with God not only during prayer and meditation, but during our mundane activities, such as washing dishes or scrubbing floors. This union brings about the mystic's *deification*, a transformation into God by direct participation in the life, power, and strength of divinity.

Unlike Eastern mystics, for whom the personal self dissolves, Christian mystics insist that self and God remain intact in the ultimate state of unity. Henry Susso, a fourteenth-century German mystic, says that in union "[the mystic's] being remains, but in another form." Writing of deification, St. John of the Cross maintains that "what is divine [is] so communicated to what is human that, without undergoing any essential change, each seems to be God."

Christianity has not been tried and found wanting; it has been found difficult and not tried.

G. K. CHESTERTON

No limits are set to the ascent of man, and to each and every one the highest stands open. Here it is only your personal choice that decides.

HASIDIC SAYING

PRAYERFULNESS

For great mystics as well as ordinary people, the heart of Christian life is prayer, defined simply as communication with God. According to Brother David Steindl-Rast, when the Bible urges us to "pray without ceasing," this means cultivating an openness to life's sacredness that is not restricted exclusively to periods of formal prayer. He calls this attitude prayerfulness, an attentive, childlike availability to moment-to-moment experience, much like mindfulness.

"It is never too late to recover that prayerfulness which is as natural to us as breathing," Steindl-Rast writes in *Gratefulness, the Heart of Prayer.* "The child within us stays alive. And the child within us never loses the talent to look with the eyes of the heart, to combine concentration with wonderment, and so to pray without ceasing. The more we allow the child within us to come into its own, the more mature we become in our prayer life. This is surely one meaning of the saying that we must 'become like children.'"

From this perspective, our formal prayers are like the poetry of prayer life. In Steindl-Rast's words: "A poem celebrates life and in that celebration becomes itself a high point of life. We look with the eyes of our heart, are overawed by the wonders we see, and celebrate that vision by a gesture that taps the very source of life. But it can be said much more simply: Prayer is grateful living."

A Rebbi's Proverb

If you always assume the person sitting next to you is the Messiah waiting for some simple human kindness—

You will soon come to weigh your words and watch your hands.

And if he/she so chooses not to reveal him/herself in your time—

It will not matter.

TRANSLATED
BY DANNY SIEGEL

MYSTICAL PRAYER

The contemplative tradition has given birth to uniquely Christian forms of mystical prayer, according to William Johnston, an Irish Jesuit who has served as a bridge-builder between East and West. The mystical journey begins with active meditation on the scriptures, a discursive activity in which we interiorize the great Christian mysteries. This matures into mystical contemplation, with what is known as its prayer of quiet, an experience of complete receptivity to Divine presence that grasps us in our core as a flame of love. Eventually, this experience deepens into the prayer of union—characterized by an undistracted focus on God—culminating in the mystical marriage, in which we become identified with God through love yet remain separate in nature and personality.

"These powerful, ecstatic experiences are the birthright of every Christian," says Mother Tessa Bielecki, a Carmelite nun and co-founder

TAKING A SPIRITUAL RETREAT

Why take a spiritual retreat? Many religious leaders point out that a period of extended introspection deepens our contact with the divine. According to Brother David Steindl-Rast, a Benedictine monk, a retreat offers a radically experiential approach to God. It also strengthens our daily practice. "It should be a booster and an accelerator of the spiritual journey—like taking a plane instead of a train or a horse to a certain destination—you go a long way in a short time," says Father Thomas Keating in *Catholic America: Self-Renewal Centers and Retreats*. Written by Patricia Christian-Meyer, *Catholic America* (1989, $13.95) gives readers instructions on finding centers and taking retreats at the more than six hundred Catholic centers in North America. Most are open to non-Catholics.

For those on an Eastern path, consult *Buddhist America: Centers, Retreats, Practices*, edited by Don Morreale (1988, $12.95). This directory includes both urban and rural meditations centers, as well as short essays on Buddhist teachings.

To find a nonsectarian listing of centers, check the *Traveler's Guide to Healing Centers and Retreats in North America*, by Martine Rudee and Jonathan Blease (1989, $11.95), which lists more than three hundred centers geared toward spiritual, mental, and physical renewal.

These books are published by John Muir Publications, P.O. Box 613, Santa Fe, NM 87404; 800-888-7504, weekdays only.

People think God has only become a human there—in his historical incarnation—but that is not so; for God is here—in this very place—just as much incarnate as in a human being long ago. And this is why God has become a human being: that God might give birth to you as the only begotten Son, and no less.

MEISTER ECKHART

of Nada Hermitage in Colorado, a monastic community of men and women. "Unfortunately, the churches don't always nourish the transcendental hunger we feel for this living experience of God. Countless Christians are starving to death because they're given stones instead of bread."

Many Westerners know a great deal about Buddhist, Hindu, and Sufi forms of meditation, she says, but very little about the Christian contemplative tradition. Yet the discoveries of the Desert Fathers, St. Francis of Assisi, Dame Julian of Norwich, and Thomas Merton in our own time have kept alive the flame of God-realization throughout the centuries, mainly in secluded monastic settings.

Today people from all walks of life—social workers, mechanics, businesspeople, homemakers, and college students—are discovering the riches in this tradition through communities and retreat centers such as Nada Hermitage that are springing up across the country. They go to these spiritual centers for weekend programs or for longer periods of retreat, then return home to integrate contemplative practices, such as mystical prayer, breathing exercises, mindful living habits, and innovative ritual, with their daily routines. In this sense, the monastic tradition, which has refined its inner technologies through centuries of practice, acts like a healer to modern society, which is suffering from an overdose of extroverted living.

Unlike monastic communities of the past that segregated the sexes, Nada Hermitage residents live as members of a celibate mixed community, an arrangement that Bielecki says makes for more balanced men and women. The community does not prescribe uniform practices for its members, but encourages an openness to other spiritual traditions. Although residents follow a basic weekly schedule of prayer, work, solitude, and play, she insists that the lively human atmosphere—not just the practicing of spiritual disciplines—leads to the unfolding of the spirit.

This unfolding has a practical social dimension. Bielecki links our problems with the environment, family stability, and education to an impoverished inner life. We are all naturally contemplative, she asserts, but when left unexercised, our innate powers of contemplation tend to atrophy, resulting in our alienated, stressful lifestyle.

Guidelines for a Contemplative Life

"Contemplation is not the privilege of the few, but the heritage of everyone—monk, mother, and business person," she says. "When action is inspired by contemplation, true renewal will take place in our religious traditions and in the social and political spheres. As Aldous Huxley said, contemplation is the only proven way of changing human behavior radically and permanently."

Bielecki offers the following suggestions for creating a spiritual foundation in our daily lives:

1. Live more closely to the rhythms of nature.
2. Live an ordered life. Many of us lose ourselves in distracting activities that obscure what is most meaningful in life. To keep our priorities straight, it is helpful to live more deliberately, with enough discipline to evoke and sustain a sensitivity to the inner life. To honor the rhythms and requirements of your life, be sure that the pattern you adopt is organic and flexible, rather than arbitrary and artificial.

I do not believe that anyone has the exclusive franchise on the Truth. What we have is a good approximation, for Jews, of how to get there. Ultimately, each person creates a way that fits his own situation. While there are differences between Jewish and non-Jewish approaches to mysticism in specific methods, observances, and rituals, there are no differences in the impact of the experiences themselves. When it comes to what I call the "heart stuff," all approaches overlap.

REB ZALMAN
SCHACHTER-SHALOMI

3. Live a balanced life. Find an equilibrium between outer and inner activity, work and play, and togetherness and solitude.

4. Consider beginning and ending the day with a tranquil, reflective practice. This may mean studying the scriptures, sitting in silence, praying some traditional prayers, doing yoga, jogging, or quietly watching the sun rise or set.

5. Live each day mindfully. Spiritual life requires no strongman acts, no glittering achievements or spectacular successes, but it does require passionate fidelity to the hundred little things of mundane life. As Jesus teaches in one of his parables, "Well done, good and faithful servant. . . . You have been faithful in the little things. Now I will entrust you with the bigger matters."

6. Try slowing down and living more leisurely. By learning the art of taking minute vacations during the workday, for example, we can neutralize the effects of the rat-race mentality.

7. Work in a tranquil, focused way. By eliminating our compulsive, frantic attitudes, we transform work into a spiritual practice.

8. Exercise the whole person—body, mind, and spirit. This may include physical exercise and reading to develop the intellectual life, along with meditation and prayer for the spirit.

9. Balance the day with poetry and play. To overcome the danger of rigid patterns of behavior, break the order of the day with disciplined wildness. Without this change of pace, we fall prey to the obsession of work and the staleness of conventional, routine piety.

10. Take a fresh look at celebrating the Sabbath. Consider spending one day a week being childlike, consciously breaking the deliberate, patterned life you have adopted. Without this destructuring, spiritual life becomes too serious and goal-oriented. Throughout the week, we live in the world of becoming, always striving to perfect ourselves spiritually. On the Sabbath, we drop all forms of becoming and inhabit the world of being, living in the end-state of all practice as if it had already occurred. From this most crucial of spiritual practices flows the inspiration to carry us through the entire week.

CENTERING PRAYER

Those who have practiced Transcendental Meditation may be surprised to learn that Christianity has its own time-honored form of mantra meditation. The technique, called Centering Prayer, draws on the spiritual exercises of the Desert Fathers, the English devotional classic *The Cloud of Unknowing,* and the famous Jesus Prayer practiced by the Eastern Christian tradition.

"In Centering Prayer we go beyond thought and image, beyond the senses and the rational mind, to that center of our being where God is working a wonderful work," writes Trappist Monk M. Basil Pennington in *Centering Prayer.* "When we go to the center, we leave behind time and place and separateness. We come to our Source and are in the Being from which we ever flow and in which we ever stand and apart from which we are not."

The technique involves focusing on a simple prayer word, such as *Jesus* or *love,* Pennington explains, then effortlessly sinking beneath discursive thought to the center where "the Spirit prays within us." His modern packaging of this ancient method has three rules:

1. At the beginning of the Prayer we take a minute or two to quiet down and then move in faith to God dwelling in our depths; and at the end of the Prayer we take several minutes to come out, mentally praying the "Our Father" or some other prayer.
2. After resting for a bit in the center in faith-full love, we take up a single, simple word that expresses this response and begin to let it repeat itself within.
3. When in the course of the Prayer we become *aware* of anything else, we simply gently return to the Presence by the use of the prayer word.

Reliance on a mantric centering device has a long history in the mystical canon of Christianity. For example, the anonymous author of the fourteenth-century work *The Cloud of Unknowing* gives this advice to a disciple: "If you want to gather all your desire into one simple word that the mind can easily retain, choose a short word rather than a long one. . . . But choose one that is meaningful to you. Then fix it in your mind so that it will remain there come what may. . . ." The author counsels that success in meditation depends on single-pointed concentration: "Let this word represent to you God in all his fullness and nothing less than the fullness of God. Let nothing except God hold sway in your mind and heart."

Centering Prayer also bears some resemblance to the Jesus Prayer practiced by the monks of the Eastern church. The technique consists of constantly repeating a simple, unvarying formula, "Lord Jesus Christ, Son of God, have mercy on me," often in coordination with the breath. The method draws the mind's normally scattered energies into the heart, where in simplicity and silence the practitioner experiences union with his or her source.

[We need] a deep mystical awakening the likes of which the planet has never witnessed before—a mystical awakening that is truly planetary, that draws out the wisdom and the mystic, the player and the justice maker from the wisdom traditions of all religions and cultures. Such a mystical awakening would surely birth that "peace on earth" for which creation longs—the promise given two thousand years ago in Bethlehem. Peace on earth cannot happen without peace with the earth and peace among all earth creatures.

MATTHEW FOX

TURNING EAST

Part of contemporary Judeo-Christian renewal involves an Eastern turn. To fill what many perceive as a spiritual vacuum, Westerners have embraced Eastern forms of meditation, such as Yoga and Zen Buddhism, with a transcendental hunger that has not been satisfied in churches and synagogues by traditional worship, sermons, and scripture reading. As Rabbi Zalman Schachter-Shalomi says in *The First Step,* "Judaism and all the other Western religions are suffering from having become ororverbalized and underexperienced."

It is precisely because Eastern meditative disciples stress direct experience and inner transformation that some Westerners have been wooed away from their churches and synagogues. Rather than break up a budding romance, however, Bede Griffiths, a Benedictine monk who has lived in India, thinks we should encourage the courtship. If the East−West dialogue continues, he says in *The Marriage of East and West,* Western religion will balance its overly rational, masculine nature with the more feminine, intuitive power of mind characteristic of Eastern religion.

In this cross-cultural dialogue, each religion must hold the fundamental truth of its own tradition, yet allow that tradition to grow as it is fertilized by other perspectives. As Griffiths explains:

> Every genuine religion bears witness to some aspect of the divine mystery, embodied in its myths and rituals, its customs and traditions, its prayer and mystical experience, and each has something to give to the universal Church. The narrow-mindedness which has divided the Christian churches from one another has also divided the Christian religion from other religions. Today we have to open ourselves to the truth in all religions. Each religion must learn to discern its essential truth and to reject its cultural and historical limitations. This may be a painful experience, a rejection of innumerable elements in religion which have grown up with the cultural and historical development of a religion and have often been identified with the religion itself. Yet this seems to be the only path open to humanity today.

COMING FULL CIRCLE

Hugo Enomiya-Lassalle, a German Jersuit priest who is also a Zen master, has experienced the reconciliation between East and West in his own life. Like Griffiths, he says that Eastern meditative disciplines help free us from the limitations of an oppressive rationalism. He also believes that the journey eastward comes full circle when we return to our Western religious

God, whose love and joy are present everywhere, can't come to visit you unless you aren't there.

ANGELUS SILESIUS

Separate yourself from all twoness. Be one on one, one with one, one from one.

MEISTER ECKHART

traditions with an awakened insight that transcends a merely intellectual assent to doctrine.

In *Living in the New Consciousness,* Enomiya-Lassalle outlines how Zen meditation can benefit Westerners:

- The development of insight—a natural by-product of Zen practice—awakens our faith as we penetrate deeper into the mystery of God beyond conventional discursive thinking.
- We experience a new appreciation of the scriptures through an intuitive understanding. Doubts based on textual disharmonies dissolve as the soul penetrates its own depths to encounter all-embracing existence.
- Our increased capacity to concentrate makes it easier to keep attentive during prayer and liturgical ceremonies.
- Increased self-control and inner freedom make it easier to serve others. As we meditate away envy, hatred, and dissatisfaction, we find it easier to make ethical progress.
- As our dedication deepens and our practice intensifies, we experience loving union with God that is typical of Christian mysticism. This brings freedom from fear and doubt, along with deep peace and joy.

God expects but one thing of you, and that is that you should come out of yourself in so far as you are a created being and let God be God in you.

MEISTER ECKHART

A NEW RELIGIOUS PARADIGM

Perhaps the most outspoken critic of mainstream Christianity in general and the Catholic Church in particular is Dominican priest Matthew Fox. The iconoclastic theologian publicly has accused the Church of being antimystical, sexist, anthropocentric, and undemocratic. Throughout most of 1989 he officially was silenced by the Vatican for being a fervent feminist, supporting the ordination of women, crusading for sexual issues not sanctioned by the Church, and denying the doctrine of original sin.

Fox's critique of contemporary Christianity revolves around what he terms "creation-centered spirituality," which offers a new religious paradigm in the West. In its obsession with original sin and salvation, he says, the Church considers nature fallen and seeks God not in nature but in the individual soul. This fall-redemption model of spirituality—patriarchal, ascetic, and guilt-ridden—distrusts the body and the senses and promotes mystical practices that mortify the flesh.

Creation-centered spirituality, which traces its roots to the biblical tradition and to a number of medieval mystics, does not stress original sin but what Fox calls "original blessing," a celebration of the natural world and its beauty. Profoundly feminist in scope, this spirituality takes a gracious, compassionate attitude toward the body, sensory life, and the Earth. Rather than mortify the flesh, creation spirituality sings its praises.

Like Mother Tessa Bielecki, Fox sees a direct relationship between the denial of mysticism by churches and synagogues and our problems with unemployment, pollution, youth despair, and social injustice. A culture that denies the mystical impulse promotes negative addictions to drugs, crime, alcohol, consumerism, and militarism. By not providing ritual initiation into transcendent states of consciousness, it encourages us to seek outside stimulants to provide the meaning in life we cannot find from within.

Fox's revolutionary prescription for breaking this addictive cycle is to awaken to the mystical revelation that God is in everything and everything is in God. Called *panentheism*, this form of mysticism proclaims that all of creation is sacred: stars, galaxies, whales, soil, water, trees, and humans. Fox calls the Western term for the Divine presence in all things the Cosmic Christ, the "I am" in every creature.

"We must all birth the Cosmic Christ in our being and doing, for that is why we exist," Fox writes in *The Coming of the Cosmic Christ*. "Is it not the purpose of incarnation in Jesus to reveal the immanence of the Cosmic Christ in the sufferings and dignity of each creature of the earth? As we discover our own 'I am' and the ecstasy and pain of the Divine One in us, we gradually grow into an 'I-am-with' others (Emmanuel, 'God-with-us'). We grow into compassion and in doing so the divine 'I am' takes on flesh once again. Since God alone is the Compassionate One, as we grow into compassion we also grow into our divinity."

THE NEW STORY

Besides uniting the "above" with the "below," the transcendent with the immanent, and the spirit with the body, creation spirituality also reconciles religion with science. While fall-redemption spirituality often opposes science, creation spirituality embraces it for revealing the ongoing story of the creation of the universe. Thomas Berry, a renowned ecotheologian, calls the 15-billion-year-old drama of our emerging universe the New Story. Reconciling empirical science with mysticism, the New Story says that the emergence of galaxies, our solar system, planet Earth, and all its life forms, including humanity, has both a physical and a spiritual dimension.

In Berry's view, the Divine reveals itself primarily through nature's manifestations: the world of wind and rain, of pineland forests and prairie grasses, of meadow flowers and flowing streams. As we diminish

The best form is to worship God in every form.

NEEM KAROLI BABA

For a man to be called a Man, he must live his life as an offering before God.

ISRAEL OF RIZHYN

the natural world, we destroy modes of Divine presence, impoverishing our inner, psychic connection to life. To reverse this devastation, he proposes a new religious orientation based on our interdependence with the Earth and the community of life species.

"Christians should seek nourishment not only from the Bible, but from the book of nature," Berry insists. "To do this, we must overcome our particular form of species selfishness, which has enabled us to separate ourselves from nature and to wantonly exploit the world's resources. We must rethink the Earth not as a collection of objects, but as a community of subjects to whom we are committed by bonds of courtesy and compassion. Without this new spiritual orientation, the devastation of the Earth will continue to lead to the devastation of religion and our souls."

JEWISH RENEWAL

Just as the winds of change are sweeping through Christianity, they are reinvigorating the practice of Jewish spirituality. This renewal involves rediscovering the Jewish mystical tradition, with its instructions for achieving ecstatic states of consciousness, redefining the meaning of traditional commandments sanctioned by the Torah (the Hebrew scriptures), and creating new forms of liturgy that address our concerns with ecology and feminism.

"Every tradition begins in the white heat of transcendent realization, then gradually over time suffers hardening of the religious arteries through the unavoidable process of institutionalization," says Rabbi Zalman Schachter-Shalomi, founder of the P'nai Or Religious Fellowship in Philadelphia and a pioneer of Jewish renewal. "By rediscovering the original divine impulse that gave birth to Judaism, we are rejuvenating it and evolving new forms to house the spirit in the modern world."

In 1987, with the encouragement of psychologist Jean Houston, Reb Zalman started the P'na Or Wisdom School, a mystery school that guides both non-Jews and Jews through the transformational work he termed "soul making." Through song, dance, prayer, movement, and celebration, Jews gain an intimacy with mystical practices that until recently were associated only with the East.

"In the past several decades, many Jews were initiated into spiritual life by excursions into Eastern religions," he points out. "A growing number of these cross-cultural explorers are now returning to their own tradition, trying to understand how their Zen, Sufi, and Vedantic experiences relate to their religious roots. Because exoteric Judaism doesn't provide the reality maps they need to explain and build on their experiences, they're embracing the mystical teachings of Judaism with all the joy and familiarity of a homecoming."

Inner Roadmap

The inner, mystical aspect of Judaism is called Kabbalah, which means "that which is received." According to Z'ev ben Shimon Halevi, a popularizer of the Kabbalah, it represents "the perennial Teaching about Attributes of the Divine, the nature of the universe and the destiny of man, in Judaic terms." Imparted by revelation and handed down over the centuries through a secret oral tradition, kabbalistic teachings, once considered strange and obscure, are now joining the marketplace of ideas as people seek out ancient wisdom to solve modern problems.

Kabbalists base their inner work on the Torah, which imparts wisdom on two levels: exoterically as codes of law, and esoterically as hidden metaphysical truths that are revealed through a deeper investigation of the

A rabbi whose congregation does not want to drive him out of town isn't a rabbi.

TALMUDIC SAYING

WALK OF THE COSMOS

According to the New Story (see page 60), which reveals the ongoing evolution of the universe, human beings have roots in a cosmological process that is 15 billion years old. To experience our cosmic identity on a personal level, Sister Miriam Theresa MacGillis, one of Thomas Berry's foremost interpreters, has created a ritual called the Walk of the Cosmos.

To do this ritual, take a piece of wool or rope about seventy feet long and arrange it on the floor in the shape of an enormous spiral. Then place a candle at the center to represent the beginning of the universe. Use other candles to measure off major events in evolution, such as the formation of the solar system, the creation of the biosphere, the emergence of unicellular life, the emergence of life from the sea, the appearance of land plants and hominids, and finally the appearance of human beings. Lights near the end of the rope commemorate significant events in human history, such as the births of Moses and Jesus, the discovery of America, the splitting of the atom, and the recent ending of the Cold War.

When everything is in place, go to the center one by one, light your candles, and then take the evolutionary walk to the accompaniment of inspiring music. When you arrive at the end of the process, call out your names: "The universe has become Mary!" or "The universe celebrates James."

"This moving ceremony drives home that each one of us was born at the conception of the universe and is integrally linked to its evolutionary unfoldment," Sister Miriam says. "Such a realization gives us a sense of cosmic identity, self-esteem, and purpose to aid us on the journey of self-actualization."

God has no religion.

MAHATMA GANDHI

texts. Traditionally, students of the path must undergo preparatory work, such as the cultivation of ethical virtues and a cleaving to God, known as *devekhut*. After sufficient purification, the seeker may choose from a wide variety of techniques, such as visualization of the letters of the Hebrew alphabet to center the mind, breathing exercises, chanting, mantra meditation, and body movement, all aimed at unifying the individual with higher levels of being.

Kabbalists chart the seeker's progress from the mundane world into higher states of consciousness by means of the Tree of Life, according to psychologist Edward Hoffman, author of *The Way of Splendor*. As seen in the diagram on page 61, each of the ten *sephirot* (or spheres) on the glyph represents the movement of Divine energy as it manifests in the cosmos and in the individual human soul. By using this inner roadmap, the meditator lifts his or her consciousness from the everyday world of Kingdom, ascends in stages to Beauty (seen by some Kabbalists as the Higher Self), then continues onward through transpersonal realms to the transcendental Crown, a point of pure, formless being untouched by the pairs of opposites. Beyond this lofty height lies the *Ein Sof*, the boundless radiance of the infinite. After dwelling briefly in this endless light, the meditator visualizes the light descending through each of the spheres, healing and transforming his or her being, from the highest to the most earthbound levels.

Inner development, Kabbalists say, consists of balancing the feminine forces on the left pillar with the masculine forces on the right, creating a harmonization of forces in the central pillar. Some commentators compare the movement of energy on the Tree to the movement of energy in the human body.

"Jewish visionaries teach that the divine force circulates through the human Sefirotic system," writes Hoffman. "In striking parallel to various Eastern viewpoints like Tibetan Buddhism, Kabbalistic thinkers have insisted that this flow of energy underlies our mental and physical health. They have taught that through conscious exercises, we can channel this flow to awaken higher potentialities."

The Kabbalah Democratized

In the eighteenth century, Rabbi Israel ben Eliezer, known as the Baal Shem Tov (Master of the Good Name), took the often abstruse practices of Kabbalah and made them available to ordinary people throughout Eastern Europe. The movement he founded, Hasidism, has become the most widely recognized form of Jewish mysticism. With its highly devotional emphasis, Hasidism invokes holiness not by mortification and fasting, but by joyous celebration of the Divine in the everyday world. The Hasid prays with an open heart, overflowing with mystical fervor that unites the world of Kingdom with the higher spheres of the Tree through a boundless love for the Absolute.

"The objective of hasidic spirituality is to become aware of God and united to God everywhere and in all things with sustained, passionate and

To love God truly, one must first love man. And if anyone tells you that he loves God and does not love his fellow-man, you will know that he is lying.

HASIDIC SAYING

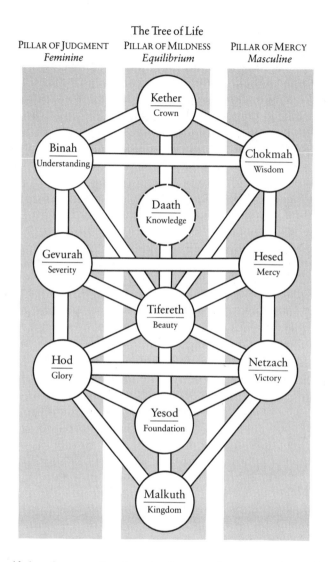

The Tree of Life

PILLAR OF JUDGMENT
Feminine

PILLAR OF MILDNESS
Equilibrium

PILLAR OF MERCY
Masculine

Inspired by the idea that not only is God necessary to man, but that man is also necessary to God, that man's actions are vital to all worlds and affect the course of transcendent events, the Kabbalistic preachers and popular writers sought to imbue all people with the consciousness of the supreme importance of all actions. . . . An architect of hidden worlds, every pious Jew is, partly, the messiah.

ABRAHAM JOSHUA HESCHEL

joyful self-abandonment," writes theology professor Monika Hellwig in *Western Spirituality: Historical Roots, Ecumenical Routes.* "For the Hasidim as elsewhere in Judaism, the quest for mystical union with God was not understood to demand a renunciation of family life. . . . It is not a matter of redeeming souls . . . out of the world of human affairs . . . but rather a matter of redeeming that world."

To bring Heaven down to Earth, Hasids cultivate a number of virtues, such as *hitlahavut,* the fire of ecstasy; *avoda,* work or service in everyday activities; *kavana,* single-minded devotion to God; and *shiflut,* humility based on an acceptance of one's uniqueness. With its emphasis on banishing melancholy and rediscovering joy, Hasidic spirituality has a particular appeal to those of us seeking what Carlos Castaneda's mentor, Don Juan, calls a "path with heart."

"The resurgence of Kabbalah and Hasidism are part of the paradigm shift affecting not only Jews, but the entire planet," says Reb Zalman. "While there are differences between Jewish and non-Jewish approaches to mysticism in specific methods, observances, and rituals, there are no differences in the impact of the experiences themselves. All the religions fit together into an organic whole, and we need the contribution of each tradition for the health and renewal of our world."

THE BIBLE: A MYSTERY TEXT

Once we learn to decipher it with the proper metaphysical understanding, the Bible can be a mystery text that reveals the secrets of existence. When read literally, Bible stories often seem puzzling and contradictory to the modern reader. When interpreted kabbalistically, however, these same stories take on archetypal significance, describing in symbolic terms the soul's journey from material bondage to the enlightened state of freedom called the Promised Land.

In *Kabbalah: Tradition of Hidden Knowledge*, Z'ev ben Shimon Halevi interprets some familiar biblical themes from *Genesis* and *Exodus* from this broader perspective. The story of Jacob's family descending into Egypt, he says, describes the soul's incarnation into physical life. The soul has a natural affinity with the Upper Worlds, but when it inhabits Egypt (which means "confined" or "limited" in Hebrew), it forgets its Divine heritage and becomes enslaved to materiality.

When the yearning for our true homeland grows strong enough, Halevi points out, Moses, the liberator, appears in our consciousness. The prince of Egypt first must kill an Egyptian, symbolic of our worldly identity, before wandering through the desert to find Jethro, his spiritual teacher. Moses's long training period involves tending Jethro's sheep, which refers to disciplining the instincts and impulses of the body and psyche. This arduous training culminates in the Burning Bush episode, the moment when we make an indissoluble inner connection and receive the calling to greater spiritual responsibility.

Moses must lead his people from bondage into a land flowing with milk and honey—in other words, into enlightened consciousness. In personal terms, this refers inwardly to educating the undisciplined parts

Holy Spirit,
giving life to all life,
moving all creatures,
root of all things,
washing them clean,
wiping out their mistakes,
healing their wounds,
you are our true life,
luminous, wonderful,
awakening the heart
from its ancient sleep.

HILDEGARD OF BINGEN

THE TEN PRINCIPLES OF SERVICE

Hasidic masters frequently impart their wisdom in unconventional ways. The following tale, retold by Martin Buber in *Tales of the Hasidim: The Early Masters,* concerns an exchange between Rabbi Dov Baer of Mezritch, the great *maggid,* or preacher, to his disciple, Rabbi Zusya, on the theme of service.

"I cannot teach you the ten principles of service," says the *maggid.* "But a little child and a thief can show you what they are."

> From the child you can learn three things:
> He is merry for no particular reason;
> Never for a moment is he idle;
> When he needs something, he demands it vigorously.
> The thief can instruct you in seven things:
> He does his service by night;
> If he does not finish what he has set out to do, in one night, he devotes the next night to it;
> He and those who work with him love one another;
> He risks his life for small gains;
> What he takes has so little value for him that he gives it up for a very small coin;
> He endures blows and hardship, and it matters nothing to him;
> He likes his trade and would not exchange it for any other.

Many great geniuses, mystics and saints—such as Walt Whitman, William Blake, Mother Teresa, Buckminster Fuller, and countless others—have had the inner resources to foster their own growth, in spite of society's obstacles. However, many more—ordinary people with ordinary levels of intelligence or unglamorous occupations—could possibly be encouraged toward healthier self-development, toward self-transcendence, if schools, churches and other social institutions were sympathetic to the values of this work.

MARSHA SINETAR

of ourselves and outwardly to instructing others seeking spiritual knowledge.

Escaping from physical and psychological bondage often precipitates a dramatic series of crises—the so-called ten plagues—as our center of gravity shifts from the ego to the spiritual self, Halevi explains. As the ego becomes progressively purified of its Egyptian identity, we may undergo changes in our personal and work relationships. After this initial housecleaning, we then cross the Red Sea, a decisive turning point indicating real commitment to spiritual development. While our old habits—symbolized by the complaining Israelites—may clamor periodically to return to the fleshpots of the unawakened condition, there is no going back. At this point, our exodus from Egypt has become a living reality, and we journey through the desert of our psyche in search of our spiritual homeland.

REDISCOVERED RICHES

After ferreting out the secrets of Eastern spirituality, many Jews are finding similar treasures within their own traditions. Rabbi Ted Falcon, the founder of Makom Ohr Shalom, a synagogue for Jewish meditation in Tarzana, California, was practicing Eastern forms of meditation in the early 1970s when he came upon these riches quite by accident.

"I had just finished praying the 'Shema Yisrael,' Judaism's most important profession of faith, which reads, 'Hear, O Israel: The Eternal is our God, the Eternal is One,'" Falcon says. "I was pondering the subsequent verses, which instruct us to love the Eternal with all our heart, soul, and strength and to keep these words in mind when we lie down and when we rise up, when we rest at home and when we walk on our way. Suddenly I realized that these verses were instructions for chanting a mantra!"

The Shema uses two Divine names to indicate the immanent and transcendent nature of God, Falcon explains. The word *Adonai* ("the Eternal") refers to the transcendent aspect of God; *Eloheynu* ("our God") stands for God manifesting within nature and ourselves. Hence the prayer/mantra proclaims the same realization uttered by ancient Vedic seers: The inside and the outside are one—as above, so below.

Falcon says that meditating on the Shema awakens us to the primordial space from which these sacred words emerge. Here are his instructions for how to proceed:

1. Find a quiet space where you won't be interrupted for fifteen or twenty minutes. At first, you might want to have a clock you can check along the way.
2. Sit comfortably. Gradually feel your body relax. Take a few deep and easy breaths and let your eyes close. Enter into your meditation with a "Shalom," with a feeling of calmness and peace.
3. Gently begin reciting the six words of the Shema in your mind: *Shema Yisrael: Adonai Eloheynu Adonai Echad* ("Hear, O Israel: The Eternal is our God, the Eternal is One"). Bring your attention back to these words when your mind wanders.
4. After a few minutes, move into the heart of the Shema, the two central words: *Adonai Eloheynu.* Stay with these two words until you are ready to conclude.
5. Then move outward to the six words again. After a few minutes, take some deep breaths and return to normal waking awareness. After stretching and resting for a few moments, you may want to record your experiences and insights in a meditation journal.

Undoubtedly, the most fundamental principle of Judaism's entire visionary way is that the cosmos is a coherent and meaningful whole. The major teachers of this longstanding body of knowledge have insisted repeatedly that each aspect of creation is vitally connected to everything else. Works like the Zohar, *the "bible" of Kabbalistic lore, stress over and over that all the various dimensions of existence . . . are intimately interwoven. . . . Indeed, perhaps the most central message of this evocative and complex volume is its often mentioned dictum that "As above, so below." A vast unseen web is said to link each of us. In its time-honored metaphor, we are all individual buds of being on the great Tree of Life, whose roots lie in heaven.*

EDWARD HOFFMAN

KEEPING ECO-KOSHER

A renewed Judaism remains fully rooted in its ancient traditions but seeks to infuse its rituals and practices with an innovative spirit appropriate to our age. For example, keeping kosher traditionally involves refraining from eating pork or shellfish and slaughtering animals in the least painful, most respectful way. But the practice of *kashrut* is evolving in our time, in part because of environmental and social issues unknown to rabbis two thousand years ago.

With this in mind, Rabbi Nahum Ward of Congregation Shir Hadash in Los Gatos, California, and Shelley Mann, a member of Guardians of the Earth, a national Jewish environmental group, have developed guidelines for keeping eco-kosher. To honor the Earth's living systems, they recommend selecting foods that are produced, transported, and packaged in a way that is environmentally sustainable. Because they view *kashrut* as governing not only how animals are slaughtered but how they are raised, they avoid the products of animals that have not been raised humanely and respectfully.

Ward and Mann have further extended *kashrut* to include the people who produce and prepare our food. They recommend using our food dollars to support growers and producers who treat their workers humanely. To promote the health of our bodies and the amelioration of world hunger, they favor a vegetarian diet of mostly whole grains, fresh fruits and vegetables, legumes, and nuts.

"Making conscious choices about the food we eat leads to an awareness of our relationship to the environment," they say. "Our practice of kashrut teaches us much about our ties to the living world and the sanctity of all life."

If the only prayer you say in your whole life is "thank you," that would suffice.

MEISTER ECKHART

FEMINIST JUDAISM

The integration of women into Judaism's patriarchal tradition is at the cutting edge of religious transformation in the West, according to Rabbi Lynn Gottlieb, one of the first women rabbis ordained in the United States and founder of Naḥlat Shalom Congregation in Albuquerque, New Mexico.

"From a feminist perspective, we approach the Torah as our sacred text, yet we stand in suspicion of it," says Gottlieb. "Jewish feminists draw on the prophetic tradition, with its emphasis on justice and the liberation of the oppressed, and seek to empower all members of the community by valuing their full humanity."

On a practical level, this means ordaining women, including them in a *minyon* (the ten adults required for a prayer service), creating rituals and liturgy that reflect feminist concerns, and including women in the process of decision-making. Perhaps the movement's most revolutionary feature involves decentralizing the rabbi's authority by drawing on the community's experience and wisdom to make decisions.

When we honor God as an exclusively transcendent power, we place the source of authority outside ourselves and relate to power in a hierarchical way, Gottlieb explains. But when we honor God as having an immanent dimension, dwelling within us, we democratize our access to wisdom by creating egalitarian forms of spirituality.

"Feminist Judaism encourages a plurality of points of view, rather than a stultifying uniformity that kills creativity," she says. "Our community gives voice to the full spectrum of religious orientation: those who are traditional, those who are secular and atheistic, and those who are 'New Age' in their attitudes. Feminist spirituality integrates all these perspectives into a harmonious community that acknowledges these differences and is enriched by them through dialogue, storytelling, and ritual drama. This non-judgmental acceptance of all points of view, without creating a monolithic standard of correct belief and practice that all must endorse, represents one of feminism's great contributions to spirituality."

LIVING IN THE PARENTHESIS PERIOD

As modern seekers rediscover their ancient traditions, a much-needed mutation in Western religion is beginning to take place, according to Rabbi Zalman Schachter-Shalomi. The new religious paradigm emphasizes planetary stewardship, the widespread dissemination of esoteric knowledge, an honoring of the feminine aspect of divinity, and an appreciation of the mystical core that unites all religions, transcending their cultural and historical differences. Once these elements fertilize Western religion, our reinvigorated traditions, with their combined wisdom and experience, can become more effective agents in promoting peace among nations and in healing our planet.

In the meantime, we are living in what philosopher Jean Houston calls a parenthesis period, a time when the old is decaying and the new spiritual values have yet to assert themselves. "We are like explorers grop-

Man is a ladder placed on the earth and the top of it touches heaven. And all his movements and doings and words leave traces in the upper world.

HASIDIC SAYING

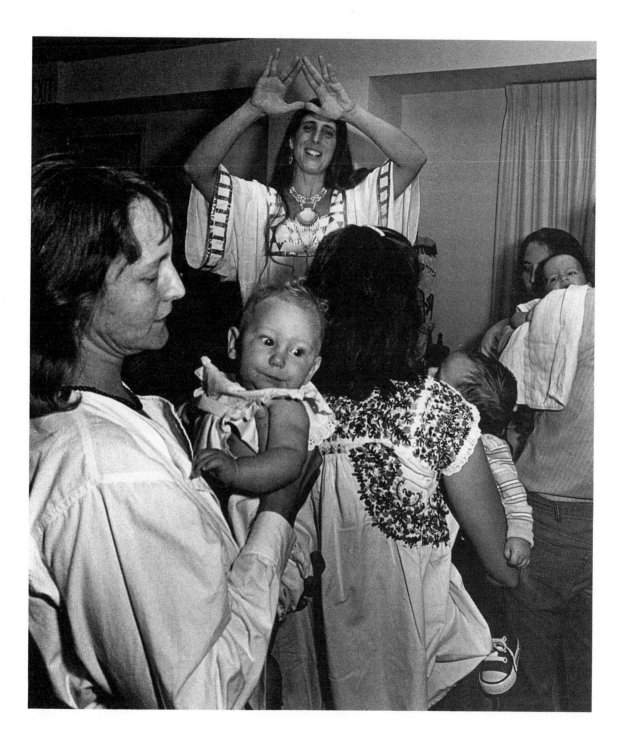

ing toward the new without blueprints to guide us," observes Sister Miriam Theresa MacGillis, director of Genesis Farm, a center for education in Earth stewardship in Blairstown, New Jersey. "We're leaving Egypt—the known—but haven't arrived yet at the Promised Land, with its fully articulated spiritual vision and practices to sustain it. As we live through this transitional age, we sense that the current flowering within our Western traditions will not negate or destroy the achievements of former ages, but carry them forward to a higher level of development."

RESOURCES

Recommended Reading

The Way of Splendor: Jewish Mysticism and Modern Psychology, Edward Hoffman (Shambhala Publications, 1981). A clear and concise introduction to the mystical wisdom of Judaism and its contemplative practices.

The Coming of the Cosmic Christ, Matthew Fox (Harper & Row, 1988). Calls for Christian renewal through creation spirituality, a mystical approach that celebrates the natural world and its beauty.

The Marriage of East and West, Bede Griffiths (Collins Sons, 1982). Explores how Western religion can be renewed through exposure to the intuitive wisdom of Eastern religion.

The First Step: A Guide for the New Jewish Spirit, Rabbi Zalman Schachter-Shalomi with Donald Gropman (Bantam Books, 1983). A guide for integrating the traditional wisdom of Judaism with the demands of the modern world.

Ordinary People as Monks and Mystics, Marsha Sinetar (Paulist Press, 1986). Explores how people seek self-transcendence in the conditions of everyday life.

Mysticism, Evelyn Underhill (Meridian Books, 1955). The classic text on mysticism in the Western tradition.

Ten Rungs: Hasidic Sayings, Martin Buber (Shocken Books, 1947). Tales and aphorisms of the Hasidim, whose approach emphasizes a joyous celebration of the Divine in everyday life.

Christian Mysticism

Friends of Creation Spirituality (160 East Virginia Street, Suite 290, San Jose, CA 95112; 415-482-4984). Matthew Fox's group runs workshops, produces and distributes audio- and videotapes, and publishes *Creation Spirituality* ($20/year), a bimonthly magazine that features essays by Fox and articles by scientists, mystics, artists, and social activists. Fox's *Institute in Culture and Creation Spirituality* at Holy Name College (3500 Mountain Boulevard, Oakland, CA 94619; 415-436-1046) offers a nine-month Master's degree program and a four-month sabbatical certificate.

The Spiritual Life Institute (Nada Hermitage, Box 219, Crestone, CO 81131; 719-256-4778). Co-founded by Mother Tessa Bielecki, the retreat offers the experience of rediscovering the mystical roots of Christianity in community.

Jewish Mysticism

P'nai Or Religious Fellowship (7318 Germantown Avenue, Philadelphia, PA 19119-1793; 215-242-4074). Founded by Reb Zalman Schachter-Shalomi, P'nai Or offers programs, retreats, and workshops for those interested in Jewish mysticism and renewal. The organization can put you in touch with others in your area who are exploring a more experiential approach to Judaism or groups that are members of the international Network of Jewish Renewal Communities.

The National Havurah Committee (9315 SW 61st Court, Miami, FL 33156; 305-666-7349) can connect you with a local *havurah* or send you information on starting your own.

The Third Jewish Catalog, compiled and edited by Sharon and Michael Strassfeld (1980, $14.95), is a comprehensive sourcebook for exploring Jewish traditions, customs, rituals, social action, and ethics. Available from Jewish Publication Society of America, 1930 Chestnut Street, Philadelphia, PA 19103; 215-564-5925.

CHAPTER 4

THE PATH OF SHAMANISM

Renewing Our Connection to Native Ways on the Earth

Lying on the floor of your room, with a companion beating a drum in the background, you leave the domain of everyday thinking and enter an altered state of consciousness for a journey into the spirit world. As the drum's monotonous rhythm continues, you visualize entering an opening in a hollow tree stump, then descending a steep tunnel that leads to a bright and marvelous landscape, shimmering with dreamlike beauty and the lure of adventure. Fully awake in the Lower World and aware of your mission, you follow a stream to flowery meadowlands, where a hawk lands on your outstretched arm and regards you with a fixed, insistent gaze. This is your power animal, the guardian spirit whose powers you consult for healing purposes and wisdom.

You pose a question about how to heal a relationship that has caused you much pain. In the wordless communion between spirit guide and seeker, a message wells up from within your heart: Be forgiving. Though simple, the message strikes you with the authority of revelation. Filled with gratitude, you release the guardian spirit, return through the tunnel to everyday reality, then "dance your animal" through a series of ritualized movements that honor your spiritual source.

In the comfort of our own homes rather than in remote jungle settings, many of us—homemakers, businesspeople, and psychologists—are

This we know. The earth does not belong to man; man belongs to the earth. This we know. All things are connected like the blood which unites one family. All things are connected. Whatever befalls the earth befalls the sons of the earth. Man does not weave the web of life, he is merely a strand in it. Whatever he does to the web, he does to himself.

CHIEF SEATTLE

making journeys like this one as we rediscover shamanism, the planet's oldest spiritual tradition. At first, we may dabble in shamanism because of its non-Western, mystical nature, its promise of bizarre, otherworldly experiences, or its eco-spiritual world view. Later, as familiarity deepens, we view it as a legitimate spiritual path, with time-honored practices for developing self-knowledge, diagnosing illness, and obtaining guidance in our professional lives and personal relationships.

TECHNICIANS OF ECSTASY

The term *shaman* refers to people in hunting-and-gathering societies who function as medicine men and women, sorcerers, witch doctors, and seers. With a tradition reaching back tens of thousands of years into the Upper Paleolithic period and perhaps further back into Neanderthal times, shamanism represents one of humanity's earliest attempts to connect with the Upper and Lower worlds, to directly experience the maxim "As above, so below."

Mystical, priestly, and political figures, described as technicians of ecstasy by scholar Mircea Eliade, shamans journey to unearthly realms, acting as intermediaries between the sacred and mundane worlds. As healers and visionaries, they minister to the sick, guide people through life's pathways, and serve as repositories of cultural history, both sacred and secular. Masters of the inner world who developed their healing arts in ancient cultures that lacked technological sophistication, they have preserved their knowledge for hundreds of generations. Today, despite the encroachment of the modern world, they carry on their sacred practices in tribal settings throughout Siberia, North and South America, Africa, and Australia.

"Shamans enter altered states of consciousness at will and journey to other dimensions to acquire knowledge and power and to help others," says Michael Harner, an anthropologist, practicing shaman, and author of the classic *The Way of the Shaman*. "They move between realities like magical athletes, manipulating spiritual power for the benefit of people whose lives are out of balance. Shamanism isn't a religion, but a methodology by which we can arrive at our own firsthand spiritual experiences about the nature of the universe."

Shamans make their journeys in what Harner calls the shamanic state of consciousness (SSC), traveling into realms that anthropologist Carlos Castaneda refers to as non-ordinary reality. Traditionally, shamans have used a wide variety of methods to alter consciousness, including halluci-

All paths lead to the same goal: to convey to others what we are. And we must pass through solitude and difficulty, isolation and silence, in order to reach forth to the enchanted place where we can dance our clumsy dance and sing our sorrowful song—but in this dance or in this song there are fulfilled the most ancient rites of our conscience in the awareness of being human and of believing in a common destiny.

PABLO NERUDA

nogenic herbs and plants, fasting, isolation in the wilderness, singing, dancing, and percussive sound, especially the monotonous sound produced by drums and rattles. Harner considers drumming the most reliable method of inducing the SSC, in part because the journey is always under personal control and can be terminated at will.

On their journeys, shamans leave the middle world of ordinary reality to explore either the Lower or Upper worlds. To enter the Lower World, they typically visualize an entrance in the Earth, such as a cave, hollow tree, or water hole. Once in the Lower World, they may obtain information to heal patients in ordinary reality or acquire *power animals*, tutelary spirits in animal form that empower the healer's capacities. They may, for example, assimilate into their own character the strength of a bear or the courage of a lion, or use various animals as tutors and guides in diagnosing and treating illnesses.

To enter the Upper World, shamans visualize ascending to the sky from special locations, such as mountains, treetops, or cliffs. In general, they journey to the celestial realm of beneficent entities to consult with teachers and enlist their help.

If your philosophy doesn't grow corn, I don't want to hear about it.

The path of power is different for every individual. . . . It is why you are here. When I speak of power, I mean a way of working and using all your energy—including your spiritual energy—in a direction that allows you to become a whole person, capable of fulfilling whatever vision the Creator gives to you.

Finding your path of power is not always easy. For me to do it, I had to tear up both the white man's and the Indian's scripts for life. If you wish to walk the path of power, you must do the same.

SUN BEAR

The ability to journey to other realms bestows on shamans not only extraordinary abilities, but the experience of ecstasy. Describing their cosmic voyages, Harner writes:

> In the SSC, the shaman typically experiences an ineffable joy in what he sees, an awe of the beautiful and mysterious worlds that open before him. His experiences are like dreams, but waking ones that feel real and in which he can control his actions and direct his adventures. While in the SSC, he is often amazed by the reality of that which is presented. He gains access to a whole new, and yet familiarly ancient universe that provides him with profound information about the meaning of his own life and death and his place within the totality of all existence. During his great adventures in the SSC, he maintains conscious control over the direction of his travels, but does not know what he will discover. He is a self-reliant explorer of the endless mansions of a magnificent hidden universe. Finally, he brings back his discoveries to build his knowledge and to help others.

OTHER JOURNEYS

Is cosmic journeying an exclusively shamanic experience? Not according to psychiatrist Roger Walsh, author of *The Spirit of Shamanism*. Although shamanic journeying requires disciplined practice, many people unfamiliar with shamanism have reported going on journeys spontaneously.

Like shamans, those who have out-of-body experiences tell about traveling at will around this or other worlds, meeting spirits, and acquiring useful knowledge. Shamanic experiences frequently occur to people undergoing near-death experiences. Patients close to death report rising above their bodies, traveling through a dark tunnel, and encountering spiritual figures or brilliant light with which they merge in ecstatic love. At the end of this dreamlike experience, the journeyer—like the shaman—returns to the world of ordinary reality.

Many of us, says Walsh, travel in our dreams to unknown lands, meet strange figures, and acquire valuable insights. In lucid dreaming—a state in which we are asleep but aware of dreaming—we can direct our activities much like shamans in non-ordinary reality.

Psychologists have harnessed the healing power of journeys in therapeutic settings. Using such popular techniques as visualization, guided imagery, and waking dreams, they guide clients on journeys to transpersonal sources of wisdom and insight. A common technique is to dialogue with a sage or inner teacher, a method not dissimilar to the

Now this is what we believe. The Mother of us all is Earth. The Father is the Sun. The Grandfather is the Creator who bathed us with his mind and gave life to all things. The Brother is the beasts and trees. The Sister is that with wings. We are the children of Earth and do it no harm in any way. Nor do we offend the Sun by not greeting it at dawn. We praise our Grandfather for his creation. We share the same breath together—the beasts, the trees, the birds, the man.

NANCY WOOD

Every human being has an obligation to return to this planet and to all our relations the sound of beauty, the power of prayer, the sense of harmony.

DHYANI YWAHOO

shamanic journey to find spirit teachers. Walsh views merging with power animals in non-ordinary reality as an empowering technique that psychologists use to help clients become self-actualized. For example, by acting as if they had the courage of a lion or the far-seeing vision of an eagle, clients can assimilate these desirable qualities through belief and identification.

Walsh's conclusion is that lucid dreaming, out-of-body experiences, and near-death experiences may have inspired the widespread belief in a soul and soul travel. They also may have inspired shamanic journeys in tribal settings and most recently in psychotherapy.

INITIATION CRISIS

The call to shamanhood may come through a dream or during a vision quest, an initiation rite in which the neophyte spends time in solitude fasting and crying for a vision from the spirit world. However, some candidates undergo a profound crisis of death and rebirth that often resembles psychosis.

The initiation crisis usually announces itself after adolescence, says Roger Walsh. The shaman-to-be exhibits bizarre, sometimes life-threatening behavior that may result in "weeks, months, or even years of unpredictable chaos that disrupts the lives of the shaman, his family, and his tribe." Western psychologists might regard this behavior as evidence of severe psychopathology, but Walsh suggests viewing it as a developmental crisis culminating in spiritual rebirth. With the guidance of an experienced shaman, community support, and insight into the nature of shamanic awakening, the shaman may turn spiritual emergency into spiritual emergence.

Joan Halifax, an anthropologist who has written widely on shamanism, has charted the stages by which the candidate moves through this developmental crisis to become a healed healer. In the first stage, *renunciation,* the shaman puts aside the everyday world, turning from the secular realm toward the cosmos. In the second stage, the *quest,* ascetic disciplines such as fasting and solitude prepare the candidate to witness unusual phenomena in the non-ordinary state of reality without losing equanimity. Then, in the *realm of hardships,* the shaman enters the underworld of suffering, disease, and decrepitude to awaken his warrior nature by battling with the spirits that cause disease. (In Jungian psychology, this stage corresponds roughly to confronting the shadow, the dark and neglected portion of the personality.)

We ourselves cannot put any magic spell on this world. The world is its own magic.

SUZUKI ROSHI

There is a world beyond ours, a world that is far away, nearby, and invisible. And there it is where God lives, where the dead live, the spirits and saints, a world where everything has already happened and everything is known. That world talks. It has a language of its own. I report what it says.

MARÍA SABINA,
MAZATEC SHAMAN

We take a handful of sand from the endless landscape of awareness around us and call that handful of sand the world.

ROBERT M. PIRSIG

In shamanism there is ultimately no distinction between helping others and helping yourself. By helping others shamanically, one becomes more powerful, self-fulfilled, and joyous. Shamanism goes far beyond a primarily self-concerned transcendence of ordinary reality. It is a transcendence for a broader purpose, the helping of humankind.

MICHAEL HARNER

"In the fourth domain, *death*, the candidate confronts not only symbolic physical death but other forms of ego death as well," Halifax explains. "From this complete dismemberment of his being, the shaman is resurrected into the realization that life and death comprise a dual unity, inseparable and complementary in nature. Finding the balance between life and death, the masculine and the feminine, pain and pleasure, is essential to a warrior's development."

In the last phase of the heroic journey, the *return to the world,* the shaman reenters society with an awakened sense of compassion, "commissioned as a spiritual social worker" to heal and serve the community. This long death-and-rebirth process usually requires apprenticeship to a master shaman, who not only guides the candidate through the inner world but transmits knowledge of the culture's mythology, ceremonial skills, and healing techniques.

"Shamans often end up as the most highly functional members of the community," writes Walsh. "They are commonly described as displaying remarkable energy and stamina, unusual levels of concentration, control of altered states of consciousness, high intelligence, leadership skills, and a grasp of complex data, myths, and rituals. So, although the symptoms and behavior of the shamanic initiation crises are unusual and even bizarre by both Western and tribal standards, shamans not only recover but may function exceptionally well as leaders and healers of their people."

MODERN RENAISSANCE

Since the 1960s, shamanism has experienced a renaissance of interest in the West, largely because of anthropologists such as Carlos Castaneda and Michael Harner, who apprenticed themselves to tribal shamans and revealed their knowledge to mass audiences. Their books have helped rescue these ancient traditions from the encroachment of missionaries, colonists, and commercial interests.

Harner, director of the Foundation for Shamanic Studies in Norwalk, Connecticut, has demystified the practice of shamanism without diluting its essential mystery. His workshops present the essential practices—journeying for knowledge and power, acquiring spirit helpers, diagnosing and treating illness—stripped of tribal and cultural baggage. To make these experiences compatible with modern lifestyles, he even recommends using a cassette tape of shamanic drumming played through headphones.

Prayer for the Healing of the Earth

We join with the earth and each other.

To bring new life to the land
To restore the waters
To refresh the air

We join with the earth and with each other.

To renew the forests
To care for the plants
To protect the creatures

We join with the earth and with each other.

To celebrate the seas
To rejoice in the sunlight
To sing the song of the stars

We join with the earth and with each other.

To recreate the human community
To promote justice and peace
To remember our children

We join with the earth and with each other.

We join together as many and diverse expressions
of one loving mystery for the healing of the
earth and the renewal of all life.

U. N. Environmental Sabbath Program

We can listen to the voice of the Earth as she shakes and sings her song expressing her tiredness. She is calling us to attention, to be alert, to recognize that now is the time to transform selfish thought and action to compassionate caretaking. Do we want a world of peace and harmony? Are we willing to make that peace within ourselves? Will we call it forth? It is your choice. Your thought and action make a difference.

Dhyani Ywahoo

Harner attributes the revival of shamanism to our hunger for first-hand knowledge of the spiritual realms; the speed and effectiveness of shamanic techniques, which are well suited to contemporary life; the growing interest in holistic health methods that emphasize the unity of mind, body, and spirit; and the wide appeal of spiritual ecology.

"In this time of worldwide environmental crisis, shamanism provides something largely lacking in the anthropocentric great religions: reverence for and communication with other beings of the Earth and with the planet itself," Harner says. "In shamanism this is not simple nature worship, but a two-way spiritual communication that resurrects the lost connections our human ancestors had with the awesome spiritual power and beauty of our garden Earth."

SHAMANIC GUIDELINES

For those interested in practicing shamanism, Harner offers the following guidelines based on three decades of experience:

Study with reputable teachers. Organizations such as the Foundation for Shamanic Studies can help beginners find them. Without this guidance, you might read books on shamanism, take workshops at various growth centers and institutes, and discover through trial and error what works for you. To reduce the risks, get informed testimony from those who have studied with shamans, much as you might research the credentials of a prospective medical doctor.

Look for your teachers in the realm of non-ordinary reality. Teachers in ordinary reality can speed up your training, but you get the specific information you need from spirit teachers. Consult with them on issues of diet, work, relationships, education, health, or whatever engages your interest. Non-ordinary teachers provide the same reliable information that guided our tribal ancestors.

Practice regularly—at least once a week—and use your journeys in search of knowledge rather than extraordinary pleasure trips. Too much journeying doesn't permit you time to integrate into everyday life the instructions you receive in non-ordinary reality. Don't be surprised if you are told to do your homework in ordinary reality before being introduced to new levels of experience and wisdom in the spirit realms.

Always expect loving, ethical guidance. Journeys to the Lower and Upper worlds take you to realms of harmony, love, and beauty. Through trial and error, you will discover that the messages you receive can be trusted for their uncanny accuracy and helpfulness.

Learn to meet fear when it arises. In fact, be thankful if you experience fear while journeying, because it means you are taking your experience seriously. After several journeys, you will discover that ordinary reality is far more dangerous, and you will appreciate the ineffable beauty of non-ordinary reality.

When they are in nature, people sense intuitively that the other kingdoms are living in harmony with universal law. In such an environment, it's much easier for the heart to open, to become softer and live in tune with the earth.

WABUN, SUN BEAR'S
MEDICINE HELPER

The shaman's work entails maintaining balance in the human community as well as in the relationships between the community and the gods or divine forces that direct the life of the culture. When these various domains of existence are out of balance, it is the shaman's responsibility to restore the lost harmony.

JOAN HALIFAX

78

The shamanic state of consciousness is safer than dreaming. In a dream you may not be able to extricate yourself from a frightening experience, while in the SSC you consciously can stop the experience at will. Unlike a psychedelic drug experience, whose length of time is chemically predetermined, you can't be locked into a bad trip.

As you advance in your practice, you will inevitably have the urge to help others. Shamanism is spiritual activism, not a system designed exclusively for self-improvement. By deepening your contact with the harmonious, hidden universe, you will automatically want to help alleviate the pain and suffering of others.

THE EARTH CONNECTION

Shamanism grows out of a world view that stresses the interdependence of all life—minerals, plants, animals, and human beings. In the Native American expression of this wisdom tradition, happiness—both personal and collective—follows from "walking in balance on the Earth Mother." To native teachers, this means honoring the Earth as a living being, living in harmony with nature, and taking care of its precious resources. They teach that by recognizing our connectedness to the sacred web of life, we can heal the twin diseases of alienation and anxiety that plague modern urban life.

We begin the healing process by giving up our illusory separateness from nature, which leads to the exploitation of the Earth in the name of profit, says Dhyani Ywahoo, a twenty-seventh-generation Cherokee teacher and founder of the Sunray Meditation Society in Bristol, Vermont. We must restore what she calls the sacred hoop, the circle of relationships that binds the individual to the greater whole with a sense of reverence.

"Earth is asking that human beings realize that the bears, the whales, the coyotes, the trees, the ants, all of these creatures are our relatives," she writes in *Voices of Our Ancestors*. "We have a duty to ourselves and the future to live correctly with all our relatives, to preserve life rather than push to extinction. The environment responds to our thought and feeling. It is for humans to be aware of how our thought, word, and deed affect the environment. One person filled with doubt and anger may wilt the flowers; another person's enthusiasm is such that cut flowers last for weeks."

Ywahoo teaches the Beauty Path, which instructs that compassionate thought and action can preserve life for future generations. Its

The shamanic initiatory crisis may reflect a deep psychological process, not limited to particular cultures or times. This process seems capable of exploding from the depths of the psyche in contemporary Westerners surrounded by cars and computers as well as in ancient shamans in tepees and igloos.

ROGER WALSH

practitioners, called peacekeepers, use prayer and meditation to purify themselves of habitual thoughts of conflict and lethargy. Holding a vision of peace, they recognize that patterns of mind manifest as our individual, family, clan, national, and planetary relationships.

"We have a short time in which to transform incorrect thinking and mental imbalance, and to clean up our rivers, our polluted atmosphere, and our denatured soil," she says. "The renewal of Mother Earth depends on our renewal; we can't transmute atmospheric pollution until we transform our mental pollution. Simple gestures performed daily with awareness and appreciation, such as blessing the air we breathe and the water we drink, can help us become more effective peacekeepers in rebuilding the sacred circle."

NATIVE CEREMONIES

Native American rituals and ceremonies also can help restore the Earth connection, according to Sun Bear, medicine chief of the Bear Tribe, an ecologically oriented community located near Spokane, Washington. For example, native people purify their bodies and minds in sweatlodges, dome-shaped structures made from saplings with heated rocks in the center pit. Water poured over the rocks causes steam to billow in the darkness. This marriage of earth, fire, water, and air, Sun Bear says, purges participants of ignorance and fear, awakening a greater intimacy with the Great Spirit and the Earth Mother. When they leave after praying and cleansing themselves, participants say "Thank you, all my relations," referring to all the rest of creation.

Before celebrations, council gatherings, and healing ceremonies, Native Americans take part in the pipe ceremony. The pipe, according to Sun Bear, represents the universe: The stone bowl comes from the mineral kingdom, the wood stem from the plant kingdom, and the fur and feather decorations from the animal kingdom. The two-legged creatures who smoke the pipe put in pinches of tobacco for these kingdoms, for the spirit world, for fellow two-leggeds, for the powers of the four directions, and for their special prayers. In this way, the pipe ceremony reminds participants of their connection with all of life.

"To restore the earth connection, I encourage people in cities to raise gardens," Sun Bear says. "When they put their hands in the earth, feel its energy, and start identifying with it, this contact restores them to a state of balance as human beings. In the same way, you can embrace a tree and feel its comforting pulse of energy. When you're in harmony with the natural

The man who sat on the ground in his tipi meditating on life and its meaning, accepting the kinship of all creatures and acknowledging unity with the universe of things, was infusing into his being the true essence of civilization. And when native man left off this form of development, his humanization was retarded in growth.

CHIEF LUTHER
STANDING BEAR

world, the connection can really strengthen you. Much like taking vitamins, it revitalizes your whole system."

To further open our hearts to nature, Sun Bear's medicine helper, Wabun (formerly Marlise James), recommends visiting a special place in nature two or three times a week. It could be by the ocean, near the mountains, in a public park, or even in a backyard. We visit not so much to catalog the plants, insects, and animals on the land, but to sit quietly and absorb what nature has to teach.

"After a while, you might start bringing gifts to your special place, such as corn meal, which represents the fertility of the Earth," says Wabun. "Soon you'll begin loving the land with the emotional force usually reserved for your dearest human friends. After a time, if you miss one of your bi-weekly meetings, you'll feel a real sense of disappointment and loss, just as if it were a human friend of yours. But soon you'll be able to transport yourself there mentally to receive the energy on a non-physical level. Once your heart has opened to that special piece of creation, you can transfer the feeling to all of creation."

This, then, is the great legacy of shamanism for the modern healer: a way to make life alive; a way to discover that the world is enchanted and not dead—a way, in essence, of resurrecting the corpse of modern medicine.

LARRY DOSSEY

SHAMANIC HEALING

As the world's first healers, shamans developed methods to treat illness based on the unity of body, mind, and spirit. This holistic approach has attracted the attention of health professionals seeking viable alternatives to Western medicine, with its mechanistic approach to diagnosis and treatment.

According to Joan Halifax, shamanic healing in some tribal cultures is based on the principle of the healer and healee becoming one. Rather than analyzing the ill person's psyche like an objective scientist, the shaman becomes the person empathetically and feels the client's afflictions.

"Shamans believe that an ill person's soul has been stolen and resides in the underworld realm of disease," she says. "We could call such a person 'dis-spirited,' because he or she has literally lost the spirit. In psychological terms, we might compare this to states of depression and melancholy, in which qualities that give life meaning dissipate and disappear. The shaman journeys to the underworld to battle for the individual's soul and to return it to the afflicted individual."

The shaman knows the underworld terrain intimately because of his initiation crisis, says Halifax. "Journeying to the underworld as a seasoned warrior, the shaman encounters his 'old buddies,' the dark spirits who are ravaging his client, and either steals the soul back or does battle, grabbing it back by right of victory."

81

Modern health practitioners can learn a great deal from shamanic healers, says Stanley Krippner, Professor of Psychology at the Saybrook Institute in San Francisco. In *Shaman's Path,* a collection of essays edited by Gary Doore, Krippner describes shamans as the world's first healers, diagnosticians, and psychotherapists: "There are shamanic healing methods that closely parallel contemporary behavior therapy, chemotherapy, dream interpretation, family therapy, hypnotherapy, milieu therapy, and psychodrama. It is clear that shamans, psychotherapists, and physicians have more in common than is generally suspected. For the shaman, however, the spiritual dimension of healing is extremely important, whereas contemporary physicians and psychotherapists typically ignore it."

Echoing the same theme, Dr. Larry Dossey, former chief of staff of the Medical City Dallas Hospital, asserts that modern physicians can draw on fifty millennia of shamanic methodology to relearn the importance of the inner life in their healing mission: "The reason the shamans placed so much emphasis on the spiritual insights and inner visions of the healer were *not* that they lacked science, and *not* that they could not reason as objectively as we, but because healing, in its highest expression, is impossible to achieve without them."

Western medicine can profit from the shamanic perspective that links disease to disharmony, fear, and soul loss, according to Jean Achterberg, author of *Women As Healer* and professor of psychology at the Institute of Transpersonal Psychology at Palo Alto, California. Shamans always have recognized that long-term feelings of meaninglessness and disharmony inevitably lead to disease. They also point out that a chronic sense of fear erodes the love and trust that make up the foundation of mental and physical health.

"Soul loss . . . is regarded as the gravest diagnosis in the shamanic nomenclature, being seen as a major cause of illness and death," Achterberg writes in *Shaman's Drum.* "Yet it is not referred to at all in our modern Western medical books. Nevertheless, it is becoming increasingly clear that what the shamans refer to as soul loss—that is, injury to the inviolate core which is the essence of a person's being—does manifest as despair, immunological damage, cancer, and a host of other very serious disorders. It seems to follow the demise of relationships with loved ones, with careers, or with significant attachments."

What these health professionals imply is that an integration of shamanic healing techniques and modern technology can bring a sense of spirituality to medicine, transforming it into a healing art. In the words of

Dr. Lewis Mehl, a Cherokee Indian and medical doctor who practices shamanic holistic medicine, "The idea is to combine the good medicines that work so each can be more effective."

TONING THE BELLY

Native American teachers stress that an unobstructed relationship between the individual and the Earth plays an important role in promoting health. In our quest for mind/body wholeness, we can use the body to strengthen our connection to the Earth, according to Brooke Medicine Eagle, a healer and teacher of Crow-Lakota descent who conducts wilderness gatherings at Sky Lodge Ranch in Montana.

Native Americans teach that we are linked to the Earth through an invisible umbilical cord centered in the belly, one or two finger-widths below the navel. By practicing a breath exercise called Toning the Belly, Brooke Medicine Eagle says, we can increase our receptivity to the subliminal messages constantly entering us from the outside world through this psychic channel. Her instructions are listed on the following page.

VISION QUEST

Throughout history individuals have retreated from civilization to seek spiritual initiation directly from the Earth through a rite of passage known as the Vision Quest. In the shamanic tradition, the seeker goes to a sacred place in nature, fasts in the wilderness on water, and cries for a vision of his or her life path and purpose. When the clamor of the candidate's internal dialogue dies down and the surface layers of accumulated knowledge recede into the background, primordial nature becomes a teacher, imparting wisdom for birthing a new self in the world.

"In traditional cultures, changes in life station were marked by regular ceremonies of passage, many like the vision quest," write Steven Foster and Meredith Little in *The Book of the Vision Quest*. "Without passage rites, individuals could not have understood their life crises, nor could they have been capable of confidently assuming the responsibilities and privileges conferred by their new life station."

This husband-and-wife team directs the School of Lost Borders, a training facility in the Eastern Sierra for individuals seeking wilderness rites of passage. The loss of such meaningful rites in contemporary life, they say, blocks our progress when going through life passages. We get

The first peace, which is the most important, is that which comes within the souls of people when they realize their relationship, their oneness, with the universe and all its powers, and when they realize at the center of the universe dwells the Great Spirit, and that this center is really everywhere, it is within each of us.

BLACK ELK

83

☆

Either standing still or walking, pull in your stomach powerfully as you expel the air from your open mouth. With your mouth closed, inhale through your nose to the bottom of your lungs, then expel the air with the snap of your belly inward. Begin the exercise by taking only a few breaths. Gradually work up to 5, 10, 20, or whatever number of breaths energizes you without causing fatigue.

Afterward, center your awareness in the belly and begin sensing the subtle impressions of the world around you. When you encounter a hummingbird or willow tree, for example, let your awareness descend from the intellectual, observing mind to "Mother's Mind" below the waist, where you will effortlessly receive intuitive knowledge that no amount of conceptual thought could ever reveal.

Toning the belly gives us a deeper perception of the world, which contributes to more efficient living. With practice, we can sense when plants are crying for nourishment, when a storm is imminent, and when our neighbors need help. Ultimately, the exercise improves our intelligent connection with all of life, providing harmonious, truly ecological solutions to the challenges we face today.

In a related exercise, says Brooke Medicine Eagle, lie in a prone position on your stomach on a favorite plot of ground for 15 minutes while visualizing a golden cord running from your belly into the heart of the Earth. Afterward, turn over on your back for the same period of time, experiencing the sky realm of wind and sunlight through the belly.

With the stomach down, you might feel the rhythmic heartbeat of the living, breathing Earth. You also might experience being loved and supported by our planet. With the back up, you might feel the immensity of life and your relationship to the greater cosmos. If you practice this exercise once a week for a number of months, your growing eco-spiritual awareness can strengthen your commitment to heal and sanctify the Earth Mother.

☆

stuck in symptoms, such as panic, hysteria, anxiety, uncertainty, anger, boredom, drug abuse, and psychosomatic illnesses, that attend these transitional times. In Foster and Little's view, these symptoms represent energy seeking transformation without a ritual vehicle to channel it.

On a Vision Quest, we go to the wilderness to formally mark the end of a life crisis, they say. The ceremony typically has three phases: *severance,* in which we separate from the context of daily life and the tem-

*With that from the earth,
  beauty I will create—
With that beauty,
  my soul I will give.*

AMADO PENA

poral world; *threshold,* in which we give birth to ourselves in a consecrated natural setting; and *incorporation,* in which we return from the sacred world of empowerment to carry out in practical terms the vision revealed to us in the wilderness.

During the first phase, we review our former life, confront fears and anxieties about undertaking such a heroic spiritual ordeal, and ready ourselves to physically survive in nature with minimal provisions. During the threshold stage, which normally lasts three or four days, we enter what Foster and Meredith call "the Great Mother's sacred cathedral." Alone in the wilderness, we confront a solitude so profound that "the absence of civilized things within the field of perception creates a huge emptiness around which the conditioned self flutters like a doomed moth."

Fasting only on water, we empty the body to cleanse and fill the spirit. Sunrise becomes our meat and noon becomes our wine. As our physical strength wanes, we cry for a vision from an empty belly and a lonely heart, and the purity of our seeking calls forth wisdom from the unconscious depths of the psyche shared by all humanity.

In the last phase of our quest, we return with both elation and trepidation to the noisy, confusing world we left behind. We must learn to live in balance with the two worlds—one visionary, consecrated, and wholly natural, the other familiar and utilitarian. Vision questers report that while the intensity of the experience may diminish over time, its impact remains permanently stamped on the psyche, always available to rekindle their sense of purpose.

We did not think of the great open plains, the beautiful rolling hills, and winding streams with tangled growth, as "wild." Only to the white man was nature a "wilderness" and only to him was the land "infested" with "wild" animals and "savage" people. To us it was tame. Earth was bountiful and we were surrounded with the blessings of the Great Mystery. Not until the hairy man from the east came and with brutal frenzy heaped injustices upon us and the families we loved was it "wild" for us. When the very animals of the forest began fleeing from his approach, then it was that for us the "Wild West" began.

CHIEF LUTHER
STANDING BEAR

AN ENVIRONMENTALIST RECONNECTS WITH THE EARTH

How are we transformed on a vision quest? We may grieve the death of a spouse and recommit to life; make the transition from adolescence to adulthood; recommit ourselves to the spiritual path; or awaken to the loving nature of the universe.

In *Dharma Gaia,* an anthology edited by Alan Badiner, environmental activist Suzanne Head writes about her vision quest in the Sangre de Cristo Mountains in southern Colorado. Worn down by the fast pace of life in San Francisco, she used her wilderness solitude to reestablish a healthy relationship with the Earth. Here are some of her insights.

Let us put our minds together and see what we will make for our children.

SITTING BULL

On being out of touch with nature: We miss her subtle signs and signals because we are just going too fast to notice. We have no space left in our minds for anything but the information, set in human signs and symbols, that demands our attention on a daily basis. . . .

With my senses opening and my perceptions expanding as I relaxed into the retreat, I realized that there is a lot more to the natural world than one can grasp through studying numbers and abstract scientific concepts. If we are to take our cues from the environment and learn how to live in harmony with our planet home, we have to go beyond the linear structures of human language to receive the messages of the elemental world more directly.

On living with a sense of wonder: I became aware of the *life* around me. . . . I felt surrounded by a world that was not only friendly, but singing to me, inviting me to a party, letting me in on its secrets, giving me a glimpse of the magical quality of our living Earth, the living quality, the power of ancient rocks and trees and stars. The aboriginal peoples convey that magic in stories, songs, and dance. And over hundreds of years, or even generations, those sacred traditions kept the magical connections between humans and the rest of Nature alive. We have lost those sacred traditions, and have been longing for the lost connections ever since.

On being a warrior for the Earth: In the morning, before I left the retreat, I stood up on the rocks above my camp. . . . With hands in prayer, I thanked the Earth for her beauty, her bounty, her balance, and her blessings. Tears poured down my face and my throat choked so that I could not speak. But silently I asked for the confidence to honor my own inner Nature, the intuition of sacredness evoked by Nature in this place, and the courage and integrity to manifest sacred outlook as a warrior for the Earth.

I prayed that the other humans of this planet would also find the confidence, courage, and integrity to honor inner Nature and outer Nature. To do so collectively would create the space within our hearts for a correct relationship with Nature. Realizing the sacredness of the Earth that supports us and

EARTH PRAYER

O Great Spirit
Whose voice I hear in the winds,
and whose breath gives life to all the world,
hear me! I am small and weak, I need your strength
and wisdom.

Let me walk in beauty, and make my eyes
ever behold the red and purple sunset.

Make my hands respect the things you have made
and my ears sharp to hear your voice.

Make me wise so that I may understand the things
you have taught my people.

Let me learn the lessons you have hidden in every
leaf and rock.

I seek strength, not to be greater than my brother,
but to fight my greatest enemy—myself.

Make me always ready to come to you with clean
hands and straight eyes.

So when life fades, as the fading sunset,
my spirit may come to you without shame.

TRADITIONAL NATIVE AMERICAN PRAYER

the sky that inspires us, and all the relationships in between, we would find ways to live that could be sustained by the biosphere. Instead of poisoning and plundering the Earth until all life expires, we could fulfill our Nature by being warriors for the Earth.

RESOURCES

Recommended Reading

The Way of the Shaman, Michael Harner (Harper & Row, 1990). The popular, clearly written guide to shamanic power and healing.

Shamanic Voices: A Survey of Visionary Narratives, Joan Halifax, editor (Dutton, 1979). Accounts of shamanic initiation, journeying, and healing from tribal practitioners around the world.

The Spirit of Shamanism, Roger Walsh (Jeremy P. Tarcher, 1990). Presents the relevance of shamanic practices to modern health professionals and to those interested in dealing with our current ecological crisis.

Shaman's Path: Healing, Personal Growth and Empowerment, Gary Doore, editor (Shambhala Publications, 1988). A collection of contemporary essays on shamanic methods of self-transformation, healing, and spiritual practice.

The Book of the Vision Quest: Personal Transformation in the Wilderness, Steven Foster with Meredith Little (Prentice Hall Press, 1988). Gives theory and practical instruction in conducting a vision quest, along with first-hand accounts of participants who have undergone this sacred ceremony.

Organizations and Publications

The Foundation for Shamanic Studies (Box 670, Belden Station, Norwalk, CT 06852; 203-454-2825). Founded by Michael Harner, the foundation disseminates information about shamanism, sponsors workshops nationwide and around the world on shamanic healing, and publishes a quarterly newsletter, available with membership ($30/year).

Shaman's Drum (P.O. Box 430, Willits, CA 95490; 707-459-0486, $15/year, quarterly). Publishes articles on shamanistic traditions around the world. Each issue also includes a calendar of workshops and events and a resource directory of organizations, centers, and individuals involved in shamanism.

Snake Power: A Journal of Contemporary Female Shamanism (5856 College Avenue, #138, Oakland, CA 94618; 415-648-0883, $23/year, quarterly). Edited by Vicki Noble, creator of the Motherpeace Tarot Deck, the magazine regularly covers feminine spirituality, astrology, rituals, herbs, poetry, and music.

Dance of the Deer Foundation/Center for Shamanic Studies (P.O. Box 699, Soquel, CA 95073; 408-475-9560) offers seminars and pilgrimages in the shamanistic tradition of the Huichol Indians of Mexico. Huichol techniques are employed for self-healing and for healing families, communities, and the environment.

Eagle Song Wilderness Camps (P.O. Box 121, Ovando, MT 59854; 406-793-5730). Held at Blacktail Ranch in Montana and led by visionary healer Brooke Medicine Eagle, these residential training programs help people deepen their relationship with nature.

THE VISION OF TRANSPERSONAL PSYCHOLOGY

The Search for Optimal Well-Being

Voyaging through the turbulent waters of a midlife divorce and her grown children's independence, Jennifer closes her eyes at her therapist's request. Cast adrift from her traditional identity as wife and mother, she grieves the past and faces a future of empty nights and unrelieved anxiety. As she attempts to relax in the darkness, inescapable questions plague her: "How will I support myself? Do I have the strength to go on alone? What purpose does my life serve?"

Following her therapist's directions, Jennifer visualizes leaving a sunlit meadow and climbing a mountain path to its summit, where she enters a temple and meets her inner guide, an embodiment of wisdom and compassion. Worried about her future, Jennifer gazes deeply into the Wise Woman's radiant eyes and feels a surge of energy pass between them, infusing her with a sense of renewed purpose. The guide then walks Jennifer to a bridge that leads across a precipice to a distant valley bathed in sunlight. "I'm afraid to cross over," Jennifer says tearfully. The Wise Woman gives her a sword for strength, a shield for protection, and winged sandals for the journey. With a hand on Jennifer's shoulder, the Wise Woman says, "The journey is arduous, but you have the tools to triumph."

When she returns to waking consciousness, Jennifer realizes that she has unsuspected inner resources with which to meet her predicament. She

Make your ego porous.
Will is of little importance,
complaining is nothing,
fame is nothing. Openness,
patience, receptivity, solitude
is everything.

RAINER MARIA RILKE

may have to brave loneliness, fear, and dependency, but she feels a renewed commitment to overcome her emotional paralysis and set out on her personal odyssey. Whenever she needs inspiration, she can reconnect with the Wise Woman in meditation and receive guidance from her own spiritual wellsprings.

In the more distant past, if Jennifer had consulted with a priest, shaman, or guru, the local soul doctor might have interpreted her suffering as a call to spiritual awakening. Today, in our secular society, the psychiatrist has displaced the priest, and being well adjusted has replaced spiritual growth as the primary focus of mental health. Like many of us, however, Jennifer senses that being well adjusted isn't enough. She finds conventional therapy incomplete because it disregards her spiritual nature (as symbolized by her Wise Woman). And so, like an increasing number of us seeking to bridge traditional therapy and spirituality, she found a transpersonal psychotherapist, the modern equivalent of a soul doctor. She feels relief not having her deepest yearnings dismissed as something pathological, irrational, or occult, and she can risk being vulnerable by sharing her spiritual experience without fear of censure or ridicule.

An Integrated Approach

The term *transpersonl* (or "beyond personal") refers to states of consciousness that transcend the normal limitations of the ego. Unlike traditional therapists who restrict their focus to ego concerns, such as personal confidence and self-image, transpersonal psychologists also recognize our capacity for expanded states of awareness and the validity of meditation and other spiritual disciplines. Because they help their clients develop strong, functional identities *and* grow beyond them toward transpersonal realization, they are expanding the field of psychological inquiry into areas associated with optimal health and well-being.

The beauty of transpersonal psychology is that it accepts the full spectrum of human consciousness, working with the body, emotions, mind, and spirit, according to Frances Vaughan, a well-known transpersonal therapist. Practitioners use dreamwork, guided imagery, and Eastern meditative practices, as well as traditional therapeutic techniques. Unlike other branches of Western psychology, however, the transpersonal approach accepts spiritual insight as a legitimate part of the healing process, so it includes realms of experience, wisdom, and creativity beyond the personality, such as mystical experience, ecstasy, and enlightenment, which were once thought to be the exclusive domain of religion.

Your task is not to seek for love, but merely to seek and find all of the barriers within yourself that you have built against it.

A Course in Miracles

We are dominated by everything with which our self becomes identified. We can dominate and control everything from which we disidentify ourselves.

Roberto Assagioli

Traditionally, says Vaughan, we have split psychological growth and the spiritual quest into separate, essentially antagonistic pursuits. "Most Western psychology has tended to dismiss spiritual searching as escapist, delusional, or, at best, a psychological crutch," she writes in *The Inward Arc: Healing and Wholeness in Psychotherapy and Spirituality.* "Spiritual disciplines, on the other hand, have tended to regard psychology as an irrelevant distraction on the path of spiritual awakening."

Robert Gerard, a clinical psychologist and pioneer in the field of transpersonal psychology, agrees with Vaughan's assessment. "In the East the guru teaches meditation to his disciples and helps them contact higher dimensions of existence," he says. "In the West psychologists work with clients' emotions. The guru without the knowledge of modern Western psychology may simply dismiss his disciples' emotional disturbances, because his traditional approach lacks ways of working effectively with them. On the other hand, the Western psychologist who repudiates the spiritual dimension is, by his limited belief system, erecting a ceiling that prevents clients from growing into that dimension."

Because of this split, Western psychology typically works in the personal dimension, helping us integrate the ego to successfully handle life's practical realities, while Eastern psychology generally cultivates transpersonal values, such as serenity, compassion, and a oneness with life. To become whole human beings, Gerard says, we need a unified psychology that encompasses both dimensions of growth.

Transpersonal therapy, Vaughan points out, does exactly that. In the first stage of therapeutic work, as we learn to *identify* our inner thoughts and feelings, we develop ego strength, raise self-esteem, and release negative patterns of self-invalidation. By acknowledging previously rejected parts of ourselves, we assume greater responsibility for our lives. As in conventional therapy, the successful completion of this stage leads to increased personal freedom and self-determination.

The second, or transpersonal, stage concerns itself with *disidentification.* After "getting ourselves together," we confront existential questions about meaning and purpose. When ego goals appear to be meaningless, we may begin to detach ourselves from roles, possessions, activities, and relationships. By going through a kind of ego death, we eventually transcend the separate self and contact the transpersonal self, which bridges the ego and the divine ground of our being. At this point, Vaughan says, "we experience ourselves as universal members of the human species, with the capacity to bring more compassion, love, and wisdom into our everyday lives."

We teach children how to measure, how to weigh. We fail to teach them how to revere, how to sense wonder and awe. The sense of the sublime, the sign of the inward greatness of the human soul and something which is potentially given to all men, is now a rare gift.

ABRAHAM JOSHUA HESCHEL

If a man devotes himself to the instructions of his own unconscious, it can bestow this gift [of renewal], so that suddenly life, which has been stale and dull, turns into a rich, unending inner adventure, full of creative possibilities.

MARIE-LOUISE VON FRANZ

AN ARDUOUS JOURNEY

While awakening to the transpersonal dimension brings joy and illumination, the process also is accompanied by mental, emotional, and even physical disturbances, according to Italian psychiatrist Roberto Assagioli, founder of Psychosynthesis, one of the most influential schools of transpersonal psychology in the West. In an essay, "Self-Realization and Psychological Disturbances," he writes: "Spiritual development is a long and arduous journey, an adventure through strange lands full of surprises, joy and beauty, difficulties, and even dangers. It involves the awakening of potentialities hitherto dormant, the raising of consciousness to new realms, a drastic transmutation of the 'normal' elements of the personality, and a functioning along a new inner dimension."

As the channel opens between the personal and transpersonal levels of consciousness, Assagioli points out, we may experience emotional upheavals, parapsychological perceptions, and prolonged periods of doubt, resistance, and melancholy called the Dark Night of the Soul in spiritual literature. We may suffer from temporary conditions, such as oversensitivity to stressful environments or loss of effectiveness in dealing with the problems and activities of normal life. Traditional therapists often view these experiences as neurotic or *regressive,* invalidating and pathologizing what they do not understand. But transpersonally oriented therapists, recognizing the *progressive* character of these symptoms, can help us move through them as we reorient from an ego-based life to a renewed spiritual orientation.

Integrating spiritual experiences into the fabric of daily life, transpersonal therapists help clients reconstruct the personality around a higher center. When this arduous process is complete, says Assagioli, the self-realized individual lives with "joy, serenity, inner security, a sense of calm power, clear understanding, and radiant love."

ORIGINS OF TRANSPERSONAL PSYCHOLOGY

Because it emphasizes exceptional mental health rather than normality or adjustment, transpersonal psychology has emerged as a new school (or Fourth Force) in modern psychology, says Roger Walsh, a transpersonally oriented psychiatrist and co-editor with Frances Vaughan of the forthcoming collection *The Awakening Mind.* The first two forces, psychoanalysis and behaviorism, focus on pathology and generally disregard our higher potential for growth. Humanistic psychology—the Third Force—

The best and most beautiful things in the world cannot be seen or even touched. They must be felt with the heart.

HELEN KELLER

To transcend mind in Spirit is not to lose mind or destroy mind but merely to include mind in the higher-order wholeness of the super-conscient.

KEN WILBER

emphasizes the importance of personal growth and self-actualization, the need for self-esteem, and the search for personal meaning. But even humanistic psychology falls short of what psychologist Abraham Maslow calls the farther reaches of human nature.

As a pioneer of humanistic psychology, Maslow articulated a groundbreaking theory of motivation called the hierarchy of needs. We all have basic needs for physical safety, love and belongingness, and self-esteem, he postulated. When we fulfill these basic needs, we move up the hierarchy to our growth needs for self-actualization. Motivated by what Maslow terms Being-values, such as truth, justice, beauty, simplicity, and wholeness, we develop our potentials and talents as a sacred calling, based on an inborn desire "to become everything that one is capable of becoming."

In his later years, Maslow expanded his growth model to include the need for self-transcendence. He observed that a number of self-actualizers, in addition to being well integrated, healthy, and effective, transcend the limitations of personal identity. He called these people who perceive the sacred dimension of life in their everyday affairs "transcendent self-actualizers."

Those who seek the truth by means of intellect and learning only get further and further away from it. Not till your thoughts cease all their branching here and there, not till you abandon all thoughts of seeking for something, not till your mind is motionless as wood or stone, will you be on the right road to the Gate.

HUANG PO

As human beings we are made to surpass ourselves and are truly ourselves only when transcending ourselves.

HUSTON SMITH

Based on his observations, Maslow wrote in 1968: "I consider Humanistic, Third Force Psychology to be transitional, a preparation for a still 'higher' Fourth psychology, transpersonal, transhuman, centered in the cosmos rather than in human needs and interest, going beyond humanness, identity, self-actualization, and the like."

Since the 1960s, the psychology Maslow envisioned has developed into a burgeoning field of inquiry that investigates human awareness without strict dogmas or creeds, according to Miles Vich, executive director of the Association for Transpersonal Psychology.

"Transpersonal therapists often use meditative disciplines and growth techniques from sacred traditions, but not as representatives of these teachings," says Vich. "Much like 'scientists of the spirit,' they gain firsthand experience of certain states of consciousness that they can bring to the therapeutic encounter in the spirit of openminded exploration. They conspicuously avoid pushing a particular brand of spirituality onto their clients."

Besides their therapeutic role, transpersonal psychologists also serve as intermediaries in the ongoing East/West dialogue, says Vich. They translate the mystical language of Eastern spirituality into psychological terms that make sense to Western students. Similarly, they help Eastern teachers communicate their teachings to Westerners with greater effectiveness.

"From a social perspective, transpersonal psychologists offer a diagnosis of our cultural problems and insights into recovery," Vich asserts. "They argue that the chronic denial of our spiritual needs results in metapathologies, such as drug and alcohol addiction, along with domestic and public violence. They see reconnecting to spiritual values as a necessary step in restoring us to essential well-being."

A human being is a part of the whole, called by us "Universe"—a part limited in time and space. He experiences himself, his thoughts and feelings, as something separated from the rest—a kind of optical delusion of his consciousness. This delusion is a kind of prison for us, restricting us to our personal desires and to affection for a few persons nearest to us. Our task must be to free ourselves from this prison by widening our circle of compassion to embrace all living creatures and to the whole of nature in its beauty.

ALBERT EINSTEIN

TRANSPERSONAL PSYCHOLOGY IN TRAFFIC JAMS

The frantic pace of modern life makes it difficult to remain centered throughout the day. During morning meditation, we may journey to realms of clear, tranquil perception. But business meetings in the afternoon may obscure whatever clarity we glimpsed briefly. How can we renew our contact during the day without withdrawing from our surroundings?

Robert Gerard, a pioneer in the development of new psychotherapeutic techniques, offers this exercise, called Energy Radiation, to save us when drowning in the sea of our daily responsibilities.

☆

Let's say that you're driving on the freeway in the middle of a traffic jam, with all the attendant negative emotions. Inwardly, become quiet, make contact with your transpersonal self and receive an influx of energy. To do this, visualize your higher self as a radiant point of light shining above your head. Then visualize a beam of light descending into your head, filling it with light, representing illumination and inspiration. As the transpersonal energy descends to your heart center of unconditional love, radiate it outward in all directions to the other drivers on the road.

Because the energy flow is transpersonal, they'll never know that you are the sender. No one will ever pat you on the back, but you will have spent your time in busy traffic developing a greater degree of calm and equanimity while serving humanity. In this way, you can transform your whole life into quiet acts of service. You also can practice service by radiation as a meditation technique in the quiet of your home.

Through this simple but powerful technique of emotional alchemy, you can transform negative energy into a constructive force with which to bless the world.

☆

THE SPECTRUM OF CONSCIOUSNESS

In the past few decades, our growing interest in self-realization has spawned a bewildering variety of therapies. We flock to bodyworkers to get Rolfed, to primal therapists to release childhood pain, to Jungian analysts for insights into our dreams, and to Zen and Yoga teachers in search of our elusive higher nature. Faced with this potpourri of therapies, we hardly know where to begin. Which one is right for us?

Even if we study the major schools of psychology and religion, we may only intensify our confusion, because they frequently contradict each other. For example, Zen Buddhists urge students to dismiss or transcend the ego, while Western therapists insist that strengthening the beleaguered ego is the royal road to happiness. Which school is right?

Transpersonal theorist Ken Wilber has a remarkable answer: They all are. Wilber has arranged the various psychotherapies and spiritual disciplines on a hierarchy he calls the "spectrum of consciousness." Much like Maslow's hierarchy of needs, this comprehensive model plots our growth from ego concerns at what is considered the higher end of the spectrum, through the middle levels of humanistic and transpersonal concerns, to the most transcendent level of mind at the lower end, called Brahman,

Eventually we'll have to confront the fact that world suffering is the result of ill-conceived thoughts taking form through misdirected action. If we're going to survive as a species, we must relinquish—to unprecedented levels—qualities such as greed, hatred, and delusion. In other words, our very survival depends on accelerated levels of psychological and spiritual maturation.

ROGER WALSH

97

Tao, Dharmakaya, or the Godhead in the various traditions. (In this schema, we descend from the periphery inward, until the self/no-self boundary ultimately vanishes in cosmic consciousness.)

"Once we become generally familiar with the spectrum of consciousness, with the various layers of our own being, we may more readily spot the level on which we now live, as well as the level from which our present suffering, if any, springs," writes Wilber in *No Boundary*. "Thus, we will be able to select an appropriate type of soul doctor, an appropriate approach to our present suffering, and thus no longer remain frozen in its midst."

In Wilber's view, conventional psychotherapy heals the split between the conscious and unconscious minds. Therapies such as Transactional Analysis and Psychodrama help reunite the persona with the shadow, the disowned parts of our personality we find unacceptable.

Humanistic therapies, such as Bioenergetic Analysis, Gestalt, and Rogerian therapy, help heal the split between the ego and the body, liberating the vast potentials of the total organism. Transpersonal therapies, such as Jungian analysis and Psychosynthesis, give us the first taste of life beyond the personal self. At the highest level, disciplines such as Zen Buddhism or Vedanta Hinduism heal the split between the total organism and the environment to reveal a supreme identity with the universe.

Seen from this perspective, the various schools complement, rather than contradict, each other. Once we resolve issues on one band of the spectrum, we then progress to the next level, with its challenges and potentials for growth.

"Growth fundamentally means an enlarging and expanding of one's horizons, a growth of one's boundaries," Wilber writes. "When a person descends a level of the spectrum, he has in effect re-mapped his soul to enlarge its territory. Growth is re-apportionment; re-zoning; re-mapping; an acknowledgment, and then enrichment, of ever deeper and more encompassing levels of one's own self."

Meditation or Psychotherapy?

Even with Ken Wilber's model to guide us, we still might not know when to seek psychotherapy and when to seek a spiritual teacher. After all, both approaches aim at relieving human suffering. As Frances Vaughan points out in a *Yoga Journal* article, both value telling the truth, releasing negative emotions, cultivating love and forgiveness, developing nonjudgmental attention, and making a consistent effort.

Given this area of overlap (and our propensity for self-delusion), we may choose a higher spiritual practice such as meditation to avoid dealing with painful childhood issues and relationship problems. If we are having trouble assuming responsibility for ourselves, we may submerge our need for autonomy by following a spiritual master who demands obedience and self-effacement. We may have idealistic flights of fancy, imagining ourselves selflessly serving the world's poor, when in fact we need to commit ourselves to a career and deal with the harsh economic realities of modern life.

Following are some suggestions on how to move along the spectrum of consciousness with greater clarity and less self-deception.

Choose Your Therapy Appropriately

Says Frances Vaughan: "It's appropriate to seek psychotherapy when you're suffering anxiety, depression, or interpersonal problems. If you're interested in spiritual development, I especially recommend transpersonal therapy during mid-life crisis, when dealing with existential issues of meaning and purpose, and when confronting issues of personal mortality or the death of a loved one. If you're not spiritually motivated, any form of conventional therapy is suitable. As for meditation, I recommend it when you're motivated by spiritual hunger, seeking a deeper experience of yourself and a sense of meaning in life."

Don't Confuse Personal and Transpersonal Issues

Again, according to Frances Vaughan: "When we've integrated our personalities, then disidentifying from them—especially from negative energies—is appropriate. But if we prematurely disidentify before resolving our personal conflicts, we experience denial rather than healing. We need to accept and deal with our anger, fear, greed, and aggression before renouncing them from a higher perspective.

"Spiritual teaching that urges us to disidentify with negativity at the right time can lead to great leaps in growth. But often such teachings advise us to disidentify with anger and sexuality at an inappropriate time on the spiritual journey. This premature renunciation only buries unacceptable impulses instead of transforming them, causing them to resurface in neurotic, sometimes harmful ways."

Don't Confuse Meditation with Psychotherapy

Psychotherapy builds up the "I," while meditation inquires into what this "I" consists of, according to clinical psychologist John Welwood. Once we have a strong sense of self, we can inquire into Eastern teachings about emptiness and selflessness without confusion.

We fear our highest possibilities (as well as our lowest ones). We are generally afraid to become that which we can glimpse in our most perfect moments, under the most perfect conditions, under conditions of greatest courage. We enjoy and even thrill to the godlike possibilities we see in ourselves in such peak moments. And yet we simultaneously shiver with weakness, awe, and fear before these very same possibilities.

ABRAHAM MASLOW

In *Awakening the Heart,* Welwood writes: "The question 'Who am I?' from a meditative point of view has no answer. Since we are never able to pin down this 'I,' meditation helps dissolve fixation on 'I' altogether. . . . Meditation can teach us how to contact a larger space or emptiness that lies beyond the constant search for personal meaning. This can effect a radical transformation in the way we live."

Don't Use Meditation to Suppress Feelings

Memories of childhood sexual abuse uncovered during meditation led Michele McDonald, a vipassana Buddhist meditation teacher, into therapy. In *Turning the Wheel: American Women Creating the New Buddhism,* by Sandy Boucher, McDonald says, "We have to learn to integrate what we call spiritual with what we call emotional. To me emotional is spiritual. I don't see any difference anymore. . . . For women and men who have been sexually abused, especially as young children, there is so much denial, there is usually so much inability to look at or even remember the story or content. I have found that meditation can be helpful to balance that denial. The detachment that one can learn in meditation can help a person finally have the strength and courage to face the truth and the feelings that arise from facing the story."

Don't Expect Transpersonal Therapy to Be a Panacea

Just as in any other significant endeavor, the path of personal evolution presents us with obstacles, dangers, difficulties, and mistakes, according to psychologist Piero Ferrucci. "A momentary euphoria may lead us to expect instant, total, and permanent results," he writes in *What We May Be.* "The magical wish to live happily ever after lurks in the back of our minds, ready to entice us into the false belief that we have achieved more than is possible. But the only way to accomplish valuable results in the work of self-realization is by being realistic about our human limitations."

We can make the adventure of self-realization safe and relatively smooth, Ferrucci says, if we respect our own rhythms and possibilities. He also advises:

- valuing times of darkness as much as periods of joy and enlightenment;
- using obstacles as stepping-stones to growth, rather than expecting their complete disappearance;

Healing comes only from that which leads the patient beyond himself and beyond his entanglements with ego.

C. G. JUNG

- appreciating the value of doubting, risking, and creative confusion rather than clutching for guaranteed safety, ecstasy, or ready-made answers; and
- valuing effort as well as effortlessness.

A Sampling of Transpersonal Therapies

When we enter transpersonal therapy, we may feel like that mythical voyager Odysseus embarking on a journey into uncharted regions. Like others who have undertaken this heroic quest, we may gaze out to sea with mixed feelings of exaltation and apprehension. Will we discover enchanting lands filled with wondrous sights, or will we do battle with Cyclopses and sorcerers of bewitching beauty?

Fortunately, a number of courageous Western psychologists have charted the regions and way stations of our inner voyage. With great candor, they have confronted many of the pitfalls that typically befall inner voyagers: the feeling of specialness that inflates the ego; the psychic powers that compensate for feelings of personal inadequacy; the doubts and disillusionments that threaten to end the voyage prematurely; and the ecstatic highs that imprison us in a complacency that makes us mistake a way station for the journey's end. The roadmaps of consciousness and growth techniques developed by these psychologists can help us avoid the tempting allurements and pitfalls of the inner path so that we can proceed with one-pointed wisdom to the "treasure hard to attain."

Here is a brief sampling of transpersonal therapies and techniques to facilitate our lifelong journeys of growth and transformation.

Jungian Analysis

Unlike Freud, who saw the unconscious as a dangerous place of repressed personal memories and experience, Swiss psychologist Carl G. Jung viewed it as the universal, creative source that gives birth to the individual self and that propels its evolution forward toward greater wholeness and integration. According to Jung, psychological growth involves an active, ongoing dialogue between the conscious mind (the ego) and the Self, the transpersonal center of the personality that lies hidden in the depths of the unconscious. Revealing itself to us through dreams and symbols, the Self guides us along a path in which we become the complete human beings we are destined to be. Jung called this path individuation.

When we work cooperatively with the unconscious, we find a deep

We put thirty spokes together and call it a wheel;
But it is on the space where there is nothing that the usefulness of the wheel depends.
We turn clay to make a vessel;
But it is on the space where there is nothing that the usefulness of the vessel depends.
We pierce doors and windows to make a house;
And it is on these spaces where there is nothing that the usefulness of the house depends.
Therefore just as we take advantage of what is, we should recognize the usefulness of what is not.

Lao Tzu

source of renewal, growth, strength, and wisdom, says Jungian writer and lecturer Robert A. Johnson in *Inner Work*. According to Johnson, neurotic behavior results when we isolate ourselves from this fathomless realm: "Our isolation from the unconscious is synonymous with our isolation from our souls, from the life of the spirit. It results in the loss of our religious life, for it is in the unconscious that we find our individual conception of God and experience our deities. The religious function—this inborn demand for meaning and inner experience—is cut off with the rest of the inner life. And it can only *force* its way back into our lives through neurosis, inner conflicts, and psychological symptoms that demand our attention."

Jungian analyst June Singer, author of *Seeing Through the Visible World*, recommends the following four approaches to establish a healthy relationship with the unconscious:

Work with your dreams, which offer glimpses into your invisible inner world. If you record your dreams regularly in a dream notebook, you will have a permanent history of your journey to consciousness.

Practice active imagination. In this technique developed by Jung, we pose a question to the unconscious, allow images to rise up spontaneously, then enter into a dialogue with them. Usually recorded on paper, these dialogues with personified inner figures can help you resolve neurotic conflicts or clarify personal values. The technique differs from guided meditation in that you don't direct the flow of imagery; you receive it in a quiet, meditative way. By engaging the unconscious as an equal partner with its own voice, you can consciously work on issues without waiting for clarification from dreams.

Engage in creative activities, such as music, dance, painting, and poetry, to bring forth your inner images.

Be sensitive to the invisible world—the depth dimension—that lies beneath the surface of the visible world. You don't have to practice esoteric techniques or take weekend workshops to do this. The marvelous reveals itself in the mundane: in the garden, the park, the vacant lot, the desert. You see it in the sudden appearance of a cluster of fungus on a tree after a week of rain or at home dusting off furniture, revealing the surface underneath. To really see through, you must believe it is possible to do so and then simply do it! Before long, life becomes an experience of constant revelation.

Psychosynthesis

Psychosynthesis, as developed by Roberto Assagioli, also recognizes the importance of unifying the conscious and unconscious aspects of our being—the worlds above and below. Assagioli distinguishes a higher un-

I am plagued by doubts. What if everything is an illusion and nothing exists? In that case, I definitely overpaid for my carpet. If only God would give me a clear sign! Like making a large deposit in my name at a Swiss bank.

WOODY ALLEN

conscious—the superconscious—from which originate our most evolved impulses, such as altruistic love, humanitarian action, and higher purpose. In the superconscious realm dwells the Transpersonal Self, an all-inclusive center of identity and being: "The experience of the Self has a quality of perfect peace, serenity, calm, stillness, purity, and in it there is a paradoxical blending of individuality and universality." This Self "is above and unaffected by the flow of the mind-stream or by bodily conditions; and the personal conscious self should be considered merely as its reflection, its 'projection' in the field of personality."

The personality, however, usually doesn't act from its center, because of false identification with subpersonalities, the multitude of semi-autonomous characters who live inside us. We don't have one monolithic personality, according to Psychosynthesis, but a full cast of characters with ambitions of their own. Therapists have given them labels, such as the Mystic, the Materialist, the Inner Child, the Critic, the Crusader, the Doubter, the Hedonist, and the Struggler. Work in Psychosynthesis involves disidentifying from the cast, unifying these characters around a personal center, then identifying with our transpersonal center of awareness and will. Specific techniques include guided imagery, movement, Gestalt, meditation, journal-keeping, and exercises to develop the will.

Therapeutic work consists of two stages. In *personal Psychosynthesis,* we integrate the personality around the personal self and attain a healthy level of functioning at work and in personal relationships. In *transpersonal Psychosynthesis,* we learn to align with the Transpersonal Self and manifest such qualities as altruistic love, social responsibility, and a global perspective. In this approach, then, the search for the Self, for God within, leads to a dedicated life of service to humanity, the planet, and ultimately all of life.

The Zen expression "Kill the Buddha" means to kill any concept of the Buddha as something apart from oneself. To kill the Buddha is to be the Buddha.

PETER MATTHIESSEN

RECOGNIZING SUBPERSONALITIES

"One of the most harmful illusions that can beguile us is probably the belief that we are an indivisible, immutable, totally consistent being," writes Piero Ferrucci, a former collaborator of Roberto Assagioli, in *What We May Be.* In reality, each of us contains an inner crowd, all claiming to be the "I" that makes decisions like a commander-in-chief. We are controlled by whichever subpersonality we are identified with at the moment—for example, the Sensible Eater when we pass up extra portions of high-cholesterol foods, or the Bon Vivant and Connoisseur when we delight in chocolate mousse and Camembert cheese. In Psychosynthesis, subpersonality work consists of recognizing, coordinating, and integrating our disparate elements around a higher order center, so that in each situation we may consciously choose which subpersonality we want to express. We increase the sense of self or center, says Ferrucci, "so that instead of disintegrating into a myriad of subselves at war with each other, we can again be one."

The exercise below from *What We May Be* can help us discover the various subpersonalities at work in our lives.

I tore myself away from the safe comfort of certainties through my love for truth; and truth rewarded me.

Simone de Beauvoir

☆

1. Consider one of your prominent traits, attitudes, or motives.
2. With your eyes closed, become aware of this part of you. Then let an image emerge representing it. It may be a woman, a man, an animal, an elf, an object, yourself in disguise, a monster, or anything else in the universe. Do not consciously try to find an image. Let it emerge spontaneously, as if you were watching a screen, not knowing what will shortly appear on it.
3. As soon as the image has appeared, give it the chance to reveal itself to you without any interference or judging on your part. Let it change if it tends to do so spontaneously, and let it show you some of its other aspects if it wants to. Get in touch with the general feeling that emanates from it.
4. Now let this image talk and express itself. Give it space, so to speak, for doing so; in particular, find out about its needs. Talk with it (even if your image is an object, it can talk back to you; anything is possible in the imaginary world). You have in front of you a subpersonality—an entity with a life and intelligence of its own.
5. Now open your eyes, and record in a notebook everything that happened so far. Then give this subpersonality a name—any name that fits and will help you to identify it in the future: the Complainer, the Artist, the Bitch, Santa Claus, the Skeptic, Jaws, the Insecure One, the Octopus, the Drunken Sailor, the Clown, I Told You So, and so on. Finally, write about its traits, habits, and peculiarities.
6. After you have identified and exhaustively described one subpersonality, you can go on to the others. But take your time and work on each one until you feel finished. The process requires merely picking a few more of your prominent traits, attitudes, or motives and going through steps 1 to 5 for each one.

☆

Holotropic Therapy

Psychiatrist Stanislav Grof and his wife, Christina, have developed holotropic therapy, which uses controlled breathing, evocative music, bodywork, and mandala drawing to evoke experiences unavailable to verbal Western therapies. This nondrug approach, they say, opens us to the spectrum of consciousness characteristic of psychedelic sessions and shamanic journeys.

During holotropic therapy, clients lie down with their eyes closed, focus attention on breathing and body sensations, and begin breathing more quickly than usual. This increase in the breathing rate loosens psychological armor, enabling the emergence of unconscious and superconscious material. Clients frequently report reliving birth experiences, having visions of the archetypal world, becoming one with all realms of nature, and experiencing transpersonal phenomena, such as telepathy and clairvoyance. (Because holotropic therapy evokes such powerful experiences, it should be practiced only with professional supervision.)

The Grofs believe that we cannot resolve our deep existential crises without accessing these powerful, non-ordinary states of consciousness. They have used their innovative therapy to treat claustrophobia, depression, suicidal tendencies, alcoholism, narcotic addiction, asthma, migraine headaches, and sadomasochistic inclinations. As Stan Grof says in a *Yoga Journal* article, "Activating the psyche through the breath induces powerful states of consciousness which can change the dynamic equilibrium underlying symptoms, transforming them into a stream of extraordinary experiences, consuming the symptoms in the process."

The curious paradox is that when I accept myself just as I am, then I can change.

CARL ROGERS

SACRED TRADITIONS

At the highest end of the spectrum of consciousness, transpersonal psychology gives way to the sacred traditions of Hinduism, Buddhism, Taoism, and Zen. These *sacred psychologies,* says Roger Walsh, train students to live ethically, discipline attention through meditation, transform negative emotions into positive ones, and transcend personal selfishness, often through the practice of selfless service. Students who master these disciplines develop what he calls exceptional mental health.

Here in the West, Eastern spirituality has seeded psychotherapy with techniques that help us calm our minds, balance our emotions, and gain detachment from neurotic personality patterns. As John Welwood points out in *Awakening the Heart,* therapists often use meditation to aid clients in reducing the hatred, greed, envy, pride, and ignorance of their personal "I." But at some point, he says, even the healthiest client will wake up and begin using meditation to let go of this "I-fixation" altogether. When pursued with single-pointed devotion, this practice can lead to the realization of our supreme identity.

About this process, Ram Dass writes in *Journey of Awakening:* "The path to freedom is through detachment from your old habits of ego. Slowly you will arrive at a new and more profound integration of your experiences in a more evolved structure of the universe. That is, you will flow beyond the boundaries of your ego until ultimately you merge into the universe. At that point you have gone beyond ego. Until then you must break through old structures, develop broader structures, break through those, and develop still broader structures."

In this constant rezoning and remapping of our souls, we can use all the tools available—both in Western psychology and Eastern meditative disciplines—to fuel our journey to liberation.

RESOURCES

Recommended Reading

The Inward Arc: Healing and Wholeness in Psychotherapy and Spirituality, Frances Vaughan (New Science Library, 1985). A comprehensive study of transpersonal psychology that maps the spiritual path, presents guidance for the journey, and offers numerous experiential exercises for personal growth.

Psychosynthesis, Robert Assagioli (Penguin Books, 1965). A classic, pioneering book that introduced the spiritual dimension into modern psychology.

What We May Be, Piero Ferrucci (Jeremy P. Tarcher, 1982). Offers a wealth of Psychosynthesis growth techniques.

Toward a Psychology of Being, Abraham Maslow (D. Van Nostrand Company, 1968). One of the classic foundational texts for the field of transpersonal psychology.

The Adventure of Self-Discovery, Stanislav Grof (State University of New York Press, 1988). Explains the principles and practices of holotropic therapy.

Beyond Health and Normality: Explorations of Exceptional Psychological Well-Being, Roger Walsh and Deane Shapiro, editors (Van Nostrand Reinhold Company, 1983). A collection of essays by noted experts in the field of transpersonal psychology.

Organizations and Publications

The *Association for Humanistic Psychology* (1772 Vallejo Street, San Francisco, CA 94123; 415-346-7929) attracts psychologists, educators, social workers, and community activists who hold that human nature is essentially positive, that physical and psychological health are interdependent, and that personal and social transformation are interconnected. Membership ($59/year) includes a subscription to the newsletter *AHP Perspective* and a discounted subscription to the quarterly *Journal of Humanistic Psychology.*

The *Association for Transpersonal Psychology* (P.O. Box 3049, Stanford, CA 94309; 415-327-2066) regards spirituality as an essential component of psychological health. General membership ($65/year) includes the quarterly *ATP Newsletter* and the biannual *Journal of Transpersonal Psychology.*

The *International Transpersonal Association* (20 Sunnyside Avenue, A-257, Mill Valley, CA 94941; 415-453-5860). Founded by Stanislav and Christina Grof, the organization hosts a cross-disciplinary conference each year, often in exotic locales, such as Bombay, India, or Kyoto, Japan.

Common Boundary (7005 Florida Street, Chevy Chase, MD 20815; 301-652-9495, $22/year, bimonthly). Explores the interface between spirituality and psychotherapy and is an excellent resource for professionals and laypeople.

THE MYTHOLOGY CONNECTION

Finding Our Roots Through Sacred Storytelling

In one of the most famous love stories of all times, a young knight, Tristan, sails from Ireland with the beautiful Isolde, who is betrothed to his uncle, King Mark of Cornwall. En route, Tristan and Isolde mistakenly drink the love potion prepared by Isolde's mother to consummate the royal union. Suddenly the young lovers are invaded by the supernatural world of love, and they yield to a passion that consumes them in the fires of ecstasy. Although before Tristan saw a young woman, he now encounters a goddess, the embodiment of his feminine ideal, whom he worships with a transcendent love that bathes his everyday world in hues of mystery and delight.

Although this tale dates from twelfth-century Europe, many of us recognize that we are modern-day Tristans and Isoldes, yearning to drink the potion of romantic love in our search for happiness. When lived unconsciously, this cultural myth can undermine relationships with unrealistic expectations of fulfillment. We may relate to our lovers and spouses as vehicles for fulfilling misty-eyed dreams of romantic bliss rather than as flesh-and-blood people, a strategy that puts terrible strains on our relationships.

Similarly, other myths may unknowingly rule our lives. Overcome by

The destiny of the world is determined less by the battles that are lost and won than by the stories it loves and believes in.

HAROLD GODDARD

feelings of powerlessness, we may reenact the myth of the Savior and search for a guru or therapist to rescue us from the uncertainties of life. Dedicated to social justice, others among us may reenact the myth of the Hero, affiliating themselves with an inspiring political leader, such as Martin Luther King or Mahatma Gandhi. Alternatively, in our desire to design a society based on spiritual values, we may live out the myth of a New Age, the Golden Era of cultural harmony that humanity has yearned for since time immemorial.

Science and the rule of reason may have banished the gods to the underworld, but as depth psychologists have pointed out, they cannot kill the overarching mythic forces that shape and inform our lives. According to the late mythologist Joseph Campbell, mythic tales reconnect us to the transcendent source that undergirds daily life, while disconnection from this realm invites the anxiety and soul sickness that characterize so much of the modern world.

Myths represent "the wisdom of the species by which man has weathered the milleniums," Campbell writes in *Myths To Live By*. By studying mythology, "we can learn to know and come to terms with the greater horizon of our own deeper and wiser, inward self. And analogously, the society that cherishes and keeps its myths alive will be nourished from the soundest, richest strata of the human spirit."

MYTHOLOGICAL THINKING

Many people today take myths to be lies, fabrications, or illusions, in large part because scientific thinking debunks mythological thinking as a primitive attempt to explain natural phenomena. But a number of psychologists, led by Carl Jung, have revolutionized contemporary thinking by showing how myths reflect psychological and spiritual processes in the human psyche. Jung, for example, took myths to be spontaneous presentations from the unconscious of humanity's inner life.

"A myth is the collective 'dream' of an entire people at a certain point in their history," writes Jungian author Robert A. Johnson in *We*. "It is as though the entire population dreamed together and that 'dream,' the myth, burst forth through its poetry, songs, and stories. But a myth not only lives in literature and imagination, it immediately finds its way into the behavior and attitudes of the culture—into the practical daily lives of the people."

Myths permeate our lives through the "interlocking stories, rituals,

A story must be told in such a way that it constitutes help in itself. My grandfather was lame. Once they asked him to tell a story about his teacher. And he related how his teacher used to hop and dance while he prayed. My grandfather rose as he spoke, and he was so swept away by his story that he began to hop and dance and show how the master had done. From that hour he was cured of his lameness. That's how to tell a story.

MARTIN BUBER

CLAN AND FAMILY

Every family has rules, customs, traditions, taboos, and ritual ways of interacting that shape each family member, according to Sam Keen and Anne Valley-Fox, authors of *Your Mythic Journey*. The following exercise, in which you reconstruct the physical setting of your childhood home, can help reconnect you to the origins of your personality and the values that shaped it:

- Draw a detailed floor plan of a house you lived in before you were ten.
- As you enter each room, imagine the furniture, pictures, smells, and events you associate with the room.
- Where were your secret places? (Where did you stash your comic books or go when you wanted to be alone?)
- Who lived in the house with you?
- What was the dominant mood in the household?
- Which rooms are you unable to reconstruct in memory? Why do you think you forgot them?
- Are there rooms you can't enter?

After you've filled in as much detail as you can remember, take someone on a tour of your house. Describe it as a novelist would so that your listener can feel the texture of the couch you lay on when you were sick, smell the bread baking, feel the emotions that permeated the house.

If you do this exercise in a group, use several persons to create a living sculpture of your family. Or pose your family members in an imaginary photograph that would represent their relative positions.

- What position did each member occupy?
- Are your parents facing each other, going in opposite directions, on the same level? Are they supportive or antagonistic? Who is leaning on whom?
- Which members are close to each other and which are distant? Where is the center of the family?
- What are the basic bonds and jealousies among the siblings?
- Who is trying to get away from the family?

You can turn your story over and over and find new perspectives on past events and emotions. You may invent a new past and open up a novel future.

The real voyage of discovery consists not in seeking new landscapes, but in having new eyes.

MARCEL PROUST

Myths inspire the realization of the possibility of your perfection, the fullness of your strength, and the bringing of solar light into the world.

JOSEPH CAMPBELL

Reality can destroy the dream; why shouldn't the dream destroy reality?

GEORGE MOORE

I think of Greek mythology as going back to a time that was the equivalent to the childhood of our civilization. These myths can tell us a great deal about attitudes and values with which we were raised. Like personal family stories or myths, they convey to the present generation something about who we are and what is expected of us—what is in our genetic memory, so to speak, and is part of the psychological legacy that shaped and invisibly affects our perceptions and behavior.

JEAN SHINODA BOLEN

rites, and customs that inform and give the pivotal sense of meaning to a person, family, community or culture," write Sam Keen and Anne Valley-Fox in *Your Mythic Journey*. Different cultural myths, they say, make Methodists munch hamburgers and Hindus worship cows. Some myths present a pantheon of heroes to celebrate, such as Ulysses and Captain America, while others offer a gallery of villains to contend with, such as the betraying Judas or the barbarous Nazis of the Third Reich.

Using an analogy drawn from computer science, Keen and Valley-Fox compare myths to the program in the systems disk of a computer. "Myth is the software, the cultural DNA, the unconscious information, the meta-program that governs the way we see 'reality' and the way we behave," they write. "By providing a world picture and a set of stories that explains why things are as they are, [mythology] creates consensus, sanctifies the social order, and gives the individual an authorized map of the path of life. A myth creates the plotline that organizes the diverse experiences of a person or a community into a single story."

Mythology recently has grown in popularity, Keen maintains, because the Old Story that sustained civilization for nearly two centuries has begun to collapse. The myth of endless material progress fostered during the Industrial Revolution is cracking under the strain of the worldwide ecological crisis. And as a culture-wide paradigm shift makes its presence felt, people are searching frantically for a New Story to give their lives meaning. If the Old Story concerned humanity's separation from nature, the New Story involves our reunion with the natural world, based on the interconnectedness of all living systems.

But the New Story, says Keen, has not yet coalesced into an effective myth that commands the large-scale support of our political and economic institutions. During this period, as the elements of change foment in the cultural cauldron, many people are feeling anxiety as they release outmoded beliefs and journey into their interior realm in an effort to discover a new guiding myth.

"It's never been more urgent to bring our underlying mythology to consciousness, because the culture's mythology is not providing adequate guidance for most people," says psychologist David Feinstein, co-author of *Personal Mythology*. "As the old guiding myths disintegrate, mythology has become an increasingly personal affair. By becoming experts in our own mythology, we can find creative guidance from within, rather than following antiquated beliefs, family codes, or cultural images. This increases our psychological freedom and strengthens our ability to cope within our rapidly changing world."

THE GRAIL—A MYTH FOR OUR TIME?

Is there a myth that reflects the modern journey from isolation and alienation to a state of wholeness and fulfillment? Some see such a unifying story in the quest for the Holy Grail, the chalice of the Last Supper that received Christ's blood when he was taken from the Cross.

According to the story, the Holy Grail resides in the castle of the Fisher King, who suffers continuously because of a wound that will not heal. His country falls barren and becomes a wasteland. The Knights of King Arthur's Round Table pledge to quest for the Grail, and one of them, the pure-hearted Parsifal, almost attains it but fails, because when he glimpses the sacred vessel in the Grail Castle, he forgets to ask the prescribed ritual question: "Whom does the Grail serve?"

Because of his personal deficiency, Parsifal must wander five more years through the wasteland. When at last he reaches the Fisher King's castle and poses the question correctly, Parsifal receives the answer: "The Grail serves the Grail King" (the Grail worshiper who lives in the castle's central chamber). The Fisher King is healed immediately, and the wasteland overflows with fertility and well-being.

How does this myth relate to our modern quest for spiritual renewal? In *Return to the Goddess,* Jungian analyst Edward C. Whitmont compares the wasteland to our planet, ravaged by runaway industrialism, ecological disaster, and the suppression of feminine values needed to heal our rupture from nature and from each other. The Grail, according to Joseph Campbell, is "the fullfillment of the highest spiritual potentialities of the human consciousness," actualized when people live authentic lives. Robert A. Johnson describes it as "the highest feminine symbol, the holy of holies in its feminine expression. . . . It gives a man everything that he asks even before he asks it. It is perfect happiness, the ecstatic experience."

Taken together, such descriptions of the Grail may offer a prescription for healing our industrial wasteland. Our culture currently suffers from an imbalance that stresses rational knowledge over intuitive wisdom, the conquest of nature over ecological awareness, competition over cooperation, masculine over feminine values. Searching for the Grail today involves readmitting exiled feminine values into our lives, rebalancing our scientific culture, and ending the alienation we feel from nature. It means pursuing inner-directed values, rather than living a carbon-copy existence that dishonors our creativity and uniqueness. It means discovering a new myth.

The Grail quest also involves finding our higher purpose, our vocation or calling, according to Lorna Catford and Michael Ray, authors of

God made man because he loves stories.

ELIE WIESEL

Myth is a kind of lensing system for the mind of God. It carries the codings of existence.

JEAN HOUSTON

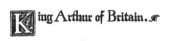

It is as psychologist Carl Jung once said: We do not believe in the reality of Olympus, so the ancient Greek gods live on for us today as symptoms. We no longer have the thunderbolts of Zeus, we have headaches. We no longer have the arrows of Eros, we have angina pains. We no longer have the divine ecstasy of Dionysus, we have addictive behavior. Even though we no longer recognize the gods, we experience their powerful forces.

ROBERT A. JOHNSON

The Path of the Everyday Hero. Early in the quest, unsure of our identity, we listen to the well-meaning advice of parents, teachers, and other authority figures, often pursuing conventional pathways that stifle our creativity. But with experience, as our Parsifal nature matures, we remember to ask penetrating questions that challenge cultural assumptions. By persisting in our inquiries, Catford and Ray write, "we might even have a breakthrough experience in which we know what our own 'Grail' is, and in fact find it and celebrate knowing our purpose in life."

If we do not pose the most important question correctly—"Whom does the Grail serve?"—then as modern Parsifals we risk the danger, sickness, and desolation that transform nature's bounty into a wasteland. Writing in *He,* Robert A. Johnson explains:

> Almost everybody in our culture thinks that the Grail is to serve us, but here there is something essential to learn. The great search for most Americans is for happiness—which of to say that we ask the Grail to serve us. We ask that this great cornucopia is nature, this great feminine outpouring, all of the material of the world—the air, the sea, the animals, the oil, the forests, and all the productivity of the world—we assume that it should serve us. And the lesson that we have to learn is that this cornucopia is nature does not serve us; it serves God.
>
> The Grail King is the image of God, the earthly representation of the divine. The myth is telling us that our task is to learn that the Grail serves the Grail King, not . . . us.

PERSONAL MYTHOLOGY

Each of us receives a mythological heritage from our culture, a legacy handed down by our families, religious teachers, educators, media purveyors, and peers. Weighed down by this collective inheritance, many of us spend a good portion of our adult lives separating the treasure from the trash. Creating a narrative account of our lives—a personal mythology that guides behavior and evolution—can help drive out the false prophets, tyrants, and money changers who rule the inner temples of our psyches.

If we remain entangled in personal myths that do not fit our individual inner nature, we experience the pain and anxiety of living an inauthentic existence. But if we forge personal myths that combine cultural and family myths with our own unique stories, we claim rulership over our lives. We become the authors of our existence, rather than victims of other people's secondhand tales. Describing the difficulties of this task, Keen and Valley-Fox write:

If we do not make the effort to become conscious of our personal myths gradually, we become dominated by what psychologists have variously called repetition compulsions, autonomous complexes, engrams, routines, scripts, games. One fruitful way to think of neurosis is to consider it a tape loop, an oft-told story that we repeat in our inner dialogues with ourselves and with others. "Well, I'm just not the kind of person who can. . . ." "I never could. . . ." "I wouldn't think of. . . ." While personal myths give us a sense of identity, continuity, and security, they become constricting and boring if they are not revised from time to time. To remain vibrant through a lifetime, we must always be inventing ourselves, weaving new themes into our life-narratives, remembering our past, re-visioning our future, reauthorizing the myth by which we live.

Myth is something that never was but is always happening. It is the nuclear cell in the entelechy, the wake-up call from Central: "It's time! Time to wake up now!"

JEAN HOUSTON

Philosopher Jean Houston offers an interesting insight into why the failure to forge a larger story causes personal suffering. In *The Search for the Beloved,* she says that people pathologize because they cannot mythologize. When we are wounded by life in some way—perhaps through physical illness, the loss of a job, or betrayal by a trusted friend—we may react to the pain by retreating into ourselves, calcifying an already established identity into permanent rigidity. But if we let the wounding crack open the boundaries of our personal self, a rebirth can occur as we connect to a larger story arising from the deep psyche that invests our suffering with archetypal meaning and significance. In our openness, we may find inspiration in the stories of Oedipus's blinding, Persephone's rape, Job's testing, or Prometheus's defiance of Zeus and subsequent punishment.

When we remain disconnected from the mythic foundations of life, we seek to relieve our pain as quickly and comfortably as possible, Houston points out. But those interested in soul-making view their wounding as a crisis by which the sacred enters into time, often shattering cherished assumptions about life.

"Wounding becomes *sacred* when we are willing to release our old stories and to become the vehicles through which the new story may emerge into time," Houston writes. "When we fall to do this, we tend to repeat the same old story over and over again. If you have a neurosis or psychosis, it probably originated in pathos that was not worked out to its source in a Larger Story. If we would only look far enough and deep enough, we would find that our woundings have archetypal power. In uncovering their mythic base, we are challenged to a deeper life."

We need to open to a Larger Story, according to David Feinstein, whenever we suffer from self-defeating patterns in intimate relationships, in jobs, or with authority figures. These are times to realign and update personal myths. Feinstein and Stanley Krippner have identified a five-step process by which personal myths evolve:

- We identify an area in which an operating myth does not serve us.
- The psyche generates a counter-myth that contains untested possibilities at the cutting edge of personal development.

FROM THE WISDOM OF JOSEPH CAMPBELL

The late Joseph Campbell, master mythologist, conveyed the wisdom of the world's myths and legends to millions of people through his books and television programs. Following is a sampling of his memorable insights.

On the nature of myth. Myth is the secret opening through which the inexhaustible energies of the cosmos pour into human cultural manifestations. Religions, philosophies, arts, the social forms of primitive and historic man, prime discoveries in science and technology, the very dreams that blister sleep, boil up from the basic, magic ring of myth.

On discovering your purpose in life. If you do follow your bliss, you put yourself on a kind of track that has been there all the while, waiting for you, and the life you ought to be living is the one you are living. When you can see that, you begin to meet people who are in the field of your bliss, and they open the doors to you. I say, follow your bliss and don't be afraid, and doors will open where you didn't know they were going to be.

On the "call" today. The modern hero, the modern individual who dares to heed the call and seek the mansion of that presence with whom it is our whole destiny to be atoned, cannot, indeed, must not, wait for his community to cast off its slough of pride, fear, rationalized avarice, and sanctified misunderstanding. "Live," Nietzsche says, "as though the day were here." It is not society that is to guide and save the creative hero, but precisely the reverse. And so every one of us shares the supreme ordeal—carries the cross of the redeemer—not in the bright moments of his tribe's great victories, but in the silence of his personal despair.

On the hero quest. We have not even to risk the adventure alone, for the heroes of all time have gone before us; the labyrinth is thoroughly known; we have only to follow the thread of the hero-path. And where we had

Ultimately, there is no way to avoid the hero's quest. It comes and finds us if we do not move out bravely to meet it. And while we may strive to avoid the pain, hardship, and struggle it inevitably brings, life takes us eventually to the promised land, where we can be genuinely prosperous, loving, and happy. The only way out is through.

CAROL PEARSON

- A new mythic vision emerges that embraces the best features of both viewpoints.
- Feeling the promise of increased creativity and freedom in our lives, we commit to the new mythic vision.
- We then anchor this vision in everyday life through behavioral changes that reflect the mythology we consciously choose to live out.

---

thought to find an abomination, we shall find a god; where we had thought to travel outward, we shall come to the center of our own existence; where we had thought to be alone, we shall be with all the world.

On the privatization of mythology in our times. In the absence of an effective general mythology, each of us has his private, unrecognized, rudimentary, yet secretly potent pantheon of dream. The latest incarnation of Oedipus, the continued romance of Beauty and the Beast, stand this afternoon on the corner of Forty-second Street and Fifth Avenue, waiting for the traffic light to change.

On the need for self-knowledge. If the person insists on a certain program, and doesn't listen to the demands of his own heart, he's going to risk schizophrenic crackup. Such a person has put himself off center. He has aligned himself with a program for life, and it's not the one the body's interested in at all. The world is full of people who have stopped listening to themselves or have listened only to their neighbors to learn what they ought to do, how they ought to behave, and what the values are that they should be living for.

On the anxiety of our age. It is possible that the failure of mythology and ritual to function effectively in our civilization may account for the high incidence among us of the malaise that has led to the characterization of our time as "The Age of Anxiety."

On the revelatory nature of mythology. Mythology is a rendition of forms through which the formless Form of forms can be known.

On mythic imagination. Whenever men have looked for something solid on which to found their lives, they have chosen not the facts in which the world abounds, but the myths of an immemorial imagination.

Whenever a knight of the Grail tried to follow a path made by someone else, he went altogether astray. Where there is a way or path, it is someone else's footsteps. Each of us has to find his own way. . . . Nobody can give you a mythology.

JOSEPH CAMPBELL

"We believe that a well-articulated, carefully examined mythology is one of the most effective devices for countering the disorienting grip of a world in mythic turmoil," they write in *Personal Mythology*. "Such a mythology also points the way back to the deeper world of the psyche."

Remembering the Myth of Your Ancestors

Nothing we ever imagined is beyond our powers, only beyond our present self-knowledge.

Theodore Roszak

The following exercise, adapted from *Personal Mythology* by David Feinstein and Stanley Krippner, demonstrates how cultural myths are passed down from generation to generation, influencing our attitudes, decisions, and pathways through life.

———————— ☆ ————————

Stand where you can move several feet in any direction. Find a comfortable posture and close your eyes. Take a backward step and imagine that you are stepping into the body and being of your father if you are a man, or of your mother if you are a woman.

After sensing this body and personality, take another step backward into the body and being of your same-sex grandparent. Repeat this process as you merge with your great-grandparent and great-great-grandparent, who might be a late seventeenth-century craftsman's wife in London, a foot soldier in the Czar's army, or the slave of a tobacco farmer in Virginia in the 1830s.

As your great-great-grandparent, reflect on your major concerns, primary sources of satisfaction, and position in society, and consider whether you look to a nonhuman authority to explain human destiny. Then step forward into the posture of your great-grandparent, your grandparent, and your same-sex parent at your current age, each time reflecting on these issues.

Finally, step into yourself. Find a posture that represents the statement your own life is making. Hear this statement as an actual phrase or sentence that you say aloud. Let your posture become animated as you continue to repeat your statement, exploring and experimenting with the movement and the statement. Then come to a resting point and reflect on your observations during this ritual.

———————— ☆ ————————

GODS AND GODDESSES WITHIN US

If, as Jung suggested, myths reflect archetypes within the psyche, then a psychology honoring the gods and goddesses might help us relate to the transpersonal forces that shape our lives. Such a psychology would tie our relationships with parents, spouses, children, and friends to the larger patterns our ancestors conceived of as the gods. As Jungian analyst James Hillman counsels, "Let us reimagine psychodynamics as mythic tales rather than physical processes; as the rise and fall of dramatic themes, as genealogies, as voyages and contests and respites, as interventions of the Gods."

Jean Shinoda Bolen, a Jungian analyst, believes that Greek gods and goddesses still operate in the psyche as images of what men and women are truly like. These images, she says, have lived in the human imagination for more than three thousand years because they correspond to psychological forces having such universal depth and power that people have personified them as gods and goddesses. By consciously relating to these universal forces, we can attune ourselves to mythic patterns that give direction and meaning to our lives.

Every era opens with its challenges, and they cannot be met by elaborating methods of the past.

CHARLES A. LINDBERGH

"Men and women are influenced by powerful images Jungians call archetypes, which are patterns in the collective unconscious that shape behavior and influence emotion," Bolen explains. "Some goddess archetypes propel women into marriage and motherhood, while others encourage them to become autonomous and career-minded. In the same way, some god archetypes propel men into positions of authority and power, while others influence them to become artists and craftsmen."

For example, the virgin goddesses—Artemis, Athena, and Hestia—represent women's needs for autonomy and their capacity to focus consciousness on meaningful goals. The vulnerable goddesses—Hera, Demeter, and Persephone—express women's need for affiliation and bonding in the traditional roles of wife, mother, and daughter. In a class by herself, Aphrodite governs women's enjoyment of love, beauty, sensuality, and creativity.

Among the male gods, Zeus, Poseidon, and Hades compel men to seek authoritarian positions by establishing dominion in a chosen realm. Apollo and Hermes, Zeus's favorite sons, help men get ahead in the patriarchal world because of their mental facility and emotional objectivity. Ares and Hephaestus predispose men to physical action, while the sensual Dionysus compels men to seek mystical, ecstatic experiences and intensity of feeling.

Some people appear to be embodiments of a single ruling archetype. For example, Gloria Steinem, founder of *Ms.* magazine, personifies the Artemis qualities of achievement, competence, independence from men and male opinions, and concern for victimized, powerless women and children. Screen goddesses Marilyn Monroe and Madonna incarnate the alluring qualities of Aphrodite. Aristotle Onassis expressed the wheeling-and-dealing Zeus qualities that built a shipping empire, while Muhammad Ali called on the aggressive instinct of Ares, the god of war, every time he stepped into the boxing ring.

"Whether we're aware of them or not, myths live through and in us," Bolen says. "When we consciously recognize and honor the gods and goddesses, they help us become who we truly are. They motivate us to lead deeply meaningful lives because our actions are connected to the archetypal layer of the psyche."

THE HERO'S JOURNEY

Throughout history, the larger-than-life exploits of heroes probably have stirred the human heart more than any other mythological tales. Whether

All the archaic images are surfacing out of the collective unconscious. The ancient ways and ancient esoteric schools have taken on a new life in the midst of a technological society. From Tibet, from the Middle East, from Scotland, from Mexico, and from the American Southwest, the archaic ways are coming back and offering themselves to us. They have lived in secret for a long time, and in secrecy they have flourished. Now, as they blaze forth into the open, they will die and, in their death, make a new life possible. Like a dying star that in its explosive end scatters the material needed for the evolution of life, the supernova of the esoteric and occult we are witnessing is both an end and a beginning.

WILLIAM IRWIN THOMPSON

as Theseus slaying the Minotaur, David battling Goliath, or Luke Sky-walker contending with Darth Vader, the hero reminds us that by meeting life's tests courageously, we can tap hidden wellsprings of strength, wisdom, and creativity to overcome personal weaknesses and prevail over challenging circumstances.

According to Joseph Campbell, the hero, aware of deficiencies in the established order, ventures into the unknown in search of germinal ideas and energies that can infuse society with the creative vigor to bring forth a new order. In *The Path of the Everyday Hero,* Lorna Catford and Michael Ray describe the journey this way: "In the course of meeting a challenge that disrupts an initial state of innocence, the hero is initiated into a realm where he or she is faced with grave danger of some sort. With the assistance of allies, the hero breaks out of that world, to successfully meet the challenge and return home with a gift of a treasure or wisdom. The hero's return is celebrated and life is resumed—somehow transformed by the Hero's Journey."

While the hero myth expresses our potential for spiritual transformation, it has flourished in patriarchal cultures that give priority to physical acts of valor and conquest. This may explain why we generally think of warriors such as Odysseus or King Arthur as exemplars of heroism rather than Jesus or Buddha, whose conquests were of an inner nature. But as the boundaries of the soul expand during this transitional age and the Grail confronts us with its call to inner adventure, we need to expand our notion of what constitutes a hero.

In Search of the New Hero

From the moment astronauts took photographs of the Earth from outer space, a global mythology began to develop that celebrates the inter-relatedness of all life forms, nations, and cultures. The very nature of global electronic communications stimulates this development. As Campbell says in *The Power of Myth,* "When you see the earth from the moon, you don't see any divisions there of nations or states. This might be the symbol, really, for the new mythology to come."

However, our hero myths do not always accord with the emerging planetary myth. They derive from an earlier age that glorified individualism, separation from nature, and a nationalism that found expression in warfare, conquest, and the imposition of the triumphant warring culture over its vanquished enemies. The contemporary hero, by contrast, faces different challenges. He or she must enter into a proper relationship with

The hero must venture forth from the world of common-sense consciousness into a region of supernatural wonder. There he encounters fabulous forces—demons and angels, dragons and helping spirits. After a fierce battle, he wins a decisive victory over the powers of darkness. Then he returns from his mysterious adventure with the gift of knowledge or fire, which he bestows on his fellow man.

JOSEPH CAMPBELL

121

nature, honor an ecology of all cultures, and temper the heroic ego by learning to live with connectedness rather than an isolating individualism.

"Being a hero is *not* the same thing as . . . being in conflict and competition with others," write Catford and Ray in *The Path of the Everyday Hero*. "Instead, the [new] hero . . . is a peaceful warrior, embodying both so-called 'feminine' and 'masculine' values of sensitivity and nurturance on the one hand, and assertiveness and strength on the other."

Sam Keen has identified four defining qualities of the new hero:

Humility. This does not refer to the traditional idea of piety. Rather, the planetary hero lives close to the humus of the Earth as a grounded creature in harmony with the commonwealth of all sentient beings.

Community. The new hero balances a hard-won sense of individuality with the needs of the larger community. Rather than being continually mobile, the new hero puts down roots and makes a commitment to home, community, city, and bio-region. Like Martin Luther, the planetary hero can proclaim, "Here I Stand!"

Compassion. By developing empathy, the planetary hero senses unity with others and guides action by this inner sense.

Love of limits. Until recently in Western history, we have been ruled by the myth of Prometheus, trying to exceed all limits through technological power. Now we must rediscover the love of limits, of joyful boundaries, so we can live appropriately with our surroundings. From this perspective, the new hero does not act larger than life, but rather life-sized, responding to challenges with a developed humanity.

THE HEROINE'S JOURNEY

To dispel our culture's negative associations with the feminine, many contemporary women have emulated the male heroic journey and have achieved hard-won successes in the academic and business world. But according to family therapist Maureen Murdock, women have paid too high a price for their advances. Adapting to male standards of behavior, in learning to live logically and efficiently they have sacrificed their health, dreams, and intuition, along with a deep relationship to their feminine nature. To redress the imbalance that has left them scarred, broken, and empty, says Murdock, they need a new model of the heroic journey that honors their uniqueness as women.

All sorrows can be borne if you put them into a story or tell a story about them.

ISAK DINESEN

122

"Women do have a quest at this time in our culture," she writes in *The Heroine's Journey*. "It is the quest to fully embrace the feminine nature, learning how to value themselves as women and to heal the deep wound of the feminine. It is a very important inner journey, toward being a fully integrated, balanced, and whole human being."

The journey to wholeness begins when women reject the feminine (seen as weak, passive, and dependent) and embrace the outer heroic journey to independence and success. At the peak of their success, however, many women feel a despair and spiritual aridity that leads to an inevitable descent to the underworld, where they encounter the fragmented, rejected aspects of their femininity sacrificed during earlier phases of the journey.

This descent, often precipitated by the loss of a significant relationship or by a life-threatening illness or accident, brings women face-to-face with confusion, grief, rage, and despair. Describing this "densely dark and unforgiving time," Murdock writes:

> A woman moves down into the depths to reclaim the parts of herself that split off when she rejected the mother and shattered the mirror of the feminine. To make this journey a woman puts aside her fascination with the intellect and games of the cultural mind, and acquaints herself, perhaps for the first time, with *her* body, *her* emotions, *her* sexuality, *her* intuition, *her* images, *her* values, and *her* mind. This is what she finds in the depths.

After the period of descent, the heroine begins to heal the mother/daughter split, which Murdock calls the deep feminine wound. Besides working on the relationship with her personal mother, she may heal herself through acts of *divine ordinariness* (seeing the sacred in the everyday), such as washing dishes or weeding the garden. She also may bond with other women through female rites of passage at women's gatherings and vision quests or establish a relationship to the inner feminine through rediscovering ancient images of female deities.

In the final stages of the journey, the heroine integrates feminine values with the masculine skills she initially learned. This sacred marriage has profound implications not only for the healing of women, but for the healing of the planet as well.

"The heroic quest is not about power over, about conquest and domination; it is a quest to bring balance into our lives through the marriage of both feminine and masculine aspects of our nature," Murdock writes.

The future is bound to surprise us, but we don't have to be dumbfounded.

KENNETH BOULDING

"[The modern-day heroine] brings us wisdom about the interconnectedness of all species; she teaches us how to live together in this global vessel and helps us to reclaim the feminine in our lives."

RESOURCES

Recommended Reading

The Hero With a Thousand Faces, Joseph Campbell (Princeton University Press, 1972). The classic work that demonstrates the commonality of the hero myth throughout all the world's cultures.

The Power of Myth, Joseph Campbell with Bill Moyers (Doubleday, 1988). A wise and witty introduction to mythology that also serves as a summing up of Campbell's work.

The Search for the Beloved: Journeys in Mythology and Sacred Psychology, Jean Houston (Jeremy P. Tarcher, 1987). A guidebook to sacred psychology that provides exercises, mythological journeys, and rituals to attune mind and body to the spiritual realm.

Personal Mythology: The Psychology of Your Evolving Self, David Feinstein and Stanley Krippner (Jeremy P. Tarcher, 1988). A comprehensive, step-by-step guide for examining and changing the personal myths that underlie our lives.

Your Mythic Journey, Sam Keen and Anne Valley-Fox (Jeremy P. Tarcher, 1973). Gives guidance and exercises for finding meaning in life through writing and storytelling.

The Hero Within: Six Archetypes We Live By, Carol Pearson (Harper & Row, 1986). Analyzes the hero's journey with insights drawn from literature, anthropology, and psychology.

The Path of the Everyday Hero, Lorna Catford and Michael Ray (Jeremy P. Tarcher, 1991). A handbook that uses myth and metaphor, along with guided exercises, to increases creativity, improve relationships, and find career fulfillment.

The Grail: Quest for the Eternal, John Matthews (Crossroad Publishing, 1981). Explores the Grail quest with highly readable scholarship and beautiful illustrations.

Ecstasy: Understanding the Psychology of Joy, Robert A. Johnson (Harper & Row, 1987). Explores the loss of ecstasy in Western culture using the myth of Dionysus as an intellectual framework.

Publications and Tapes

Parabola (656 Broadway, New York, NY 10012-2317; 212-505-6200, $22/year, quarterly). Each issue of the magazine is devoted to a specific theme, such as addiction, money, demons, pilgrimage, Earth and spirit, forgiveness, and the child. Contributors include Joseph Campbell, Peter Matthiessen, Ursula LeGuin, and Robert Bly.

Anima: The Journal of Human Experience (c/o Harry Buck, 1053 Wilson Avenue, Chambersburg, PA 17201; 717-267-0087, $9.95/year, published semiannually). Explores women's spirituality, Asian religions and culture, Jungian and Teilhardian thought, and myth and psychology. Contributors include Jean Houston, Thomas Berry, Joanna Macy, Starhawk, and June Singer.

Joseph Campbell and the Power of Myth, the six-hour video series of interviews with the legendary mythologist conducted by Bill Moyers, is also available on audiocassette. Information: Mystic Fire Video, P.O. Box 9323, South Burlington, VT 05407; 800-727-8433.

Big Sur Tapes (3C Mercury Avenue, Tiburon, CA 94920; 415-435-5511). Features one of the largest tape archives of Joseph Campbell's work, recorded live primarily by Dolphin Tapes over the last twenty years at Esalen Institute. Tapes of other speakers also are available.

The Art of Dreamwork

Unlocking the Gates to the Inner World

After completing an undergraduate degree with honors, Erica worked as a waitress for ten years, then returned to school for an MBA. Just before graduation, facing the unnerving prospect of job interviews, she had the following dream:

"I am on top of a mountain, being forced to jump from my mountain to the top of another mountain. There is a steep valley below, so it is very dangerous. I know I have to take a chance. I imagine that I'm jumping and finally take a great leap and make it. I am aware of all my movements and how I'm breathing as I land."

As a dramatization of her current situation, the dream suggests that Erica can succeed in making the transition from graduate school (her current "mountain") to the business world (the other peak). By taking a great leap, she can rise above her lesser job and humble origins, symbolized by the steep valley, and reach new heights in her career.

In another case, Joel, a computer programmer, began working overtime to provide financially for the arrival of his first child. When his wife was five months pregnant, he had the following dream about attending a baseball game:

"In the middle of the game, I get up to get some beer. When I return, I can't find my seat. I look around for a new one, but many of the women in

Dreams are real while they last. Can we say more of life?

Havelock Ellis

127

the stands are pregnant, and they are taking up two seats. I have to go to the back of the stadium and stand. I am very annoyed."

This dream, which portrays Joel as an outcast in a traditional male setting, expresses common emotional issues among expectant fathers: the fear of being excluded during pregnancy and of being displaced by the arrival of the baby. Once he deciphered the dream's message and owned up to his unacknowledged feelings, Joel cut back on overtime hours to spend more time with his wife preparing for her baby's arrival.

These cases, recounted by psychologist Alan B. Siegel in *Dreams That Can Change Your Life,* illustrate how dreams can provide X-rays of our inner life and give valuable guidance during times of crisis or critical change. By opening a window to the unconscious mind, dreams can help us unearth hidden feelings and unexpressed needs; explore and resolve conflicts in our professional lives and close relationships; confront our greatest fears; and deal with the challenges of illness and the loss of loved ones.

"When you remember your dreams, you remember your Self, your hidden wounds, fears, desires and joys," Siegel writes. "When you explore your dreams, you begin to make yourself whole: you take back the powerful feelings of grief, rage, and love that you've denied or avoided. When you share your dreams, you are sharing deeply personal feelings that create bonds of intimacy and help you receive the love and support needed to heal and grow at times of change."

THE MYTHOLOGY OF OUR DREAMSCAPE

Each night in falling asleep, we temporarily put aside the linear logic of our waking minds and journey into the theater of our personal mythology. Like a movie director reflecting on the day's successes and failures, its moments of confidence and self-doubt, the dreaming mind creates minipsychodramas that are projected onto the inner screen of consciousness, waiting for critical reviews from the audience. When we fail to understand the picture language projected onto the screen, then, as the Talmud suggests, our dreams remain like unopened letters. But if we master our dream mythology, we receive valuable insights and wise counsel about every aspect of life, including the accomplishment of goals and the clarification of values, along with our pretensions and self-deceptions.

Depth psychologists believe that myths and dreams express what Carl Jung called archetypes, the primordial images or universal patterns found in the unconscious. In archetypal dreams, which generally have a mythical quality, we may descend to the underworld to battle with monsters guard-

When men dream, each has his own world.
When they are awake, they have a common world.

HERACLITUS

In dreams we see ourselves naked and acting out our real characters, even more clearly than we see others awake.

HENRY DAVID THOREAU

128

ing the treasure of our individuality. Like Odysseus, we may set sail on a voyage, meet goddess figures, and undergo initiatory rites. As dreamers, we also may witness the birth of a divine child or receive guidance from a sage who symbolizes the inner self.

Dreams record the process of *individuation,* the ongoing journey by which the ego moves into a relationship with the Self, the center and organizing principles of the psyche, Jungian analyst Marie-Louise von Franz points out in *Man and His Symbols.* When considered in sequence and arranged as a pattern, they reveal the slow, sometimes meandering, but always purposeful way in which the psyche communicates with and leads the personality toward integration.

In the journey to wholeness, we encounter archetypal dream figures who represent unconscious parts of ourselves that we either welcome into conscious life or struggle against in our resistance to growth. These figures include the *shadow,* the same-sex figure who represents unknown or repressed parts of the psyche, often perceived as dark or frightening; the opposite-sex soul image, called the *anima* for men and *animus* for women, which guides us into and through the inner world; and the *Self,* the innermost nucleus of the psyche, symbolized for women as a priestess, sorceress, or Earth mother and for men as a wise old man, guru, or masculine initiator. The Self also is symbolized by a royal couple, a circle, a mandala (a circle divided into four parts), or any symbol of quaternity.

Dreams are like people: they respond to attention and retreat when neglected.

SAM KEEN AND
ANNE VALLEY-FOX

There have been times when I have fallen asleep in tears; but in my dreams the most charming forms have come to cheer me, and I have risen fresh and joyful.

GOETHE

THE PERSONAL NATURE OF DREAMS

Not all dreams present us with archetypal characters and situations, however. According to psychologist Ann Faraday, author of *The Dream Game,* most of them focus on themes of a more mundane nature, acting as sensitive barometers of the daily pressures of our domestic and professional lives.

In her view, dreams express the "thoughts of the heart," our honest, uninhibited responses to life's challenges, which our self-image, prejudices, and social pressures often prevent us from seeing in waking life. For example, a cheerful, self-effacing woman who represses her anger may dream that her stove is exploding. The woman's waking mind might reject her angry feelings as being bad, but the dreaming mind bypasses cultural conditioning, revealing that unless she expresses her bottled-up feelings, an emotional explosion is imminent.

To Jung, dreams balance one-sided conscious attitudes with more realistic appraisals. For example, he cites the case of a young man who dreamt that his normally proper, self-controlled father was behaving like a drunken brute. Because the youth idealized his father, inferiority feelings prevented his own growth into manhood. The dream compensated for his distorted view by portraying the father in a deprecatory manner, as if to say, "He has feet of clay like other men. Give up worshiping a man with human faults and think more highly of yourself." As Jung writes in *Man and His Symbols:*

> The general function of dreams is to try to restore our psychological balance by producing dream material that re-establishes, in a subtle way, the total psychic equilibrium. This is what I call the complementary (or compensatory) role of dreams in our psychic make-up. It explains why people who have unrealistic ideas or too high an opinion of themselves, or who make grandiose plans out of proportion to their real capacities, have dreams of flying or falling. The dream compensates for the deficiencies in their personalities, and at the same time it warns them of dangers in the present course.

DREAM GROUPS

To contact the guidance and inspiration of dreams, some people meet in ongoing dream-work groups. These groups, run on an egalitarian basis, often with rotating leadership, strengthen the influence of dreams in our lives, much as an audience can validate an artist's creative endeavors.

"To know any particular dream well requires patience and perseverance as well as skill," writes Eva Renee Neu in *Dreams and Dream Groups: Messages from the Interior.* "Several people working together can do more and do it more quickly than one. With our combined waking intelligence, we approach more easily these difficult, shy, or even intimidating fragments of non-objective reality."

To form a dream group, Neu offers the following guidelines:

- Review at the first meeting each member's experience and expectations of dream groups.
- Arrange for a certain set number of meetings. Six is a typical number. The idea is to pledge yourselves to attend a short series of meetings and then have the chance to decide whether you wish to continue with a second limited commitment.

A dream *is a theater in which the dreamer is himself the scene, the player, the prompter, the producer, the author, the public, and the critic. . . . Such an interpretation conceives all the figures in the dream as personified features of the dreamer's own personality.*

C. G. JUNG

Dreams also compensate for low estimations we hold of ourselves and others, according to Jungian analyst Frieda Fordham. If, for example, we habitually undervalue someone, we may have a dream in which this person behaves with the grandiloquence of a king or queen granting audiences to commoners. "Dreams also bring hidden conflicts to light by showing an unknown side of the character," Fordham writes in *An Introduction to Jung's Psychology*, "as when a mild, inoffensive person dreams of violence, or an ascetic of sexual orgies." They also express hidden wishes, point toward future personality development, and warn of imminent danger.

Spiritual Guidance Through Dreams

Because dreams portray our individual journeys to wholeness, they also have a spiritual dimension. Ancient people looked to their dreams for spiritual guidance, and most religions regarded dreamwork as a legitimate

Just as in night-dreams the first symptom of waking is to suspect that one is dreaming, the first symptom of waking from the waking state—the second awakening of religion—is the suspicion that our present waking state is dreaming likewise. To be aware that we are only partially awake is the first condition of becoming and making ourselves more fully awake.

A. R. ORAGE

- Set a fixed place for those meetings. Agree on the frequency and duration of sessions and set a regular time. The sessions should accommodate at least two dreams, allowing at least half an hour for a dream (even for a fragment that takes only ten seconds to tell).
- Agree on confidentiality. The group must realize that what is revealed in dreams is the private business of the dreamer.
- Allow for flexibility of format in your meetings. Besides working with dreams verbally, the group may decide to dramatize, sculpt, paint, or dance the dreams. These ways of tapping the unconscious may give a pleasant respite and invite new dream awareness later.

"The dream group does not set itself the task of problem-solving and definitely avoids the 'what's wrong with you' stance associated with diagnosis," Neu says. "Instead of finding its historical roots primarily on the couch or in one-to-one confrontation, the dream group acts as a descendant of other gatherings that search for information, celebrate mystery, reveal secrets, make strategy, give importance to metaphor, and receive inspiration. . . . We gather to receive some ultimate wisdom that we cannot get by ourselves when we are alone."

The dream is the royal road to the unconscious.

Sigmund Freud

The alternative to recalling and interpreting dreams is not always pleasant. Individuals cannot expect to drift forever. If they do not puzzle out their identity, and the direction of their lives by the aid of their dreams, then they may be brought, by the relentless action of their own pent-up souls, into some crisis which requires that they come to terms with themselves. It may be a medical crisis. It may be the end of a marriage or of a job. It may be depression or withdrawal. . . .

Edgar Cayce

spiritual practice. To the ancients, dreams provided individual and collective guidance, as illustrated by the biblical story of Joseph, whose dream interpretations helped the Egyptians avoid famine.

"The dream is, among other things, a spiritual event," writes Louis Savary in the anthology *Dreamtime & Dreamwork,* edited by Stanley Krippner. "The dream can provide healing and wholeness. It is, in part, the dream's purpose to put you in touch with your ultimate values."

Dreamwork opens a line of communication between the waking ego and the inner self, Savary says. Establishing this relationship can help bring people to spiritual maturity, provided they ground the insights they receive in appropriate action. To keep the energy of dreams alive, we can reflect on dream symbols, dialogue with dream figures, bring unfinished dreams to resolution, and use artwork to give shape to dream images. We also can translate our insights into concrete action. If, for example, a woman contacts the energy of courage in one of her dreams, she can express it through an appropriate act of assertiveness to anchor this positive quality in her personality.

"If you don't use the energy released in the dream, it will slip back into the unconscious and no longer be as readily available," writes Savary. "How many of us have had insights about our lives that we recognized as important, intended to do something about them, but never turned those insights into concrete tasks? Consequently, our lives were never changed." The more we exercise our dream *muscles* in the arena of daily life, Savary concludes, the more energy we have available to keep our dreams alive and growing.

Dream Recall

Researchers say that we dream periodically throughout the night, especially during periods of rapid eye movement (REM) sleep. Many of us, however, awaken in the morning with vague nocturnal impressions that quickly dissolve. Some of us even proclaim that we never dream. Given the elusiveness of dreams in what Ann Faraday calls our pragmatic, "dream-thieving society," whether we remember dreams or not seems to depend on personal interest and motivation.

As dream researcher Stephen LaBerge writes in *Lucid Dreaming:* "For the most part, those who want to remember their dreams can do so, and those who do not want to do not. For many people, simply having the intention to remember, reminding themselves of this intention just before bed, is enough. One effective way to strengthen this resolve is to keep a dream journal . . . and record whatever you can remember of your dreams every time you wake up. As you record more dreams, you will remember more dreams."

In general, dream psychologists recommend keeping recording equipment, such as a journal and pen, close to the bed. Because dreams are so elusive and nocturnal memory so unreliable, experts urge dreamers to commit their narratives to paper as soon as they awaken, no matter how trivial or bizarre the incidents may appear. An apparently senseless dream fragment may contain hidden insights that can resolve long-standing problems or cast light on our unsuspected motivations.

Once we reclaim our lost dreamworld, we need to unlock the mystery of dream symbolism. In general, it is better to avoid ready-made interpretations that ascribe universal meaning to certain symbols. A snake that appears in one dream may refer to sexual temptation, while in another context it may indicate the need for regeneration of the personality. "No dream symbol can be separated from the individual who dreams it, and there is no straightforward interpretation of any dream," observes Jung in *Man and His Symbols*. "Each individual varies so much in the way that his unconscious complements or compensates his conscious mind that it is impossible to be sure how far dreams and their symbols can be classified at all."

Still, there are some general principles that can help in deciphering dreams without violating our uniquely personal symbolism. Here are some of Ann Faraday's suggestions from *The Dream Game*:

1. The dream should always be considered literally in the first instance and examined for signs of objective truth, such as warnings or reminders, before moving on to metaphorical interpretation.
2. If the dream makes no sense when taken literally, then (and only then) see it as a metaphorical statement of the dreamer's feelings at the time of the dream.
3. All dreams are triggered by something on our minds or in our hearts, so the primary objective must be to relate the dream theme to some event or preoccupation of the previous day or so.
4. The feeling tone of the dream usually gives a clue as to what this particular life situation is. For example, if the feeling tone of the dream is miserable, then the dream was sparked by some miserable situation in the dreamer's current life.
5. Common dreams themes [such as falling, flying, appearing naked, losing money and valuables] are likely to indicate common areas of human feeling or experience. But within these broad limits each theme can mean quite different things to different dreamers, according to the individual's life circumstances at the time of the dream.

The dream is the small hidden door in the deepest and most intimate sanctum of the soul, which opens into that primeval cosmic night that was soul long before there was a conscious ego and will be soul far beyond what a conscious ego could ever reach.

C. G. JUNG

133

We in the contemporary west may wake each morning to cast out our sleep and dream experience like so much rubbish. But that is an almost freakish act of alienation. Only western society—and especially in the modern era—has been quite so prodigal in dealing with what is, even by the fictitious measure of our mechanical clocks, a major portion of our lives.

THEODORE ROSZAK

6. The same dream may recur from time to time in the dreams of the same dreamer and have a different specific meaning each time, according to his life circumstances at the time of each dream.
7. Dreams do not tell us what we already know (unless, of course, it is something we know but have failed to act upon, in which case they will recur, often in the form of nightmares, until we do). If a dream seems to be dealing with something you are quite aware of, look for some other meaning.

8. A dream is correctly interpreted when and only when it makes sense to the dreamer in terms of his present life situation and moves him to change his life constructively.

9. A dream is incorrectly interpreted if the interpretation leaves the dreamer unmoved and disappointed. Dreams come to expand, not to diminish us.

"Dreams reflect not only actual happenings, but also a whole host of thoughts and feelings that passed us by during the day because we were too busy or unwilling to catch them," Faraday writes. Besides expressing the "thoughts of our heart," dreams function as "powerful revealers of hidden talents, buried beauty, and unsuspected creative energy. They urge us to recognize that we are actually a lot nicer than we have hitherto realized."

DREAM INCUBATION

William, a struggling artist who charged students twenty dollars a month for drawing lessons, was tempted to give up his vocation as a painter for a regular job and a more financially secure lifestyle. One night he went to sleep repeating the following question much like a mantra: "Should I get a job to earn money, or is there a better way for me?" He dreamed:

"I see a $20 admission ticket to financial well-being. I somehow understand that this will hold me over until bigger and better things come my way. In the dream, I think this means I should continue to teach my drawing classes even though the going will not be easy."

William awoke in the morning certain of his decision: He would continue with his present course, even with its temporary privations, encouraged that bigger and better opportunities eventually would come his way. Within a year and a half, his classes had grown in popularity and his paintings were on display in several reputable galleries.

This incident, reported by dream psychologist Gayle Delaney in her book *Living Your Dreams*, illustrates how we can target our dreams for help. Besides receiving unplanned, spontaneous dreams, we can consciously elicit—or incubate—dreams to solve specific problems. For example, we can incubate dreams to receive inspiration for creative projects, such as poetry or painting, or to solve more pragmatic problems, such as getting along with a business partner, parent, or spouse.

According to Delaney, many scientists and mathematicians have solved problems in their sleep. After working three days and nights

Our revels now are ended. These our actors,
As I foretold you, were all spirits, and
Are melted into air, into thin air;
And, like the baseless fabric of this vision,
The cloud capp'd towers, the gorgeous palaces,
The solemn temples, the great globe itself,
Yea, all which it inherit, shall dissolve;
And, like this insubstantial pageant faded,
Leave not a rock behind. We are such stuff
As dreams are made on, and our little life
Is rounded with a sleep. . . .

WILLIAM SHAKESPEARE

without rest, the Russian chemist Dmitri Mendelyev fell asleep and saw a representation of the periodic table of elements that turned out to be unerringly accurate in waking life. Inventor Elias Howe dreamed the solution to a design problem that led to the lock-stitch sewing machine. Writers and composers, such as D. H. Lawrence, Robert Louis Stevenson, Beethoven, Brahms, and Stravinsky, have drawn upon their dreams for inspiration and problem-solving.

Here are Delaney's recommendations, adapted from her essay in *Dreamtime & Dreamwork*, for incubating dreams to solve personal and professional problems:

1. *Choose the right night,* when you are neither intoxicated nor overtired. Get a full night's sleep followed by enough time to record your dreams in the morning.

2. *Record your day notes.* Before going to sleep, write down the day's highlights in a dream journal kept beside your bed. Record in four or five lines the emotional highlights of the day.

3. *Have an incubation discussion.* In no more than a page, write about the issues you would like to dream about. Describe the problems, your willingness to consider them from a fresh perspective, and the emotional payoffs that you might have to give up if you resolved them.

4. *Formulate an incubation phrase.* Now write a simple, one-line question or request that expresses the desire to understand your predicament. Examples include "Why am I afraid of heights and what can I do about it?" and "What are the dynamics of the relationship between X and me?"

5. *Repeat the phrase as you fall asleep,* as if it were a lullaby or mantra. Each time your mind wanders, bring it back to your phrase. You will fall asleep quickly, because you are not allowing yourself to ruminate or worry about your problem.

6. *Record whatever is on your mind when you awaken.* Whether you awaken in the middle of the night or in the morning, record in detail all your dream memories. Keeping the incubation phrase in mind, try to draw meaning from your dreams in a way that seems appropriate.

Why does dream incubation work in solving our problems? In *Living Your Dreams,* Delaney observes:

Dreams are like a microscope through which we look at the hidden occurrences in our soul.

ERICH FROMM

Since you dream every night, there is never a dearth of material for spiritual growth.

LOUIS SAVARY

136

In the dream state, we seem to be more exploratory, more playful. We seem to allow ourselves more freedom to experiment with different solutions to problems and to try different creative responses to our questions. In the dream state, we are freed from the constant distractions of sense data and daily concerns. We are able to focus intently and seem to have recourse to all the history of our feelings, actions, and life experience. Some dreamers feel strongly that in sleep we can even have experiences in other planes of existence, receive spiritual guidance, as well as glimpse the nature of the universe. . . . An understanding of dreams proves that we are less defensive, more open to new ideas, larger perspectives, and new combinations of ideas while asleep than while awake.

LUCID DREAMS

In the vast majority of dreams, we remain unconscious of the fact that we are dreaming. An independent force—what we might call the dream director—gathers the principal actors, sets the stage, and then provides the script for the ensuing drama. However, occasionally we wake up from our unconsciousness and realize that we are dreaming. Recognizing our freedom from all restrictions of time, space, and ordinary thinking, we assume the role of dream director, and with an exhilarating sense of power we orchestrate our own self-directed adventures. These powerful experiences are called lucid dreams.

"When you become lucid you can do *anything* in your dream," writes Patricia Garfield, author of *Creative Dreaming*. "You can fly anywhere you wish, experience love-making with the partner of your choice, converse with friends long dead or people unknown to you; you can see any place in the world you choose, experience all levels of positive emotions, receive answers to questions that plague you, observe creative products, and, in general, use the full resource of the material stored in your mind."

Lucid dreams appear more realistic than ordinary dreams, which may take place in surreal landscapes peopled by bizarre creatures, Garfield explains. Animals or objects rarely start talking, and other dream figures act in psychologically realistic ways. (There are some notable exceptions, however: Many lucid dreamers miraculously can fly under their own power or rearrange the environment at will.) Perceptions generally appear vivid; thought processes operate more realistically than in ordinary dreams; and emotional excitement often accompanies the realization that the rules governing everyday dream reality have been suspended.

The tendency to revel in emotional highs, though understandable, can abort lucid dreams. "If you have strong awareness, there is a danger

God gives us songs in our sleep.

JOB

I can never decide whether my dreams are the result of my thoughts, or my thoughts the result of my dreams. It is very queer, but my dreams make conclusions for me. They decide things finally. I dream a decision. Sleep seems to hammer out for me the logical conclusion of my vague days and offer me them as dreams.

D. H. LAWRENCE

that excitement over the joy of your freedom and power will wake you," Garfield writes. "If you relax your awareness, you lose it and fall into ordinary, uncontrolled dreaming. You must exercise your will not to become overexcited and wake, yet at the same time not become distracted and slip into ordinary dreaming. Like crossing a narrow board, you must keep your balance to avoid falling one way or the other."

Like dream recall, mastering lucid dreaming requires motivation, effective techniques, practice, and perseverance. According to dream researcher Stephen LaBerge, author of *Lucid Dreaming,* we can induce lucid dreams in two ways: from either the dream state or waking consciousness.

While dreaming, for example, we can let nightmarish images and figures snap us into lucidity, enabling us to confront fears rather than fleeing from them. We can develop critical thinking during dreams, so that the incongruities we witness trigger the thought, "That's impossible! I must be dreaming." Dreamers also can use predetermined memory cues—such as trees, streets, or familiar parts of the body—to trigger lucidity, or program themselves to fly during their dreams, an experience that frequently precipitates the desired awareness.

We can program ourselves from the waking state by repeating a suggestion throughout the day, such as "Tonight, I will have a lucid dream." We also can focus attention on a mental object or thought as we fall asleep, allowing body awareness to diminish and finally vanish while mental awareness continues without interruption into the dream state.

Once familiar with our lucid dreamscape, we can use nighttime awareness to work on creative projects, experiment with ESP, or resolve problems in personal relationships, Garfield points out. We also can rehearse skills needed in waking life—anything from perfecting a golf swing to mastering assertive behavior at work.

"Being 'awake in your dreams' provides the opportunity for unique and compelling adventures rarely surpassed elsewhere in life," writes LaBerge in *Lucid Dreaming.* As a skill, it "has considerable potential for promoting personal growth and self-development, enhancing self-confidence, improving mental and physical health, facilitating creative problem-solving, and helping you to progress on the path of self-mastery."

God speaks in one way, and in two, though man does not perceive it. In a dream, in a vision of the night, when deep sleep falls upon men, while they slumber in their beds, then he opens the ears of men. . . .

THE BIBLE

LEARNING LUCID DREAMING

Stephen LaBerge, who has done pioneering research at the Stanford University Sleep Laboratory, developed a number of techniques to produce lucid dreaming. One such technique uses a memory aid to precipitate the desired result. The exercise takes place during the early morning, because most lucid dreaming occurs during REM periods in the later part of a night's sleep. Here are LaBerge's directions.

1. During the early morning, when you awaken spontaneously from a dream, go over the dream several times until you have memorized it.
2. Then, while lying in bed and returning to sleep, say to yourself, "Next time I'm dreaming, I want to remember to recognize I'm dreaming."
3. Visualilze yourself as being back in the dream just rehearsed; only this time, see yourself realizing that you are, in fact, dreaming.
4. Repeat steps two and three until you feel your intention is clearly fixed or you fall asleep.

The second technique involves maintaining conscious awareness during the transition from waking to sleep at night. Here are the instructions:

1. Count to yourself ("one, I'm dreaming; two, I'm dreaming," and so on) while drifting off to sleep, maintaining a certain level of vigilance as you do so.
2. At some point—say, "forty-eight, I'm dreaming"—you will find that you *are* dreaming! The "I'm dreaming" phrase helps to remind you of what you intend to do, but it is not strictly necessary. Simply focusing your attention on counting probably allows you to retain sufficient alertness to recognize dream images for what they are, when they appear.

STANLEY KRIPPNER'S FAVORITE DREAM BOOKS

The following are among the favorite dream books of Stanley Krippner, a professor of psychology at Saybrook Institute in San Francisco and former director of the Dream Laboratory at Maimonides Medical Center in Brooklyn.

What the psychoanalysts stress, the relation between dreams and our conscious acts, is what poets already know. The poets walk this bridge with ease, from conscious to unconscious, physical reality to psychological reality.

ANAÏS NIN

We are so captivated by and entangled in our subjective consciousness that we have forgotten the age-old fact that God speaks chiefly through dreams and visions.

C. G. JUNG

A Little Course in Dreams: A Basic Handbook of Jungian Dreamwork, R. Bosnak (Shambhala, 1988). My favorite introduction to Jungian dreamwork.

The Dream Workbook: Discover the Knowledge and Power Hidden in Your Dreams, J. Morris (Little, Brown, 1985). My favorite introduction to keeping a dream workbook.

Dreams and Spiritual Growth: A Christian Approach to Dreamwork, L. M. Savary, P. H. Berne, and S. K. Williams (Paulist Press, 1984). My favorite book about the spiritual aspect of dreams.

Dreams: Tonight's Answers for Tomorrow's Questions, M. Thurston (Harper & Row, 1988). My favorite discussion of dreams from the Edgar Cayce viewpoint.

Working with Dreams: Self-Understanding, Problem-Solving, and Enriched Creativity Through Dream Appreciations, M. Ullman and N. Zimmerman (Jeremy P. Tarcher, 1979). My favorite introduction to group dreamworking.

Living Your Dreams: Using Sleep to Solve Problems and Enrich Your Life, G. Delaney (Harper & Row, 1988). An excellent introduction to solving practical problems through dreams.

Let Your Body Interpret Your Dreams, E. T. Gendlin (Chiron, 1986). An excellent introduction to body-based dream interpretation.

The Dream Game, A. Faraday (Harper & Row, 1974). An excellent introductory book to dreamworking, with a combination of theoretical and practical approaches.

Dreamtime & Dreamwork: Decoding the Language of the Night, S. Krippner, editor (Jeremy P. Tarcher, 1990). An excellent compilation of material by several dream explorers.

Dream Life, Wake Life: The Human Condition Through Dreams, G. Globus (State University of New York Press, 1987). My favorite philosophical approach to dream interpretation.

FEMININE SPIRITUALITY

Reawakening to the Goddess

Throughout the world, in literature and the arts, in psychology and religion, in politics and the rising ecological movement, we are witnessing a reawakening of the feminine as a cultural force. Revered by the ancients as the Goddess, the divine source of life, the feminine is an archetypal pattern in the psyche that affects men and women's capacity for love, relatedness, receptivity, and connectedness to the Earth and cosmos. After being devalued and repressed for millennia, the Goddess is returning to a world desperately in need of the feminine values of harmony and cooperation.

The Greeks have a mythological tale that illuminates how this reunion takes place in our lives. One day Persephone, the virginal daughter of Demeter, goddess of the grain, is gathering flowers in a meadow when suddenly the ground splits open. Hades, god of the underworld, bursts forth in his regal chariot and abducts the helpless maiden to his dark kingdom. When Demeter learns of her daughter's abduction and rape, she wanders the world in grief and rage. As goddess of the harvest, she withholds the bounty of the Earth, and everywhere famine threatens the human race.

Finally, because of the goddess's uncompromising anger, Zeus commands Hades to release Persephone, who eventually is reunited with her mother in a tearful embrace. As Queen of the Underworld, Persephone

The present moment is a
powerful goddess.

GOETHE

*One is not born a woman,
one becomes one.*

SIMONE DE BEAUVOIR

Not until I said Goddess *did I
realize that I had never felt
fully included in the fullness
of my being as* woman *in
masculine or neuterized
imagery for divinity.*

CAROL CHRIST

must return to Hades one-third of the year; but during the remainder of
the cycle, when mother and daughter celebrate their unity, the earth yields
its bounty in abundance.

Some psychologists view the rape of Persephone as an young woman's initiation into sexual experience and the potential for motherhood;
others regard her abduction and rape as inner events that open women to
life's transformative, transpersonal dimensions. But from a cultural perspective, we can view Persephone as an embodiment of the feminine
values of love, cooperation, and reverence for life that have been systematically devalued in modern life. In our patriarchal society, she is carried underground (into the unconscious) and held captive by Hades, who
emphasizes the masculine values of individuality, rational thinking, competition, and the conquest of nature. The absence of feminine values
eventually makes life barren and meaningless, prompting us, like Demeter, to weep, then search for our missing wholeness.

When at last Persephone returns above ground, she brings with her
the riches she has gained in the underworld. No longer a powerless, dis-
honored maiden, she brings the spiritual wisdom and experience needed
to help heal our technologically ravaged world.

A NEW MOVEMENT

"When the Goddess returns from exile," says Jungian analyst Jean Shinoda
Bolen, "feminist women encounter patriarchal religious systems that elevate the masculine without including much mention of the feminine.
They feel resentful when told to worship God the Father, without including his feminine counterpart, God the Mother. Hence a new movement
has developed that consciously elevates the feminine principle as something divine and nourishing."

As this grass-roots movement grows, feminist spirituality groups are
springing up all over the country. Some women, writes theologian Carol
Christ in *The Laughter of Aphrodite,* are working to reform biblical traditions to reflect a feminist vision of the equality of women. Others, such
as Merlin Stone in *Ancient Mirrors of Womanhood,* search among the
ruins of old traditions, seeking to rediscover a spiritual vision based on
ancient Goddess religion.

In their disenchantment with the Father God of the Judeo-Christian
tradition, other women hope to escape their spiritual oppression by turning eastward. However, although Eastern spiritual teachings speak of the

highest truth as beyond gender, the teachers and traditions from which they come generally reflect and maintain a patriarchal bias that hierarchically ranks men over women and tends to assign women a lower spiritual status.

What unites all these women is their vehement objection to patriarchal religious traditions that portray the divine in exclusively masculine terms. In *Wisdom's Feast: Sophia in Study and Celebration,* Susan Cady, Marian Ronan, and Hal Taussig give voice to this dilemma:

> A woman whose only symbol for God is male may be able to pray to him and be comforted and strengthened by him, but there is a level which is beyond her reach: she can never identify with him. She may believe that she is created in his image, but what does it mean to be like someone who is called "Father"? Only by denying her own sexuality or by placing it in a sphere that is totally out of reach, beyond sexual identification, can she relate as one who is created in the image of a male god. She can never have the experience that is open to every male in our society: to have her sexual identity affirmed by God, and to identify directly with "him."

Fundamental Separation

Religions centered on the worship of an exclusively male God, says Carol Christ in *The Laughter of Aphrodite,* keep women in a state of psychological dependence on men and male authority. Besides disempowering women, these systems also create an unbridgeable chasm between the created world and its divine source.

In patriarchal religions, says Bolen, we experience God up in the heavens, removed from the Earth like a monarch who rules with hierarchical authority. Human beings are down on the lowly Earth, cut off in some fundamental way from God's transcendent splendor. By separating the divine from nature, we then exploit the Earth's resources without regard for the health of natural systems.

"In religions that honor the feminine, people experience the divine as love and compassion present both in nature and culture," Bolen says. "As spiritual realization expresses itself in political action, people work on changing social systems that sanction inequality and injustice. Because there is less emphasis given to hierarchies, there is a broader distribution of power among the downtrodden in society, including women, oppressed races, the handicapped, and the elderly. And because the divine is immanent—embodied in all of life's forms—people also tend to value the Earth as a sacred vessel in which spirit indwells."

The task of feminist religion is to help us learn those things that seem so simple, yet are far more demanding than the most extreme patriarchal disciplines. It is easier to be celibate than to be fully alive sexually. It is easier to withdraw from the world than to live in it; easier to be a hermit than to raise a child; easier to repress emotions than to feel them and express them; easier to meditate in solitude than to communicate in a group; easier to submit to another's authority than place trust in oneself.

STARHAWK

By resacralizing the body and sexuality, feminine, Earth-based spirituality heals the split between the above and the below, between spirit and matter, and between mind and body, which has haunted the Western religious imagination. Rather than supporting spiritual hierarchies that have power over people, feminine spirituality focuses on shared power, power that comes from within. Instead of looking to external sources for spiritual authority, we find it within ourselves. This emphasis on personal experience rather than on doctrinal assent tends to promote personal responsibility and to reduce uniformity of belief and practice.

"Traditional religion, with its hierarchical organization and 'one true' approach to the divine, destroys the creativity in spiritual life," says Christine Downing, author of *The Goddess*. "In feminist spirituality, we respond with our uniqueness, creating rituals from many traditions—Jewish, Christian, Greek, Buddhist, Wiccan—that truly stir us in our depths. By democratizing and individualizing spiritual expression, we rely less on ideology and more on our own inner experience."

Seen from the larger perspective of world religion, the cultures of Western civilization are like the children of a family that has suffered a terrible divorce. The children now live only with the father and are forbidden to mention their mother's name or remember those warm and happy times they once spent in her embrace.

JENNIFER AND ROGER WOOLGER

Every mother contains her daughter in herself, and every daughter her mother.

C. G. JUNG

CELEBRATING TREES

Members of the burgeoning women's spirituality movement often meet outdoors to enact their own rituals, which usually are connected to natural cycles, such as the phases of the moon, the equinoxes, and the solstices. Women's rituals also celebrate an appreciation of growing things, such as vegetables, herbs, plants, and trees. Ancient Europeans revered trees as symbols of the motherhood principle and the goodness of nature, writes Barbara Walker in *Women's Rituals*. They recognized their dependence on trees for natural beauty, fruits and nuts, materials for shelter, tools, household articles, and fuel for cooking and warmth.

"Today, when the world's few remaining forests are being ruthlessly destroyed, we need more than ever to redevelop some of the ancient reverence for trees," Walker writes. Here are her instructions for a group ceremony to help restore our lost reverence for trees.

——————— ☆ ———————

Find a private space outdoors with flat ground surrounding a sizable free-standing tree. The group sits in a meditation circle around the tree, and when ready, each woman in turn stands up and puts her arms around the trunk for as long as she wishes. When all have taken a turn hugging the tree, they share their feelings about the experience. The group may pass around a talking stick made of one of the tree's fallen twigs or a scrap of loose bark.

Then group members join hands, rise, and dance counterclockwise around the tree, chanting

> Hail, Forest Mother,
> Beautiful tree,
> Gracious protectress,
> We honor thee.

After the dance, the group may sit in a tighter circle around the tree, either facing it or placing their backs to it in star formation, with legs extended and touching the neighbor's foot. In this formation, group members may speak about their feelings or hold another meditation period.

Before bidding farewell to the tree, each woman may pick a single leaf from its branches or from the ground to take home and press. After celebrating the life of a mature tree, some members also might want to plant a young tree to conclude this ancient ritual.

——————— ———————

The women are speaking. Those who are identified as having nothing to say, as sweet silence or monkey chatterers, those who were identified with Nature, which listens, as against Man, who speaks—those people are speaking. They speak for themselves and for the other people, the others who have been silent, or silenced, or unheard, the animals, the trees, the rivers, the rocks. And what they say is: We are sacred.

URSULA K. LeGUIN

THE GODDESS

In the beginning, says Merlin Stone, God was a woman. Throughout western Asia and Asia Minor, the chief deity for many centuries was a Great Mother goddess. In whatever form she was worshiped—as Ishtar, Astarte, Isis, Cybele, or Demeter—her celebrants honored the changing seasons of the year, the agricultural cycle, and the ongoing rhythms of life, death, and regeneration.

Our ancestors worshiped the Goddess as a personification of the life-giving and life-destroying powers of nature, writes Jungian scholar M. Esther Harding. As the mother of all, she gives birth to and nurtures all life, including plants, animals, and human beings. As the wielder of nature's destructive powers, like the Hindu goddess Kali, she dissolves physical form as a prelude to the regeneration of life. In her refusal to separate death from life, she embraces both poles of existence in a vision of organic wholeness.

According to transpersonal philosopher Ken Wilber, the Great Mother sheltered humanity in a state of preconscious unity with nature, which prevented the emergence of the individual ego as a center of independent will and action. By breaking free of the Great Mother's smothering protection, the individual ego gained control over the fluctuations of nature, emotion, instinct, and environment—a feat dramatized in the hero myths of world literature, such as Perseus's slaying of the gorgon Medusa or Theseus's slaying of the Minotaur.

"But in its zeal to assert its independence, [the ego] not only *transcended* the Great Mother, which was desirable; it *repressed* the Great Mother, which was disastrous," writes Wilber in *Up From Eden*. "And there the Western ego . . . demonstrated not just an awakened assertiveness, but a blind arrogance."

The religion of the Goddess never completely died out in the West, however. Despite the persecutions of the Inquisition and the witch burnings, the old religion went underground and recently has reemerged in the Wiccan movement, one of the strongest goddess-centered streams within feminine spirituality.

Witches—the followers of Wicca—consider themselves to be priests and priestesses of an old European shamanic nature-based religion that worships a goddess related to the ancient Mother Goddess. Unlike God the Father, who rules the world, writes Starhawk in *The Spiral Dance*, the Goddess *is* the world, manifest in moon and Earth, stone and seed, flowing river, and the budding and blossoming fruits and plants in nature.

As our religions embrace feminine values, we will honor the earth, harmonizing with nature rather than seeking to conquer it. We will live with a sense of completion, acceptance, and forgiveness rather than with a competitiveness that divides nations. With this sensibility, we will give birth to a planetary civilization based on cooperation and goodwill.

JUNE SINGER

The Goddess also presents an image of empowerment for modern women. As Starhawk explains:

> For women, the Goddess is the symbol of the inmost self, and the beneficent, nurturing, liberating power within woman. The cosmos is modeled on the female body, which is sacred. All phases of life are sacred: Age is a blessing, not a curse. The Goddess does not limit women to the body; she awakens the mind and spirit and emotions. Through Her, we can know the power of our anger and aggression, as well as the power of our love.

According to Naomi Goldenberg, author of *Changing of the Gods,* practitioners worship the Goddess in three forms: as maiden, mother, and crone (the old, wise woman past menopause who is full of life experience and wisdom). "The triple Goddess," she writes, "allows the witch to envision herself as a regal, valuable being even when she feels unattractive or old—even when she is unattached to any man or to any child."

Witchcraft has no dualism of body and soul, no concept of original sin, no rigid law of discipline to keep so-called base human instincts in control, and no sacred texts, writes Goldenberg. The craft does, however, acknowledge the threefold law of return, which states that what we send out returns to us three times over. This injunction introduces a strong ethical element into Wiccan rituals.

Although these doctrines hardly seem compatible with Western religion, Wicca—along with other forms of feminine spirituality—appears to be introducing a human, life-affirming impulse into our decaying traditions. Recognizing the sacred in the secular, it honors the spiritual dimension of sexuality, parenting, and emotional vulnerability. "Because the Goddess is manifest in human beings, we do not try to escape from our humanness, but seek to become fully human," writes Starhawk. To transform our culture, she concludes, we need to drop the dehumanizing ideals of patriarchal religion and accept "all the muckiness and adventure of being human."

WHO NEEDS THE GODDESS?

Women need the Goddess, writes Carol Christ in *The Laughter of Aphrodite,* because she affirms the legitimacy of female power. In addition, she affirms the female body and its life cycles, encourages women to assert their personal will, and promotes women's relationship to other women through sisterhood.

But do men need the Goddess? Clearly, they do, writes Starhawk in *The Spiral Dance:*

> The oppression of men in Father God-ruled patriarchy is perhaps less obvious but no less tragic than that of women. Men are encouraged to identify with a model no human being can successfully emulate: to be minirulers of narrow universes. They are internally split, into a "spiritual" self that is supposed to conquer their baser animal and emotional natures. They are at war with themselves: in the West, to "conquer" sin; in the East, to "conquer" desire or ego. Few escape from these wars undamaged. Men lose touch with their feelings and their bodies, becoming . . . "successful male zombies."

The symbol of the Goddess, she writes, enables men to experience and integrate the feminine side of their nature:

> For a man, the Goddess, as well as being the universal life force, is his own, hidden, female self. She embodies all the qualities society teaches him not to recognize in himself. His first experience of Her may therefore seem somewhat stereotyped; She will be the cosmic lover, the gentle nurturer, the eternally desired Other, the Muse, all that he is not. As he becomes more whole and becomes aware of his own "female" qualities, She seems to change, to show him a new face, always holding up the mirror that shows what to him is still ungraspable. He may chase Her forever, and She will elude him, but through the attempt he will grow, until he too learns to find Her within.

According to Christine Downing, the healing of men's relationship with the feminine also has profound implications for the healing of the Earth. "Earth-based spirituality, with its emphasis on living in harmony with the natural world, speaks powerfully to men as well as women," she says. "Although men and women relate differently to the Goddess, we all need to embrace the emerging consciousness to avoid ecological catastrophe. In this endeavor, no one sex has exclusive rights to the Goddess' blessings."

THE CHALICE AND THE BLADE

Feminine spirituality, with its emphasis on ecological awareness, plays a crucial role in healing the Earth of its technological wounds. But ultimately, says feminist theorist Riane Eisler, it does something far more revolutionary: It gives us a historical foundation on which to rebuild the modern world on principles of egalitarianism rooted in ancient Goddess religions.

In her ground-breaking book *The Chalice and the Blade,* Eisler pre-

Self-affirmation for women means, first and foremost, acceptance of their differentness from men, rather than identification, imitation, and competitiveness with them. Only by first finding this basic feminine stance can they also claim their Yang element and give expression to their masculine drives and capacities, in their own ways, as women.

EDWARD C. WHITMONT

sents archaeological evidence that seems to show that Neolithic (agrarian) societies that worshiped the supreme deity as female enjoyed a partnership between women and men. These societies, she says, did not rank people hierarchically, engage in warfare, or promote the senseless violence, looting, and rape that we generally associate with so-called primitive civilizations. Eisler calls the cultures of Old Europe and Minoan Crete "partnership societies," because they based social organization on linking rather than ranking, on equality of the sexes rather than dominance of one group over another.

This peaceful state of affairs, which lasted for thousands of years, came to an abrupt halt during the late Neolithic and early Bronze Age, Eisler says, when Indo-European and other invaders destroyed or radically altered the peaceful civilizations that worshiped the nurturing powers of the universe (symbolized by the ancient chalice or grail). These invaders worshiped what University of California archaeologist Marija Gimbutas calls the "lethal power of the blade"—the power to take life and to establish power through domination.

Overrunning Old Europe, Mesopotamia, and Palestine, these invaders suppressed Goddess worship and its life-affirming values. In its place, they eventually substituted a transcendent male deity that sanctioned social systems in which male dominance, violence, and authoritarian rule became the norm. Implacable foes of the Goddess, the victors then rewrote history, portraying Goddess religion as evil and heretical. Women, identified with the Goddess, were denied full participation in society. Across the world there arose what Eisler calls "dominator societies" whose religious, political, and social practices were based on the hierarchical ranking of men over women.

"In the past several thousand years, dominator thinking has obscured most references to our egalitarian past, exiled the divine feminine from our religions, and brought us to an evolutionary dead-end as evidenced by our global ecological crisis," Eisler says. "Yet there is cause for optimism. The partnership resurgence of the '60s has spawned international movements promoting women's rights, peace, social justice, and ecological consciousness. Feminist spirituality reinforces these movements by emphasizing that we cannot graft a peaceful, ecologically balanced global system onto social structures that permit one-half of humanity to dominate the other half."

In fact, argues Eisler, without the feminine spiritual perspective, progressive ideological movements alone cannot move us from a dominator

Which of These Forms Have You Taken?

This year I have been
*   growing*
down into the tree
against my will
making nothing happen.
Across the woods
through the bare branch haze
of bars against the light
someone is coming with an
*   axe.*

I have known this all my life.

DEENA METZGER

to a partnership system. "The transformation of society cannot occur until the power to give and nurture life takes precedence over the power to dominate and destroy," she says. "Only then will we have the temporal and spiritual foundations for a more balanced, just and peaceful world."

LIVING THE PARTNERSHIP WAY

The dominator mentality seems so deeply entrenched in our culture that changing it sometimes appears tantamount to Sisyphus's task of pushing an enormous boulder up a steep hill again and again. Our culture still worships at the altar of violence, domination, and conquest, as evidenced by the movie heroes we glorify, such as Rambo and Dirty Harry. Given the pervasiveness of this model, argue Riane Eisler and David Loye, authors of *The Partnership Way,* we need to infuse the world with softer, more feminine values that nurture and heal, rather than brutalize and destroy.

Because there is no better place to begin than at home, Eisler and Loye offer the following suggestions for revolutionizing our personal relationships and family life:

> To consciously work on developing a partnership relationship with someone you live with, consider keeping a progress journal that you review periodically with your loved one. In it, you record when your communications, attitudes, and actions were based on dominator dynamics and when they were based on the more egalitarian partnership way. As a spouse or lover, this means taking a close look at the prison of the "macho" role, which goes along with the manipulative, subtly controlling, and devious female stereotype of the "Total Woman." As a parent, this means observing when your actions with children bear the imprint of authoritarianism, or when they encourage open communication, power sharing, and cooperation. The awareness generated by this journal-keeping exercise can help strengthen your commitment to more enlightened ways of relating to each other.

THE GODDESS WITHIN

The reemergence of the Goddess in the contemporary world has given birth to goddess psychologies that define women in their own right, rather than as adjuncts to men. These psychologies draw on archetypal goddess images culled from Greek and Roman mythology that personify ways in which women typically respond to life's challenges. According to Jungian psychologists, these archetypes govern how we think, feel, and behave in ways that we call feminine.

I found God in myself and I loved her fiercely.

NTOSAKE SHANGE

The association of the Masculine with what is above and the Feminine with what is below serves to maintain a dominator mentality by unconsciously reinforcing the idea that the rule of men and masculinity over women and femininity is simply "the way it is."

RIANE EISLER

Hymn to Ishtar

I pray unto thee, Lady of Ladies, Goddess of Goddesses!
O Ishtar, Queen of all peoples, directress of mankind!
O Irnini, thou art raised on high, mistress of the spirits of heaven;
Thou art mighty, thou has sovereign power, exalted is thy name!
Thou art the light of heaven and earth, O valiant daughter of the Moon-
    god.
Ruler of weapons, arbitress of the battle!
Framer of all decrees, wearer of the crown of dominion!
O Lady, majestic is thy rank, over all the gods it is exalted!
Thou art the cause of lamentation, thou sowest hostility among brethren
    who are at peace;
Thou art bestower of strength! (friendship)
Thou art strong, O Lady of Victory, thou canst violently attain my desire!
O Gutira who art girt with battle, who are clothed with terror,
Thou wieldest the sceptre and the decision, the control of earth and
    heaven!
Holy chambers, shrines, divine dwellings and temples worship thee!
Where is thy name not (heard)? Where is thy decree not (obeyed)?

FROM THE "SEVEN TABLES OF CREATION"
IN *Women's Mysteries* BY M. ESTHER HARDING

Man enjoys the great advantage of having a god endorse the code he writes; and since man exercises a sovereign authority over women it is especially fortunate that this authority has been vested in him by the Supreme Being. For the Jews, Mohammedans, and Christians, among others, man is Master by divine right; the fear of God will therefore repress any impulse to revolt in the downtrodden female.

SIMONE DE BEAUVOIR

In *The Goddess Within,* psychotherapists Jennifer and Roger Woolger refer to a goddess as "a complex female character type that we intuitively recognize both in ourselves and in the women around us, as well as in the images and icons that are everywhere in our culture." For example, they view today's independent, hard-working career women as embodiments of the goddess Athena, revered by the Greeks as the patron deity of civilization. The Woolgers have identified six major Greek goddess archetypes that are most active in the contemporary psyche.

1. Athena, the goddess of wisdom and handicraft, helps urban
    women succeed in the partriarchal world. At home with logic,
    goal orientation, and competition, Athena women work along-

Oh, what a catastrophe, what a maiming of love when it was made a personal, merely personal feeling, taken away from the rising and the setting of the sun, and cut off from the magic connection of the solstice and equinox! . . . [W]e are bleeding at the roots, because we are cut off from the earth and sun and stars, and love is a grinning mockery, because, poor blossom, we plucked it from its stem on the tree of Life, and expected it to keep on blooming in our civilized vase on the table.

D. H. Lawrence

side men not as girl Fridays, but as colleagues and companions worthy of respect and equal responsibility. Ruled more by their heads than their hearts, they often need to cultivate a closer relationship with sensual Aphrodite and maternal Demeter.

2. Artemis is the goddess of nature in its virgin or untamed form. In contrast to Athena, who represents nature tamed and civilized, Artemis rules over women's instinctual life and practical outdoor ac-tivities, including athletics and dance. As goddess of the hunt and the moon, she personifies the independent feminine spirit that encourages women to express their self-reliance and will to achieve.

3. Aphrodite, ruler of love and eros, governs the domain of sexuality, intimacy, and personal relationships. As the goddess of beauty, she inspires creative liaisons between the sexes, artistic inspiration, and the visual arts, such as painting, sculpture, and architecture as well as poetry and music. Aphrodite women value relationships that have heart and intensity more than the status and safety of conventionally good marriages.

4. Hera, wife of the god Zeus, rules over marriage and public roles in which women exercise power or leadership. As a defender of social morality, Hera upholds the integrity of the family and carries on the traditions that lend cohesiveness to the community. When her power is limited to the family, she becomes the undisputed family matriarch.

5. Persephone, as queen of the dead, mediates between the spirit world, the realm of transpersonal experience, and the everyday mind. Persephone women have a receptivity to the deeper unconscious mind, the dreamworld, paranormal or psychic phenomena, and mysticism. Because she unites the dark and light sides of the Goddess within herself, in her maturity Persephone may become a wise woman—or crone—who imparts wisdom to others seeking initiation into their depths.

6. Demeter, goddess of motherhood, governs the nurturing of children, as well as women's menstrual and childbearing cycles. Sometimes called the Lady of Plants, she symbolizes a deep connection to the growth, harvesting, and preservation of crops. Demeter women find fulfillment through pregnancy and through providing physical and psychological nourishment to infants, children, and growing creatures.

Because our culture has worshiped the father principle and devalued the feminine, when we begin to become aware of the various goddesses, they initially appear to be weak, confused, and wounded, say the Woolgers. They write:

> This woundedness is due to the harsh treatment they have received at the hands of patriarchal repression. Aphrodite is ashamed of her sexuality; Athena questions her own ability to think; Hera doubts her own power; Demeter mistrusts her fertility; Persephone denies her visions; Artemis misunderstands her instinctive bodily wisdom. This . . . is the legacy of the psychic exile of the feminine.

To heal ourselves, the Woolgers recommend identifying which goddesses are active in our lives, then attending to those goddesses that are weak, neglected, or deeply wounded. A woman can sabotage her growth by developing her wifely Hera energy, yet neglect her professional life (Athena) or ignore her sexuality (Aphrodite) or inner development (Persephone). Similarly, a man can undermine his development if he seeks only motherly women (Demeter), while avoiding intellectual women (Athena) or strong women (Hera).

One way to heal a wounded or excluded goddess is to engage her in a written dialogue with the reigning goddesses with whom she is in conflict. If, for example, a dutiful but unromantic Hera woman discovers that the fire has gone out of her marriage, she may contact passionate Aphrodite through journal writing. Much as in the Jungian practice of Active Imagination, engaging the Goddess in dialogue may release romantic feelings and longings that were repressed on the altar of marriage, monogamy, and fidelity. Similarly, a woman in whom scholarly Athena predominates may need to be reconciled with Demeter's instinctive call to motherhood, whereas a woman ruled by nurturing Demeter may need to contact the independent energies of Artemis and Athena.

The Conscious Feminine

Generations of women raised in our patriarchal value system have pursued the masculine values of power, perfection, and success rather than discover their own feminine natures, writes Jungian analyst Marion Woodman in *Addiction to Perfection*. Today, however, as women break free from cultural stereotypes about masculinity and femininity, they are exploring the deep nature of the feminine when it is liberated from male idealizations. They are giving birth to the conscious feminine.

Like Jacob with the angel . . . women will struggle with God, and perhaps at the end of the night, both women and God will emerge with new names and the power of new being. At dawn women may hear a still, small voice speaking to them saying, "God is woman like yourself; she, too, has suffered and ceased to exist through the long years of patriarchal history." With that sister God, and the sister earth she once represented, women will perhaps make a new covenant: promising to liberate her and the earth as they liberate themselves.

CAROL CHRIST

155

In *To Be a Woman,* Connie Zweig outlines the psychohistorical process that culminates in conscious femininity. In the first stage, *matriarchal consciousness,* we exist in a preconscious state of unity within the womb of the Great Mother. In the second stage, *patriarchal consciousness,* we break away from containment within the Great Mother as we strive for autonomy and independence. Devaluing the feminine, we collectively identify with masculine values, such as domination, competition, and the rule of objectivity, that give modern civilization its decidedly patriarchal orientation. In the third stage, *emerging consciousness,* we readmit into our lives the exiled feminine values of relatedness, receptivity, and love that were abandoned in the heroic journey from preconscious wholeness to individuality. Now, with fully developed egos, we can delight in our individual differences without sacrificing a sense of unity with nature, our communities, the planet, and the cosmos.

This new stage in human consciousness, says Zweig, with its transpersonal perspective, breathes vitality into a world threatened by the imbalanced technological reign of the masculine. "Today, with the coming end of the patriarchy, the feminine is like a root shooting up through the cracked concrete surface of the culture," she writes. "The evidence for her reappearance is apparent in our growing concerns with deep ecology, the Goddess, even the newly forming men's movement. Therefore, the Conscious Feminine is the next image to pull us forward on the human journey."

Marion Woodman suggests re-visioning the feminine as the archetype governing receptivity, process-orientation, and a grounded presence in the body. She sees the masculine as the archetype governing independent action and goal-orientation. As women raise the feminine to a new level of consciousness, Woodman writes, they build feminine ego-containers strong enough to relate with vibrancy and creativity to the emerging masculine consciousness without losing their hard-won identities.

In the process, women must first break an unconscious identification with their mothers and give birth to what Woodman terms the "conscious virgin," a mature femininity uncontaminated by other people's projections and expectations. To do this, women need to forgive their mothers for providing a wounded model of femininity and motherhood, then take responsibility for mothering themselves. No longer an unconscious victim, the virgin lives her own essence by drawing on the power of the archetypal feminine within her, alive to her personal needs, values, and possibilities.

Such a woman "lives by the spirit, not by the law," writes Woodman. "Therefore she demands constant awareness and spontaneity. She loves the potential in things: the possibilities in the growing plant, the growing child, the growing hopes and dreams. She trusts life, trusts change, trusts love and holds nothing static. She loves and lets go. She loves with her whole Being so that her vulnerability becomes her greatest strength."

CRADLING THE WORLD

The Goddess not only helps us re-vision psychology; she also brings her nurturing presence to the practice of meditation. As a contribution to the new spirituality, Deena Metzger, a poet, novelist, playwright, and therapist, offers the following exercise, which can be practiced by itself on a daily basis or following zazen, meditation, or prayer. The exercise appears in *Healing the Wounds: The Promise of Ecofeminism*.

In the late twentieth century there is a growing awareness that we are doomed as a species and planet unless we have a radical change of consciousness. The re-emergence of the Goddess is becoming the symbol and metaphor for this transformation of culture.

ELINOR W. GADON

What would it mean to live in a nurturing society, one where even men nurtured self, one another and others? . . . From a theological point of view [it would mean] the recovery of the tradition of God as Mother.

MATTHEW FOX

✰

Proceed, as in Zen meditation, by sitting quietly and following your breath. However, instead of clearing your mind, allow images of everything you love to pass across the screen of your mind and through the cradle of your heart. Allow people—faces, living and dead, known and unknown—places, plants, animals, stones, memories, dreams, activities, ideas—whatever you love—to pass through without attaching to them. As they enter your heart, imagine that you are protecting them. Allow yourself to be the protector. Do this for as long as you wish, and for the last minute of the meditation, allow yourself to hold the Earth itself in this protective cradle.

✰

THE GODDESS IN JUDAISM AND CHRISTIANITY

Men and women working within Judaism and Christianity to reform their patriarchal one-sidedness have discovered little-known but vital underground traditions that honor the feminine aspect of God. In Judaism, the Goddess appears as the *Shekinah*, the female aspect of divinity that is immanent in the world to balance God's transcendence. She appears in the Book of Proverbs, writes Rabbi Leah Novick in *The Goddess Re-Awakening*, as Wisdom, present at the time of creation as the loving consort and co-architect with Yahweh. Conspicuously absent during much of Jewish history, the *Shekinah* reemerged in twelfth-century Europe, then later in sixteenth- and seventeenth-century Palestine as a central focus of kabbalistic thought and practice. As part of their response to our planetary crisis, Jewish feminists are rediscovering and reinventing her as they search for a feminine presence within their own tradition.

"Jewish women carry the imprint and the images of the Goddess within them," writes Novick. "Because this generation is serving as the midwife for the rebirth of the Shekinah, we will have to be familiar with the ancient knowledge and traditional prayers which invoke her, at the same time that we are creating new forms. In this ancient/future subculture, we will need poets and prophets, rebels and rabbis, musicians and mothers."

Christianity—most specifically Roman Catholicism—venerates and at times appears to worship the feminine through devotion to the Virgin

Our Western heroic achievements are the envy of the rest of the world, but they were won at the cost of our capacity for warmth, feeling, contentment, and serenity. We are so rich in things and so poor in feminine values!

ROBERT A. JOHNSON

Mary. Many feminists, however, object to Mary as the feminine image of God, because Christianity never recognizes her as being equal with her son. They also object to her as a role model for modern women because of her denial of sexuality and exclusive identification with motherhood.

In the past few decades, however, voices from within and outside the tradition have been seeding Christianity with alternatives to its rigidly patriarchal theology. Dominican priest Matthew Fox, for example, believes that a creation spirituality that redeems fallen nature—long associated with women—and that honors the Motherhood of God could infuse Western civilization with new life.

The patriarchal tradition, which has repressed and devalued the maternal within our psyches, religions, and political institutions, has severely limited our capacity to extend compassion to the suffering Earth and its people, Fox argues in *Original Blessing*. As the feminist movement urges us to recover traditions that honor God's motherhood, and as creation-centered spirituality replaces the fall/redemption model that emphasizes a transcendent male deity removed from the Earth, the Mother's return may usher in an era of more fulfilled, creative living.

"A return to the motherly side of God would be a return to compassion as a way of life," Fox writes. "It would be a return to wisdom as distinct from mere knowledge or information-gathering. Wisdom and compassion: wouldn't such energy revitalize Western religion and civilization, forge new links with non-Western traditions, create gentler and more dialectical relationships to earth, to body, to pleasure, to work, to the artist within and among us?"

While reintroducing the motherhood of God may help revivify patriarchal religion, some theologians quietly argue that Christianity needs to elevate Mary to the position of avatar, an incarnation of God. In *Wisdom's Feast,* Susan Cady, Marian Ronan, and Hal Taussig call for the recovery of the goddesslike figure Sophia, called Wisdom in the Old Testament, who as the link between heaven and Earth is identified with Jesus in the New Testament. In their view, "Sophia bridges the gap between feminist spirituality's need for transforming images and the demand of the biblical traditions that such images be congruent with their history and experience."

If, indeed, Sophia—the female face of God—is making a comeback in our Western religions, the second coming of the Goddess may inspire us to find the skillful means to heal the world's misery, despair, poverty, and spiritual emptiness.

The moon, the feminine principle, is ruler of the night, of the unconscious. She is goddess of love, controller of those mysterious forces beyond human understanding, which attract certain human beings irresistibly to each other, or as unaccountably force them apart. She is the Eros, powerful and fateful, and incomprehensible.

M. ESTHER HARDING

Our whole culture—with its endless violence, homeless people on the streets, colossal nuclear arsenals, and global pollution—is sick. It is sick because it is out of harmony with itself; it suffers from what the Hopi Indians call koyaanisqatsi, *which is rendered in English, "crazy life, life in turmoil, life out of balance." What is missing is the feminine dimension in our spiritual and psychological lives; that deep mystical sense of the earth and her cycles and of the very cosmos as a living mystery. We have lost our inner connection to that momentous power that used to be called the Great Mother of us all.*

JENNIFER AND ROGER
WOOLGER

KORE CHANT: SPRING AND FALL EQUINOX

Her name cannot be spoken,
Her face was not forgotten,
Her power is to open,
Her promise can never be broken.

(Spring)
All sleeping seeds She wakens,
The rainbow is Her token,
Now winter's power is taken,
In love, all chains are broken.

(Fall)
All seeds She deeply buries,
She weaves the thread of seasons.
Her secret, darkness carries,
She loves beyond all reason.

She changes everything She touches, and
Everything She touches, changes. [Repeat—chant.]
Change is, touch is; Touch is, change is.
Change us! Touch us! Touch us! Change us!

Everything lost is found again,
In a new form, In a new way.
Everything hurt is healed again,
In a new life, In a new day.
[Repeat any and all verses.]

FROM *The Spiral Dance*
BY STARHAWK

RESOURCES

Recommended Reading

The Chalice and The Blade: Our History, Our Future, Riane Eisler (Harper & Row, 1987). The ground-breaking work that contends that Goddess-worshiping Neolithic cultures were egalitarian before the rise of partriarchy.

Return of the Goddess, Edward C. Whitmont (Crossroad Publishing, 1982). A seminal work by a Jungian analyst about the return of the feminine principle in today's world.

The Heroine's Journey, Maureen Murdock (Shambhala Publications, 1990). Outlines the healing process by which modern women can reclaim thir feminine wholeness.

Women's Mysteries, M. Esther Harding (Bantam Books, 1971). Explores the mythological foundations of the feminine principle, with insights into modern romance, the experience of motherhood, and spirituality.

The Spiral Dance, Starhawk (Harper & Row, 1979). Gives an overview of the rebirth of Goddess religion, as well as a wealth of rituals and exercises for personal empowerment.

To Be a Woman, Connie Zweig, editor (Jeremy P. Tarcher, 1990). A striking collection of essays by psychologists, Jungian analysts, and scholars of Goddess cultures on how to awaken the conscious feminine.

The Goddess Within: A Guide to the Eternal Myths That Shape Women's Lives, Jennifer Woolger and Roger Woolger (Ballantine Books, 1987). Promulgates a new psychology of women based on archetypal patterns from Greek mythology.

Addiction to Perfection: The Still Unravished Bride, Marion Woodman (Inner City Books, 1982). Explores the wounding and healing of the feminine principle in our patriarchal culture.

Femininity Lost and Regained, Robert Johnson (Harper Perennial, 1991). A readable account of the loss of feminine values in modern culture and its impact on our lives.

The Once and Future Goddess, Elinor Gadon (Harper & Row, 1989). A scholarly, readable, and visually rich chronicle of the reemergence of the Goddess in our times.

Female Saints and Mystics

Matthew Fox, the proponent of creation spirituality, has made available the works of women Christian mystics, whose emphasis on personal healing and social justice makes them surprisingly relevant for women today. Bear & Company (P.O. Drawer 2860, Santa Fe, NM 87504-2860; 800-932-3277) publishes a *Meditation With* series that includes the writings of Hildegard of Bingen, Julian of Norwich, Teresa of Avila, and Mechtild of Magdeburg.

Women Saints: East and West, edited by Swami Ghanananda and Sir John Stewart-Wallace (Vedanta Press, 1979, $7.95), contains moving biographies of twenty-five women from the Buddhist, Jewish, Christian, Hindu, and Sufi traditions. The book is available from the Vedanta Society, 1947 Vedanta Place, Hollywood, CA 90068; 213-465-7114.

Meetings with Remarkable Women (Shambhala Publications, 1987, $13.95) profiles thirteen Buddhist women, including Joanna Macy and Ruth Denison.

Publications

Womanspirit Sourcebook, Patrice Wynne (Harper & Row, 1988, $16.95). This definitive guide to women's spirituality contains recommendations on books, music, publications, and audio- and videotapes.

Circle Network News (P.O. Box 219, Mt. Horeb, WI 53572, $13/year, quarterly), an international newspaper serving the pagan community, includes articles, rituals and invocations, meditations, herbal formulas, book and music reviews, and resources.

Daughters of Sarah (3801 N. Keeler, Chicago, IL 60641; 312-736-3399, $18/year, bimonthly). This magazine for Christian feminists covers issues such as eco-feminism, aging, incest, spiritual wisdom, and spiritual child-rearing.

Lilith (P.O. Box 3000, Dept. LIL, Denville, NJ 07834, $14/year, quarterly). Offers a feminist perspective on Judaism.

Octava (P.O. Box 8, Clear Lake, WA 98235; 206-856-5469, $10/year). This spiritual feminist gazette, published to correspond with the eight pagan feasts, includes articles on Wiccan spirituality, poetry, book reviews, and a calendar listing of events.

Of a Like Mind (P.O. Box 6021, Madison, WI 53716, $13–$33 on a sliding scale, quarterly). An international newspaper and networking tool for women interested in Goddess religion, paganism, and Wiccan spirituality that includes resource listings and letter exchanges.

Woman of Power (P.O. Box 827, Cambridge, MA 02238; 617-625-7885, $26/year, quarterly). A magazine on feminism, spirituality, and politics that explores themes such as ritual and magic, women of color, women in community, woman as warrior, and Goddess spirituality.

THE MEN'S MOVEMENT

Exploring the New Masculinity

Under a harvest moon, in a redwood lodge located far from the clutter and clockwork regularity of urban life, a community of men has gathered for the weekend to rediscover the ancestral roots of the male spirit and to re-vision masculinity in our changing era. These men have gone through a traditional Native American sweat lodge ceremony, which purifies the body of toxins. Using ceremonial arts, such as chanting, drumming, and dancing, they loosen the bands of their emotional armoring and with un-suspected depth of feeling share their pain and grief as fathers, sons, and lovers. Listening to fairy tales about male initiation, they retrieve wisdom from the past to guide them through the perplexing, painful, and often solitary process of growing to manhood in our post-industrial culture.

This evening, one of the groups is enacting a ritual drama, complete with Greek chorus, about the woundedness inflicted on men by our so-ciety. A young boy, who scrapes his knee while skateboarding, runs to his father for comfort and receives his first wound when the chorus an-nounces an axiom of the heroic mentality, "Big boys don't cry." The boy receives further wounding when he implores his father to play a game with him, and the chorus responds in a cold, distant tone, "Not now, I'm busy." When the young boy announces that he wants to be a musician, the father confiscates his violin and replaces it with a rifle as the chorus casts a spell

Nobody expects a man and a woman to reach the same corner at the same time.

Marta Lynch

It doesn't matter who my father was; it matters who I remember he was.

ANNE SEXTON

Our fathers did love us; they worked hard, they provided, they were in many ways on the outside of the family, and in their silent doing was the expression of their love.

SAMUEL OSHERSON

on him: "Give up your dreams and be sensible. Father knows best." Finally, after receiving the command to "Be a man!" the boy falls to his knees in pained confusion, mirroring the unresolved tensions carried by both the actors and onlookers.

This ritual drama, full of self-invalidation, also contains the seeds of healing for the assembled men. In this safe, nonjudgmental community, they abandon masks of invulnerability to reveal their shame and rage, their broken dreams, and their relentless search for an often distant or absent father. If, as poet Robert Bly suggests, "Grief is the doorway to a man's feelings," these men emerge from the weekend purged of the burden of bearing their pain alone. Having lost some of their armoring, they have gained in return a reconnection with their spiritual depths, a greater compassion for other men, and—perhaps the greatest gift—a newfound respect for maleness.

THE MYTHOPOETIC APPROACH

All across the country men are flocking to weekend workshops and retreats or forming their own support groups to deal with what the men's movement perceives as an erosion of masculinity in contemporary society. "Feminism has encouraged women to demand equality in the work world, in childrearing and housework, and in personal relationships," says Shepherd Bliss, who teaches men's studies at John F. Kennedy University in Orinda, California. "But in adapting to women's demands, men experience a conflict between the old masculinity, with its Marlboro Man image of the tough guy who hides his feelings while remaining in control, and the more realistic expectations of wives, lovers, and co-workers. The feminist critique of industrial society has put men on the defensive and masculinity itself on trial, as if there's something innately destructive in masculinity. The men's movement helps us reclaim and honor the beauty of healthy masculinity, which includes its generative, earthy, and nurturing qualities."

While the more political arm of the movement deals with feminist issues and men's rights, the mythopoetic approach, with its unique brand of spirituality, has most captured men's hearts and souls. Based on Jungian and archetypal psychology, this approach uses ancient mythology and fairy tales, poetry, ritual, drumming, and ecstatic dancing to build masculine consciousness.

For example, storytellers might entertain a men's gathering with the exploits of the Greek god Zeus, who embodies a male authority that is used to benefit the community, or Dionysus, who embodies men's more sensuous, feeling-oriented qualities. These stories of the ancient gods bypass the mind's rational defenses, enabling listeners to contact the archetypal energies represented by these images. Once these energies are activated, men express them through group rituals and eventually through concrete activity in their everyday lives, including working on the father–son connection, building male friendships, and developing male modes of intimacy.

Behind this inner work, men are struggling to contact and assimilate the energies of the deep masculine, which Robert Bly calls the Wild Man. When men dropped their macho personas in the '70s and '80s, Bly contends, they became soft or naive males, gentle but unhappy men who were "life-preserving but not exactly life-giving" because they had surrendered a male vitality necessary for self-assertion. In addition, the weakening of the father–son bond, caused when the Industrial Revolution forced men to seek their livelihood outside the home, has further deprived men of the modeling and emotional nourishment required to strengthen their masculine identity.

To overcome their emotional numbness and naïveté, Bly says, contemporary men must pursue the path of what he terms "endarkment," descending through their woundedness into the shadow self that houses their instinctual life energy—the Wild Man. Here they will find a hidden source of masculine power, which is dark and undomesticated, capable of rage as well as love and generativity. The encounter with primordial masculinity fills many men with feelings of dread. As Bly writes in *Iron John: A Book About Men:*

> When a man welcomes his responsiveness, or what we sometimes call his internal woman, he often feels warmer, more companionable, more alive. But when he approaches . . . the "deep male," he feels risk. Welcoming the Hairy Man is scary and risky, and it requires a different sort of courage. [It] requires a willingness to descend into the male psyche and accept what's dark down there, including the *nourishing* dark.

When men journey into their depths in community, this descent becomes less frightening. Community, writes Sam Keen in *Fire in the Belly: On Being a Man,* provides a missing ingredient as necessary to the health of the male psyche as vitamin C is to the health of the body. "There is no way we can recover a secure sense of manhood," he writes, "without rediscovering the bonds that unite us to others and reaffirming our fidelity to the 'We' that is an essential part of the 'I.'"

Star Wars has a valid mythological perspective. It shows the state as a machine and asks, "Is the machine going to crush humanity or serve humanity?" . . . When Luke Skywalker unmasks his father, he is taking off the machine role that the father has played. The father was the uniform. That is power, the state role.

JOSEPH CAMPBELL

As soon as these bonds are secure, Keen says, men will give up exploiting the world's resources and will care for them as guardians of the future. In touch with the generative depths of their masculinity, they will work passionately and with commitment for the healing of the earth.

WHO IS THE WILD MAN?

The Wild Man motif derives from a Grimm's fairy tale called "Iron John." In the tale, hunters have been disappearing from a remote area of the forest near the king's castle. A courageous hunter, who volunteers to look into these mysterious disappearances, drains a pond in the forest and dis-

In short, all good things are wild and free. . . . Give me for my friends and neighbors wild men, not tame ones.

HENRY DAVID THOREAU

THE NEW MALE MANIFESTO

1. Men are beautiful. Masculinity is life-affirming and life-supporting. Male sexuality generates life. The male body deserves to be nurtured and protected.
2. A man's value is not measured by what he produces. We are not our professions. We need to be loved for who we are. We make money to support life. Our real challenge, and the adventure that makes life full, is making soul.
3. Men are not flawed by nature. We become destructive when our masculinity is damaged. Violence springs from desperation and fear rather than from authentic manhood.
4. A man doesn't have to live up to any narrow, societal image of manhood. There are many ancient and modern images of men as healers, protectors, lovers, and partners with women, men, and nature. This is how we are in our depths: celebrators of life, ethical and strong.
5. Men do not need to become more like women in order to reconnect with soul. Women can help by giving men room to change, grow, and rediscover masculine depth. Women also support men's healing by seeking out and affirming the good in them.
6. Masculinity does not require the denial of deep feeling. Men have the right to express all their feelings. In our society this

covers the culprit, a fierce man covered with hair from head to foot. He captures this Wild Man, who is then imprisoned in a cage in the king's courtyard.

One day the golden ball belonging to the young prince rolls into the Wild Man's cage. In exchange for his freedom, Iron John returns the golden ball to the prince, then hoists him onto his shoulders and carries him away into the forest. The boy goes through a series of initiatory tests, then has a series of adventures in the world that in time transform him into a man. (In this context, the Wild Man represents the initiator who separates a boy from maternal comfort, exposing him to the trials and tasks from which masculine identity is forged.) According to Bly, we also may think of the Wild Man as:

The true vocation of men [is] to guard the earth, love it, care for it. . . . Men are called to be warriors for the earth. You love this earth so much you would defend it to the death. . . . If men will awaken to that call, everything else follows. When a man walks in nature, his humanity is turned on and he becomes complete.

JOHN STOKES

takes courage and the support of others. We start to die as human beings when we are afraid to say or act upon what we feel.

7. Men are not only competitors. Men are also brothers. It is natural for us to cooperate with each other. We find strength and healing through telling the truth to one another—man to man.

8. Men deserve the same rights as women for custody of children, economic support, government aid, education, health care, and protection from abuse. Fathers are equal to women in ability to raise children. Fatherhood is honorable.

9. Men and women can be equal partners. As men learn to treat women more fairly, they also want women to work toward a vision of partnership that does not require men to become less than who they authentically are.

10. Sometimes we have the right to be wrong, irresponsible, unpredictable, silly, inconsistent, afraid, indecisive, experimental, insecure, visionary, lustful, lazy, fat, bald, old, playful, fierce, irreverent, magical, wild, impractical, unconventional, and other things we're not supposed to be in a culture that circumscribes our lives with rigid roles.

FROM *Knights Without Armor*
BY AARON R. KIPNIS

The spontaneity preserved from childhood. When we are in a boring conversation, we could, instead of saying something boring, give a cry. Little dances are helpful in the middle of an argument, as are completely incomprehensible haikus spoken loudly while in church or while buying furniture.

Friendliness toward the wildness in nature. The Wild Man protects endangered species, such as the Spotted Owl. As guardian of the Earth, he protects its creatures, the waters, the air, the mountains, the trees, the wilderness. He also keeps track of the wild animals inside us and warns us when they are liable to become extinct.

The positive side of male sexuality. The hair that covers his whole body is natural, like a deer's or a mammoth's; he has not been clean shaven out of shame, and his instincts have not been suppressed as to produce the rage that humiliates women.

Trust in what is below. The Wild man encourages a trust of the lower half of our body, our genitals, legs and ankles, our inadequacies, the soles of our feet, the animal ancestors, the earth itself and the treasures long buried there. Honoring what is below encourages us to follow our own desires, which we know are not restricted to sexual desire but include desires for the infinite—for the woman at the edge of the world, for the firebird, for the treasure at the bottom of the sea.

The Wild Man, writes Bly, does not represent macho energy, which does great damage to soul, Earth, and humankind. By contrast, it leads to forceful action undertaken, not with cruelty, but with resolve. When men develop this energy, they will effectively meet its similar expression in women and take a decisive step in reconciling the relationship between the sexes.

> *If contemporary men can take the task of their own initiation from Boyhood to Manhood as seriously as did their tribal forebears, then we may witness the* end *of the* beginning *of our species, instead of the* beginning *of the* end.
>
> ROBERT MOORE AND
> DOUGLAS GILLETTE

MALE INITIATION

When modern men descend into their woundedness, many of them discover that they were never adequately initiated into manhood. Throughout history, initiation rites performed in a sacred space and in the company of wise male elders helped prepare a young man for the joys and responsibilities of adult life. In the presence of spiritual fathers or mentors, a young boy would receive instructions in becoming an independent person, undergo a quest for his life purpose, and return to society, connected to his inner self and aware of his place in the social order.

Our ancestors knew that growth into manhood requires ritual, effort, and the active intervention of older males. Unfortunately, say Jungian ana-

The problem is that patriarchal attitudes and values are no longer obviously true. Unless masculinity is differentiated from patriarchy, both will go down the drain together.

EUGENE MONICK

lyst Robert Moore and mythologist Douglas Gillette, the breakdown of the modern family and the disappearance of ritual processes for initiating boys into men have led to a "crisis in masculine identity of vast proportions."

"A man who 'cannot get it together' is a man who has probably not had the opportunity to undergo ritual initiation into the deep structures of manhood," they write in *King, Warrior, Magician, Lover: Rediscovering the Archetypes of the Mature Masculine.* "He remains a boy—not because he wants to, but because no one has shown him the way to transform his boy energies into man energies. No one has led him into direct and healing experiences of the inner world of the masculine potentials."

Genuine initiation ceremonies, they observe, rip the boy from his childhood cocoon by slaying his ego through ritual actions that connect him to a previously unknown power. By submitting to this archetypal process, the youth gives birth to a new masculine personality characterized by calm, compassion, clarity of vision, and generativity.

Most initiation rites share certain features in common, write psychologists John A. Sanford and George Lough in *What Men Are Like.* Typically, the elders separate the boy from his mother's household and take him to a sacred area reserved for initiation. They then systematically alienate the boy from his family, especially his mother, through intimidating physical and psychological ordeals that put an end to his childhood identity and replace it with the imprint of his male ancestors.

"The boy's ability to endure the pain and fear is a hallmark of his readiness to enter into the world of men," they write. "His entry into the world of men provides him with a new set of relationships to replace the ones he has severed. He is also initiated into the 'men's mysteries,' a body of myth and culture known only to the men, and this gives him a new spiritual orientation."

Our culture lacks initiation rites that carry this kind of transformative energy, they observe. Ceremonies such as confirmations or bar mitzvahs contain only pale vestiges of once-living spiritual experience, while fraternal initiations generally fulfill unmet social needs. Conscription into the military or into a street gang, as Moore and Gillette point out, does initiate men—but through pseudorituals that produce a patriarchal manhood, which is skewed, stunted, and abusive of others. They call these initiations *pseudo* because "real men are not wantonly violent or hostile."

Moore and Gillette believe that the lack of meaningful ritual and scarcity of ritual elders can be corrected. Perhaps such a correction takes place every time men congregate to celebrate male mysteries. By being in the company of other male initiates and receiving spiritual instruction through the ancient form of storytelling, men of all ages are fulfilling a yearning embedded in the deepest strands of their cultural DNA. And in some profound way, through an ancestral link stretching from the Paleolithic era to the Information Age, a much-needed healing is taking place in the male psyche.

CREATING YOUR OWN RITUAL

Those of us who have missed certain age-appropriate initiations in our development can take heart. According to Jungian therapist Edith Sullwold, we can create personal rituals to finish growth processes from earlier peri-

Since boys are taught not to cry, men must learn to weep. After a man passes through arid numbness, he comes to a tangled jungle of grief and unnamed sorrow. The path of a manly heart runs through the valley of tears.

SAM KEEN

ods in life. "Because we have the possibilities of unlimited creativity," she says, "we can complete our lives, no matter how old we are."

Here is an example of an adolescent rite of passage designed by one of Sullwold's adult workshop participants, who had almost drowned while swimming with friends at age eleven and who wanted to test his courage in water:

To create a sense of support, the men and women in the group stood around him near a swimming pool. When he was ready, the men gave him practical instruction in entering the water, relaxing, navigating his way through the depths, and emerging safely when he had completed his test. The men then wrapped him in a robe and threw him into the deep end of the pool. His ritual task was to extricate himself from the robe and emerge from the water at the other end.

When the man performed his task successfully, he jumped out of the pool ecstatically. Having died to a fear-ridden adolescent image of himself, he dug a hole in the ground and planted a young palm tree to celebrate his newfound courage. Then, much to his surprise, a spontaneous sound, similar to that of a baying coyote, issued from his throat. Afterward, he quietly dressed himself in new clothing and received gifts from the women, including fruits and flowers.

"We have within our psyches the same inner images and impulses that gave birth to the great rituals that have sustained our civilization over the millenia," Sullwold says. "To create personal rituals, we need group support, meaningful dramatic action, and trust that the ritual-maker is alive and well in us. To be successful, modern rituals also must invoke the spiritual dimension of life, contain some teaching and learning, along with the element of risk-taking."

When these conditions are fulfilled, she says, we can create rituals that enable us to die to an old form of being and to be reborn into an expanded sense of self.

MALE SPIRITUALITY

Like feminine spirituality, masculine spirituality has no monolithic belief system, no Ten Commandments carved in eternal stone. Nor does it have universally accepted practices. Some men's groups honor Dionysus and Orpheus through drumming and dancing, while those with a more Christian orientation relate to the Wild Man energies of the Hebrew prophets and John the Baptist. Yet no matter how diverse its expressions, wherever male spirituality takes root, it appears to have certain key features that distinguish it from other approaches.

The deep masculine is a way of being that includes both the sword and the shield, the ability to strike and take action, be potent and active, and yet at the same time know when to shield not only ourselves from violence and abuse, but others as well.

JOHN LEE

Fathers and families need new images of what a father can be, images that go beyond the idea of father as outsider, father as provider, or father as intruder in the home. There is a need for images that acknowledge father as a potent nurturant force within the family as well as a creative liaison with the world outside the family.

ARTHUR AND LIBBY
COLMAN

Because it is Earth-based, male spirituality reveres nature, animals, and the physical world, according to Chris Harding, editor of *Wingspan,* a journal that chronicles the men's movement. With its ecological focus, it promotes an attitude of guardianship toward the natural world.

Male spirituality also affirms the uniqueness of male experience, he points out. With its emphasis on depth psychology, it accesses men's inner life through intense and frequent ritual process enacted in community. As an embodied spirituality, it focuses on experiencing joy and reverence through nonverbal means, rather than through strictly introspective techniques.

"Masculine spirituality emphasizes action over theory, service to the human community over religious discussion, truth-speaking over social graces, and doing justice over looking nice," says Franciscan priest Richard Rohr. "Without this masculine element, our spirituality in its inwardness will lack the vigor to carry out effective social change."

STARTING A MEN'S GROUP

"In one sense the voyage of self-discovery is solitary, but that doesn't mean you have to take it all alone," writes social critic and men's-group veteran Sam Keen in his book *Fire in the Belly: On Being a Man.* "In matters of the psyche and spirit, taking the journey and telling the story go hand in glove, and that is why we need a listening community to make our solitary pilgrimage. The most powerful resource we have for transforming ourselves is honest conversation between men and men, women and women, men and women."

Keen, who has participated in an ongoing men's group for more than thirteen years, says that the most important qualities of such groups are confidentiality, candor, regularity, and fun. "We don't just sit around and constantly bare our souls," he says. "We also express our closeness through laughter and good-natured jokes." Keen offers the following advice for starting a leaderless men's group:

- Reach out to one person who seems ripe for friendship and risk being candid about your feelings and needs. Men who you sense are in trouble with romance, marriage, family, alcohol, drugs, or work

Proponents of this nascent spirituality often refer to their practices as soul work, to distinguish them from more traditional spiritual approaches. "Unlike Christian and Eastern spiritual practices, which seek light, ascension, and transcendence, soul work deals with the descent into darkness, reconciliation with the shadow self, and connection to earth and soil," says Forrest Craver, a board member of the Men's Council of Greater Washington. "Too often spiritual practices such as meditation prematurely separate men from their grounded, instinctual selves, giving them a false sense of 'all is well,' when in fact it's just repressed. When soul can mediate between body and spirit, we can express our spiritual intentions in the world without losing touch with our instincts and intuitions."

When Craver refers to soul, he conceives of it in masculine terms, rather than in its conventionally feminine form. This radical re-visioning of the psyche, popular in the men's movement, makes approaching the inner world less apprehensive to those in search of a renewed masculinity.

The warrior energy of men now has to be used paradoxically to destroy the warrior psyche and the politics of warfare. It will require more courage and aggression than we've ever seen on the battlefield.

SAM KEEN

are good candidates. Go slowly in gathering your community. It is important to collect a group of men with whom you can be honest.

- Keep the group small enough to allow for in-depth sharing by all members, with no more than twelve or fifteen, and large enough to give you some diversity, with no fewer than six. To build intimacy and trust, regular, frequent meetings are important. It is essential to include only men who are willing to make a long-term commitment to meeting either once a week or every other week.

- The agenda of the group will emerge naturally from the concerns of the members. Most weeks, one or more men will be wrestling with some problem that becomes the focus of discussion. Gradually, the group will share experiences, stories, and feelings, and learn how to challenge, pursue, and nurture. In time, questions about sex, money, work, authority, power, competition, loneliness, death, guilt, addictions, fathers, mothers, children, goals, and the pains and pleasures of being male will arise.

- Beware of unrealistic expectations when you commit to a men's group. Remember that at its core, a men's group is about friendship.

According to Jungian analyst Eugene Monick, when men seek their roots in the unconscious, they encounter phallos, the archetypal god image that underpins their gender identity, sexuality, and spiritual orientation. As the fundamental mark of maleness, phallos is characterized by determination, effectiveness, penetration, and strength.

The presence of this masculine archetype gives men safer passage into the unconscious when they begin moving beyond their conscious ego identities, Monick says. If the unconscious is seen only as the realm of the Great Mother, men may dread descending into their depths, fearing an encounter with the totally Other. But with the support of phallos, men more confidently can undertake the inner journey, knowing they will encounter energies that are friendly and primordially familiar.

"If origin is understood only as feminine, male resistance [to the unconscious] is understandable, given the energy that has been expended in establishing masculinity as independent from the matrix," Monick writes in *Phallos: Sacred Image of the Masculine.* "Phallos as masculine source offers a man a way to return to the unconscious without surrendering his phallic identity."

Reverence for phallos in its earthy manifestation—as the Wild Man—enables men to move beyond ego limitation to ecstatic merger with the archetypal world in sexuality, Monick says. If men lose touch with the "hot breath" of phallos, their spirituality becomes "brittle and technical . . . rational and without inspiration."

But grounded in their instinctual energies, men can help heal the mind/body split that has plagued the Judeo-Christian religious tradition, says Craver. On a personal level, they will relate to women with an integrity and trust forged in the fires of gender-affirming inner work. "Together," he says, "women and men will then give birth to an immensely creative energy necessary for solving our global problems."

Having no soul union with other men can be the most damaging wound of all.

ROBERT BLY

THE MATURE MASCULINE

In their hunger to construct a viable masculine psychology, some men have turned to the archetypes of Greek mythology to reclaim images of mature manhood. Olympian gods, such as kingly Zeus, knowledge-seeking Apollo, and mystical, ecstatic Dionysus, provide men with time-honored patterns for manifesting their energy in uniquely masculine ways. Archetypal psychologists insist that whether they are honored consciously or entirely repressed, these powerful, innate patterns continually affect a man's personality, work, and relationships.

Perhaps the greatest price men have paid for the obsession with fearlessness is to have become tough on the outside but empty within. We are hollow men. The connection between fearlessness and feelinglessness should be obvious.

SAM KEEN

Besides turning to the universal patterns contained in Greek mythology, men recently have been focusing on the archetypes of King, Warrior, Magician, and Lover, which according to Robert Moore and Douglas Gillette constitute the deep structures of the mature male psyche. In their view, patriarchy blocks men's connection to mature masculinity by sanctioning the expression of the immature masculine, which confuses controlling, threatening, and hostile behavior with strength.

"Patriarchy is based on fear—the boy's fear, the immature masculine's fear—of women, to be sure, but also fear of men," they write in *King, Warrior, Magician, Lover.* "In the present crisis in masculinity, we do not need, as some radical feminists are saying, less masculine power. We need more. But we need more of the mature masculine. . . . We need to develop a sense of calmness about masculine power so we don't have to act out dominating, disempowering behavior toward others."

Moore and Gillette believe that the following four archetypes hold the key to decoding the male psyche and empowering men to celebrate authentic masculine power and potency:

The King. As the central archetype of male authority, the King establishes law and order in his kingdom (both inner and outer). Undeveloped King

177

energy seeks power over others; while in its more mature expression, motivated by the welfare of all beings, it seeks to empower them. When the King manifests in a man's life, it brings order to his affairs, stabilizes chaotic emotions, gives centeredness, and mediates vitality, life force, and joy. Examples of well-known Kings include Winston Churchill, John F. Kennedy, and Franklin Delano Roosevelt.

The Warrior. Focused, disciplined, and clear-thinking, trained to wield power skillfully, the Warrior channels his aggressiveness, expressing it as brute force in its lowest manifestation and as service to a transcendent cause in its highest. The Warrior prizes courage, fearlessness, and an unconquerable spirit. When this archetypal energy is activated, a man acts energetically, decisively, and courageously, loyal to some greater good beyond his own personal gain. Examples include generals George Patton and Douglas MacArthur, Japanese samurai warriors, and police officers who do their job without using unnecessary force.

The Magician. A master at containing and channeling power, the Magician governs the realm of secret and hidden knowledge that takes special training to acquire. The Magician archetype also predisposes a man to awareness and insight gained through introspection. At his least developed, the Magician manipulates knowledge for personal gain; at his most highly developed, he uses knowledge as a holy man or shaman to heal his people. Men who access this energy express clear-sightedness, technical skill, and self-knowledge in their professional and personal lives. Examples include Merlin, King Arthur's magician; psychologist Carl Jung; scientist Albert Einstein; and astronomer Carl Sagan.

The Lover. Much maligned by Western religion, the Lover encourages a healthy sensuality, an unbounded connectedness to life through powerful feelings, an aesthetic awareness, and a longing for mystical oneness. The Lover represents the masculine side of eros, which promotes love and gentleness. At his least developed, the Lower is ruled by an addictive quest for sensual experience; at his most mature, because he celebrates the beauty of nature and the physical world, he becomes a guardian of the Earth. When men access this energy, they feel alive, enthusiastic, and compassionate about their work and relationships. Without the Lover, the other three archetypal energies lose much of their warmth and relatedness. Well-known Lovers include entertainer Frank Sinatra, actors Richard Burton and Kevin Costner, opera singer Luciano Pavarotti, and singer Michael Jackson.

Men have been depressed now for many years in their male and resplendent selves, depressed into dejection and almost abjection. Is that not evil?

D. H. LAWRENCE

Writing passionately, Moore and Gillette call for men to act "with the benevolence of ancient kings, the courage and decisiveness of ancient warriors, the wisdom of magicians, and the passion of lovers" in defense of our ailing world. They conclude: "How well we transform ourselves from men living our lives under the power of Boy psychology to real men guided by the archetypes of Man psychology will have a decisive effect on the outcome of our present world situation."

TECHNIQUES TO EVOKE THE MATURE MASCULINE

By getting in touch with archetypes of mature masculinity, men can become genuinely stronger, more centered, and generative toward themselves and toward other men and women. To begin, Moore and Gillette recommend the exercises shown on pages 180 and 181.

HEALING OUR FATHERS, OURSELVES, AND THE EARTH

One of the most memorable scenes in the *Odyssey* occurs when Odysseus returns to Ithaca after fighting in the Trojan War for ten years, to be followed by another decade of adventure-filled wandering. As translated by Robert Fitzgerald, here is how the great warrior king reveals himself to his teenage son, Telemachus:

> "I am the father whom your boyhood lacked and suffered for lack of. I am he. . . . This is not princely to be swept away by wonder at your father's presence. No other Odysseus will ever come, for he and I are one, the same."
>
> Throwing his arms around this marvel of a father, Telemachus began to weep. Salt tears rose from the wells of longing in both men, and cries burst from both as keen and fluttering as those of the great taloned hawk, whose nestlings farmers take before they fly. So helplessly they cried pouring out tears, and might have gone on weeping till sundown.

Like Telemachus, many men in our society have undertaken a quest to discover the Odysseus figure they never knew in their childhood. They often are confused about masculine strength, having grown up without strong, nurturing fathers to provide them with a confident model of manhood. Because their fathers were often shadowy presences, distant and emotionally unavailable, these men suffer from a father hunger experienced as resentment, sorrow, and a sense of loss.

According to psychologist Samuel Osherson, they also carry a wounded father within, an internal sense of masculinity based on their

Authentic initiation is marked by the compassion, generativity, and ethical action which issues out of it.

ROBERT MOORE

The unique character of this male journey is that . . . there can be no maps, no certitudes, no short-cuts. It can't just be talked through, imitated, or role-played. The male journey must be done—by me.

FATHER RICHARD ROHR

fathers as rejecting, incompetent, or absent. The women's movement compounds the problem, because in their zeal to end patriarchal oppression, many men as children and adolescents formed unconscious alliances with their mothers to exclude their fathers. The guilt caused by this betrayal further widens the breach between fathers and sons.

"All sons need to heal the wounded fathers within their own hearts," Osherson writes in *Finding Our Fathers.* "At bottom, healing the wounded father is a process of untangling the myths and fantasies sons learn growing up about self, mother, and father, which we act out every day with bosses, wives, and children. It means constructing a satisfying sense of manhood both from our opportunities in a time of changing sex-roles and by 'diving into the wreck' of the past and retrieving a firm, sturdy appreciation of the heroism and failure in our fathers' lives."

Men can start the healing process, counsels Osherson, by exploring their fathers' lives and empathizing with their pain. This requires sacrific-

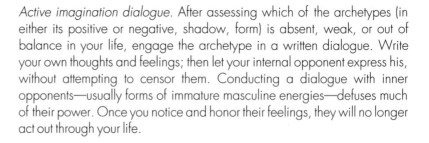

Active imagination dialogue. After assessing which of the archetypes (in either its positive or negative, shadow, form) is absent, weak, or out of balance in your life, engage the archetype in a written dialogue. Write your own thoughts and feelings; then let your internal opponent express his, without attempting to censor them. Conducting a dialogue with inner opponents—usually forms of immature masculine energies—defuses much of their power. Once you notice and honor their feelings, they will no longer act out through your life.

Invocation. Spend time looking for images of the King, Warrior, Magician, and Lover. Then find a quiet place, clear your mind, and consciously invoke an image of a masculine archetype. If you invoke the King, seek to merge your deep unconscious with him. In your imagination, make your ego his servant, and feel his calm strength and his benevolence toward you. Imagine yourself before his throne, having an audience with him. Tell him that you need his help—his power, favor, orderliness, and manliness. Count on his generosity and kind disposition. This technique is comparable to what religions have always called prayer, when it was accompanied by ritual connection to the god.

ing the illusion of finding the perfect, all-powerful father and relating to the flesh-and-blood figure who was idealized and feared in childhood. "Seeing our fathers as human, accepting their frailties and lapses," he writes, "allows us to accept our own frailties and imperfections in this world." By identifying with the good and strong qualities in their fathers, men can grow into a fuller, more trustworthy sense of masculinity which, in Robert Bly's words, is both life-preserving and life-giving.

Perhaps the most powerful work of reconciliation occurs when men become fathers themselves. In recent years, some men, disillusioned with the image of father as outsider, provider, or intruder in the home, have been searching for new ways to parent children. As part of the radical re-structuring of masculinity now under way, they acknowledge the father as both a nurturing force within the family and as a creative bridge to the outside world.

Psychologists Arthur and Libby Colman call this new parent an

Admiring men. Read biographies of men who embody qualities you want to develop. If you need more King energy, study the life of Abraham Lincoln or Ho Chi Minh. If you need more warrior energy, read about the Egyptian pharoah Ramses II or Roman emperor Marcus Aurelius. For Magician energy, look into the lives of Sigmund Freud or Jonas Salk; for the Lover, read about Sir Richard Francis Burton, the eighteenth-century explorer and translator of the *Arabian Nights,* or Alan Watts, who popularized Eastern mysticism in the West.

Method acting. Learn to get into character by adopting the movements, speech patterns, and thoughts of an archetype, even if you don't really feel the character. Simply act as if you do. If, for example, you have just been fired from your job and your wife has left you, pick up the King's script, read his lines, sit on his throne, and declare, "The show must go on!" Pretty soon, believe it or not, you will start to feel like a king. To access the Lover, act as if you really appreciate sunsets by paying particular attention to the shifting colors. Pretty soon, strange as it may seem, you really may find yourself becoming interested in the sunset!

Without other men, especially older men, to "bless" him and to affirm him, . . . a man is inordinately vulnerable to what he experiences as the overwhelming and life-threatening power of the feminine. Without realistic self-esteem, facilitated by his experiences with the nurturing masculine, no man can form a fully intimate relationship with a woman. He cannot because he experiences himself as too weak to exercise, or even to claim, his legitimate power.

DOUGLAS GILLETTE

"earth father," because he makes the family his primary focus by involving himself in the intimate activities of child-rearing. The traditional "sky father," on the other hand, lives on the outskirts of the family, committed to his role as breadwinner in the outside world.

While a sky father nurtures his children intermittently, an earth father routinely will take off from work to accompany his sick child to a doctor's appointment or pass up a business conference to tuck his children into bed. Such a man heals himself by providing his children with what he himself never received. In *The Father: Mythology and Changing Roles,* the Colmans describe the challenges of being an earth father:

> Of all the images of parenting, earth father is farthest removed from the values and ambitions instilled in growing boys in America. It may be the hardest image for a man to feel truly enriched by, and yet it represents a most fundamental level of parenting. Rather than being a hero, a disciplinarian, a bridge to the outside world, or a force to be overcome, the earth father takes on the job of providing his children with the basic trust and inner security with which to grow up and out of the family toward independence and a unique identity.

When it comes time for a young male to talk with the Wild Man, he will find the conversation quite distinct from a talk with a minister, a rabbi, or a guru. Conversing with the Wild Man is not talking about bliss or mind or spirit or "higher consciousness," but about something wet, dark, and low—what James Hillman would call "soul."

ROBERT BLY

If earth fathering represents a mutation in male identity, it may promise more than just a revolution in the family. For if by family we mean the commonwealth of creatures on the Earth, then men have an opportunity and a responsibility to become nurturing fathers and caretakers of our ailing planet. When men transmute their fierce warrior energies and learn to husband rather than conquer nature, says Sam Keen, they will "treat air sheds, watersheds, the humus, the myriad species of mammals and plants, to say nothing of beetles and earthworms, as kinfolk."

EXPRESSING THE NEW MASCULINITY

Here are Forrest Craver's practical guidelines for developing a healthy masculinity in our everyday lives:

Link up with a local men's council or get together with a number of male friends on a regular basis. Topics for discussion might include fatherhood, child-rearing, intimate relationships, marriage, and parents.

Bless younger men, who have a deep yearning to be admired and encouraged. Even if you have an excellent relationship with your son, shower your kingly blessing on others who need your generosity of spirit.

Revere and respect older men. Often denigrated by our ageist society, older men need to be appreciated for their contributions to life on our behalf. You might express your appreciation for someone who has taken a courageous political stand or who has dedicated himself to community service.

Bury the cultural stereotype of the silent, unexpressive man who is cut off from his feelings and his body. Affirm in attitude and action men's capacity to communicate with others—including women and children—from the heart level.

Speak out against male-bashing images in the media that present men as inept, weak, or foolish. Show your respect for masculine integrity by making complaints to television stations, programmers, and advertisers who purvey these damaging images.

Consider other men as valuable resources for healing your emotional wounding. Just as women have strengthened themselves through sisterhood, men can find emotional and spiritual nourishment through brotherhood.

The process of reconciliation with the father is never-ending and continues through death and beyond.

ARTHUR AND LIBBY COLMAN

RESOURCES

Recommended Reading

Iron John: A Book About Men, Robert Bly (Addison-Wesley, 1990). Presents a new vision of a mature, vigorous masculinity using the Grimm's fairy tale "Iron John" as its framework.

Fire in the Belly: On Being a Man, Sam Keen (Bantam Books, 1991). Explores the difficulties of being a modern man and the need for a new masculine consciousness.

King, Warrior, Magician, Lover: Rediscovering the Archetypes of the Mature Masculine, Robert Moore and Douglas Gillette (HarperCollins, 1990). Sets forth a new masculine psychology based on four archetypes that connect men to deep sources of empowerment.

Finding Our Fathers, Samuel Osherson (Fawcett Columbine, 1986). How healing the father/son relationship frees men to have fuller, more fulfilling lives.

Gods in Everyman: A New Psychology of Men's Lives & Loves, Jean Shinoda Bolen (Harper & Row, 1989). Presents a masculine psychology based on archetypal images drawn from Greek mythology.

Knights Without Armor: A Practical Guide for Men in Quest of Masculine Soul, Aaron R. Kipnis (Jeremy P. Tarcher, 1991). Centered around the intimate experience of a men's group, this book offers a broad look at the sociological and mythological bases of the new masculinity.

To Be A Man: In Search of the Deep Masculine, edited by Keith Thompson (Jeremy P. Tarcher, 1991). The best collection of psychology and literature on male issues.

Fathers, Sons, and Daughters, edited by Charles S. Scull (Jeremy P. Tarcher, 1992). An anthology of inspirational readings.

The Flying Boy: Healing the Wounded Man, John Lee (Health Communications, 1987). An autobiographical account of a man's journey through grief to masculine strength.

A Warrior's Bookshelf

To Chinese Taoists and Japanese samurai, the true way of the warrrior involves mastery of both pen and sword, according to Rick Fields, author of

The Code of the Warrior: In History, Myth, and Everyday Life. No warrior should go into battle without first having contemplated the lessons distilled from the literature of the warrior. Here are Fields's suggestions of ancient and modern texts to study.

The Iliad by Homer. Godlike Achilles died victorious and young, setting the pattern for the heroic warrior of the West. Homer's poetry looks unflinchingly at both the glory and gore of warfare. My favorite translation is by Robert Fitzgerald.

The Bhagavad Gita. Arjuna's refusal to fight a bloody war against his relatives is resolved by his charioteer Krishna, who expounds on the duties of a warrior and on how to fight (or do anything) with non-attachment. S. Radhakrishnan's translation gives a useful word-for-word gloss on the original Sanskrit.

The Art of War by Sun Tzu. This work by an ancient Chinese general turns the teachings of the *Tao Te Ching* into a practical field guide for action. It is still so up-to-date that during the Persian Gulf war the Marines issued ten thousand audiotapes of Sun Tzu to their troops. I like to consult translations by Samuel Griffith and Thomas Cleary.

The Destiny of the Warrior by Georges Dumezil. This classic of comparative mythology is scholarly, difficult, dense, and indispensable for understanding the stormy Indo-European warrior.

The Warriors: Reflections on Men in Battle by Glenn Gray. This is an unsentimental meditation on the terrors and exhilarations of battle by a philosophy professor who served as a combat soldier in World War II.

Shambhala: The Sacred Path of the Warrior by Chogyam Trungpa (Bantam Books, 1986). This modern adaptation of an ancient Tibetan tradition explores warriorship as the path of bravery and open-hearted vulnerability in everyday life.

In Search of the Warrior Spirit: Teaching Awareness to America's Military Elite by Richard Strozzi Heckler (North Atlantic, 1989). A modern samurai meets the Green Berets in this gripping, real-life account of a California aikido teacher who tries to bring his version of the new warrior to a U.S. Army top-secret training program.

Organizations

The following are regional men's centers that can put you in touch with or help you start a men's group in your area:

The Austin Men's Center (1611 West Sixth Street, Austin, TX 78703; 512-477-9595) focuses on recovery programs and publishes the quarterly magazine, *Man! Men's Issues, Relationships & Recovery*. The publication ($11/year) covers health, addiction and recovery, and the mythopoetic movement.

The Boulder Men's Council (P.O. Box 385, Boulder, CO 80306) publishes the quarterly *Men's Council Journal*, which includes upcoming workshops, descriptions of council ceremonies, and interviews with leading figures in the men's movement.

The National Men's Resource Center (P.O. Box 882, San Anselmo, CA 94960; 800-658-1212) offers a Men's Resource Hotline Calendar, which lists events primarily in northern California, although some national events are included.

The Men's Council of Greater Washington (P.O. Box 185, Cabin John, MD 20818; 301-593-8182) meets monthly and publishes a newsletter.

Seattle M.E.N. (Men's Evolvement Network), 602 West Howe Street, Seattle, WA 98119; 206-285-4356. The organization publishes a monthly newsletter and makes referrals to men's groups, wisdom councils, and workshops in Washington.

The Twin Cities Men's Center (3255 Hennepin Avenue South, Suite 45, Minneapolis, MN 55408; 612-822-5892) publishes the quarterly *Men Talk: A Source for Emerging Male Expression* ($14/year).

Publications

Wingspan: Journal of the Male Spirit (P.O. Box 1491, Manchester, MA 01944; 617-282-3521, free but donations welcome, quarterly). The largest men's publication in the country features articles by leading figures in the men's movement, interviews, and a resource directory of publications, organizations, workshops, events, and support groups nationwide.

Men's Friends: How to Organize and Run Your Own Men's Support Group by Bill Kauth is a self-published manual that also contains resource listings for men's groups and events. It costs $15 plus $2 postage. To order, write E.Q.L.S. Publishing, 4913 North Newhall Street, Milwaukee, WI 53217; 414-964-6656.

Inroads: Men, Creativity, Soul (P.O. Box 14944, University Station, Minneapolis, MN 55414, $7.50/year, biannual). This somewhat scholarly journal includes poetry and art critiques inspired by the work of Robert Bly, James Hillman, Michael Meade, and Joseph Campbell.

Man, Alive! New Mexico's Journal of Men's Wellness (Men U Network Press, P.O. Box 40300, Albuquerque, NM 87196; 505-255-4944, quarterly). This newspaper documents the male experience through poetry, articles, and essays, and serves as a good networking resource in the Southwest.

Men's Resources Northeast (New Views Educational Services, P.O. Box 137, Little Ferry, NJ 07643; 201-848-9134). Lists 150 men's groups in the Northeast and contains a nationwide calendar of conferences and retreats, updated quarterly. The publisher provides consultations by phone for those starting men's groups.

CHAPTER 10

ADDICTIONS, CO-DEPENDENCE, AND RECOVERY

Applied Spirituality for Self-Healing

An alcoholic, who clings to the idea that his drinking is manageable, suddenly goes on a binge that destroys his flimsy illusion of self-control, along with the last shreds of his self-respect. Having bargained and cajoled with and broken every promise he has made to God to stop drinking, he returns to his AA program humbled and contrite. He has exhausted every strategy of personal will to overcome alcoholism, and in his powerlessness he cries out, "Oh, dear God, where am I going to find the strength to overcome my disease?"

Suddenly from within him the answer comes, calm and sweet beyond description: "You have the strength. All you have to do is use it. I am with you. Use *Me.*" With the dawning of this realization, the man awakens from the tomb of his captivity to alcohol and is reborn into a life of sobriety founded on daily contact with his inner source.

This experience of an AA member, related in *Came to Believe,* illustrates why Twelve Step programs may be the country's fastest-growing spiritual path. They give people in recovery from substance abuse and dysfunctional families the spiritual principles, daily tools, and group support needed to heal a disorder that is at root spiritual. As Carl Jung once observed, "The craving for alcohol [is] the equivalent, on a low level, of the spiritual thirst of our being for wholeness; expressed in medieval language: the union with God." Because addicts and alcoholics displace the

Life is like a game of cards. The hand that is dealt you represents determinism; the way you play it is free will.

JAWAHARLAL NEHRU

search for self-transcendence onto physical substances, Twelve Step programs stress that real healing occurs by connecting with a higher power discovered through prayer and meditation.

APPLIED SPIRITUALITY

"Twelve-Step programs represent a down-to-earth application of the spirituality practiced in ashrams and monasteries over the centuries," explains consciousness researcher John White, author of *The Meeting of Science and Spirit.* "Throughout the ages, spiritual teachers have taught that attaching ourselves to external sources of pleasure inevitably leads to dependency and suffering, especially when these sources of gratification are withdrawn. People in the recovery movement, who are victims of a severe form of attachment, are learning to make the leap from outer-directed addiction to inner-directed freedom."

The recovery movement traces its origins to Bill Wilson, an alcoholic who had a spiritual awakening, stopped drinking, and co-founded Alcoholics Anonymous in 1935. In 1951, Wilson's wife, Lois, founded Al-Anon, an AA-related support group that uses the Twelve Steps to help family members and friends recover from the damaging effects of other people's alcoholism. In the past decade, self-help groups for adult children of alcoholics (ACAs) and adult children of other types of dysfunctional families have been springing up at an estimated rate of one new group per day in the United States. At the same time, other Twelve Step-related groups have been proliferating: Overeaters Anonymous, Gamblers Anonymous, Sex Addicts Anonymous, and Narcotics Anonymous, to name a few.

"Twelve-Step programs apply spiritual methods to heal the addictive, compulsive behavior caused by growing up in dysfunctional families," says Jacquelyn Small, a transpersonal psychotherapist and author of *Awakening in Time: The Journey from Codependence to Co-Creation.* "As more and more people wake up to their woundedness, they're discovering that transpersonal approaches to healing work faster and more effectively than approaches that deny the spiritual dimension."

To enter what Small calls "the path of direct knowledge," people first need to redefine their years of addictive behavior as a training ground that can provide insight into the causes of human suffering. By viewing their seeming failures as undigested lessons of the soul, she says, they develop the right attitude to embark on the Twelve Step spiritual path with its three distinct stages:

In the first stage, *surrender,* we become painfully aware of the ego's

---

It is a terrible thing
To be so open: it is as if my
heart
Put on a face and walked into
the world.

SYLVIA PLATH

God allows us to experience
the low points of life in order
to teach us lessons we could
not learn in any other way.

C. S. LEWIS

powerlessness in effecting permanent change, and we decide to allow a higher power to assume control over our unmanageable lives. In the second stage, *purification,* we undertake a comprehensive self-review that becomes the basis for establishing healthier personal relationships. In this process, we draw on the nurturing support of our higher power, forgive ourselves for our human failings, and then make amends to the people we have injured in the past. In the third stage, *right relationship,* we move out into the world with a service orientation, living and sharing the principles that have transformed our lives.

Small characterizes the Twelve Step path as a movement from the personal to the interpersonal, culminating in the transpersonal. "We have to develop a fully integrated ego before transcending it," she says. "And we can only transcend the ego by working through its needs at the personal and interpersonal levels, not by denying or attempting to bypass them. Otherwise, we become addicted to the highs of altered states of consciousness as a defense against our neurotic compulsions."

Twelve Step spirituality helps people develop healthy egos by drawing on practices taught by the world's great spiritual traditions, according to Christina Grof, co-author of *The Stormy Search for the Self.* Like most approaches, this "inspired Western yoga" emphasizes surrender of the personal ego, self-purification, and introspection through prayer and meditation, along with selfless service in the world. Most programs place an emphasis on developing detachment, or the art of living in the moment without trying to control relationships and events to fit our preconceptions about how life should be. Twelve Step programs also stress the beneficial effects of doing spiritual work in a community of like-minded people.

"What makes this approach special is that it communicates the eternal truths in non-esoteric language that people can understand," Grof says. "As this down-to-earth approach begins to influence the field of transpersonal psychology, health professionals will increasingly bring a spiritual perspective to the treatment of addiction."

Such an approach may help uproot the epidemic of addictive behavior afflicting our culture. In *When Society Becomes an Addict,* psychologist Anne Wilson Schaef argues that the vast majority of our population suffers either from addictions to substances, such as alcohol, nicotine, or food, or addictions to processes, such as gambling, work, relationships, obsessive sex, or quick-fix brands of religion. Although society exhibits all the characteristics of the individual alcoholic or addict, Schaef believes that collective recovery is possible once we give up living in denial of our diseased condition.

In every man there lies hidden a child between five and eight years old, the age at which naïveté comes to an end. It is this child whom one must detect in that intimidating man with his long beard, bristling eyebrows, heavy mustache, and weighty look—a captain. Even he conceals, and not at all deep down, the youngster, the booby, the little rascal, out of whom age has made this powerful monster.

PAUL VALÉRY

THE TWELVE STEPS

"The spiritual life is not a theory. We have to live it," counsels Alcoholics Anonymous's basic text. Here are AA's world-famous guidelines—remarkable in their simplicity and universality—for following this sound advice:

1. We admitted we were powerless over alcohol—that our lives had become unmanageable.
2. Came to believe that a Power greater than ourselves could restore us to sanity.
3. Made a decision to turn our will and our lives over to the care of God as we understood Him.
4. Made a searching and fearless moral inventory of ourselves.
5. Admitted to God, to ourselves, and to another human being the exact nature of our wrongs.
6. Were entirely ready to have God remove all these defects of character.
7. Humbly asked Him to remove our shortcomings.
8. Made a list of all persons we had harmed, and became willing to make amends to them all.
9. Made direct amends to such people wherever possible, except when to do so would injure them or others.
10. Continued to take personal inventory and when we were wrong promptly admitted it.
11. Sought through prayer and meditation to improve our conscious contact with God as we understood Him, praying only for knowledge of His will for us and the power to carry that out.
12. Having had a spiritual awakening as a result of these Steps, we tried to carry this message to others, and to practice these principles in all our affairs.

Perfect love means to love the one through whom one became unhappy.

SØREN KIERKEGAARD

It is the Child that sees the primordial secret in Nature and it is the child of ourselves we return to. The child within us is simple and daring enough to live the Secret.

LAO TZU

"It is possible to see the Twelve Steps operating on a systems level," she writes. If, like the recovering alcoholic, we collectively equate spirituality with sobriety and make sobriety our top priority, the widespread practice of the Twelve Steps might help our addictive culture reverse its moral and spiritual deterioration.

ADDICTION AS SPIRITUAL EMERGENCY

When we think of spiritual life, images of Mother Teresa feeding the poor or disciplined meditators practicing zazen stereotypically come to mind. In our self-righteousness, we might exclude an alcoholic vomiting in the toilet stall of a bar or a heroin addict shooting up in a squalid room from the ranks of legitimate spiritual seekers. Yet evidence is mounting that the addict's self-destructive behavior, seemingly devoid of redeeming value, is often a case of spiritual emergency, a transformative crisis involving psychological death and rebirth.

"Behind the craving for drugs and alcohol in many people lies the craving for transcendence or wholeness," explains Christina Grof, who is herself a recovering alcoholic and founder of the Spiritual Emergence Network. "Many addicts and alcoholics have a highly developed sensitivity and mystical nature that cause them trouble in our rational, scientific culture. During episodes of spiritual emergency, they sometimes turn to alcohol and drugs to escape from the pressures, pain, and chaos of the inner world and from the alienation they may feel in their outer life."

During a transformational crisis, says Grof, a person sinks into the depths of addiction and hits bottom. This depression, experienced as the dark night of the soul, brings the terrifying realization that every former strategy for achieving a workable life has failed. Stripped of defenses and illusions, face-to-face with fear and loneliness, the addict exhausts personal resources for controlling his soul sickness and surrenders to a higher power. In this moment of victorious defeat, the ego dies a devastating death, breakdown becomes breakthrough, and a reborn self rises tentatively from the ashes, carrying the seeds of a spiritually oriented life.

The newly awakened self, which previously may have resisted even casual reference to spiritual subjects, can now openly embrace a Twelve Step recovery program, not as a luxury, but as a matter of life or death. "What we really have is a daily reprieve contingent on the maintenance of our spiritual condition," according to the *Big Book,* the basic text for Alcoholics Anonymous. "Every day is a day when we must carry the vision of God's will into all of our activities. 'How can I best serve Thee—Thy will (not mine) be done.' These are thoughts which must go with us constantly."

When people enter Twelve Step programs, they encounter a democratic form of spirituality without hierarchies or gurus. "There is no doctrine, no orthodoxy, no 'right way' to do the program, no 'right way' to believe," writes Jacob Barrington, a former Zen monk and a child of an

In every adult there lurks a child—an eternal child, something that is always becoming, is never completed, and calls for unceasing care, attention, and education. That is the part of the human personality which wants to develop and become whole.

C. G. JUNG

The violation of the natural weakness and simplicity of the young child not ready for autonomy can turn into a protective infantilism that lasts through one's life. These wounds may be redeemed through the natural simplicity of loving; indeed, they may offer the gateway through which love may enter.

JEAN HOUSTON

alcoholic family, in *Yoga Journal.* "Your higher power may be God, mine may be the Big Silence, somebody else's may be the Original Self or Brahman or the Divine Within." This practice, he says, shows respect for each person's particular spiritual understanding.

Because the group environment is so supportive, often with rotating leadership, members may freely share their stories, discuss successes in working the Twelve Steps, or confess to personal difficulties with relationships. No one is compelled to participate; however, because programs re-

Do You Suffer from Religious Addiction?

Like alcohol and other addictive substances, humankind has used religion to escape from pain, according to Father Leo Booth, an Episcopal priest, recovery counselor, recovering alcoholic, and author of *When God Becomes a Drug.* "Religious addiction is using God, the Church, or a belief system as an escape from reality, in an attempt to find or elevate a sense of self-worth or well-being," he writes. "It is using God or religion as a fix. It is the ultimate form of co-dependency—feeling worthless in and of ourselves and looking outside for something or someone to tell us we are worthwhile."

Religious addicts often feel judged by God, so they learn to judge others, says Father Leo. Believing themselves fallen and dirty, they inflict their self-hatred onto others, making them feel inherently defective as well. Suffering from low self-esteem, a sense of inadequacy, shame, and guilt, they take refuge in religious practices and rituals that anesthetize themselves from inner pain.

People who are religiously addicted, says Father Leo, display the following symptoms:

- Inability to think, doubt, or question information or authority
- Black-and-white, simplistic thinking
- Shame-based belief that they aren't good enough or that they are failing in the practice of their religious rituals
- Magical thinking that God will fix them
- Perfectionism: rigid, obsessive adherence to rules, codes of ethics, or guidelines

The healing energy of God, the Universe, life, and recovery surrounds us. It is available, waiting for us to draw on it, waiting for us to draw it in. It's waiting at our meeting or groups, on the words of a whispered prayer, in a gentle touch, a positive word, a positive thought. Healing energy is in the sun, the wind, the rain, in all that is good.

Melody Beattie

create the intimacy and self-acceptance that are lacking in dysfunctional families, many members slowly shed layers of defensiveness and denial to reveal—and embrace—the inner self they abandoned in childhood in order to survive.

"I've been able to admit my rage, and the hurt and sadness underneath, to myself and a roomful of people," writes Barrington. "I've been able to talk frankly about my inability to take criticism, my compulsive need to perform and achieve for approval, my defensiveness and eager

- Uncompromising judgmental attitudes
- Compulsive praying, going to church, or quoting scripture
- Unrealistic financial contributions to church
- Belief that sex is dirty—that our bodies and physical pleasures are evil
- Compulsive overeating or excessive fasting
- Conflict with science, medicine, and education
- Progressive detachment from the real world, isolation, and breakdown of relationships
- Psychosomatic illness: back pains, sleeplessness, headaches, or hypertension
- Manipulating scripture or texts, feeling chosen, or claiming to receive special messages from God
- Trancelike states or a glazed, happy face
- Cries for help; physical, mental, and emotional breakdown; hospitalization

To recover from religious addiction, first we need to recognize that we are spiritually unhealthy, after which we must work on changing our beliefs and behaviors. "Recovery means discovering divinity in one's own life," says Father Leo. "We are co-creators with God, not puppets on a string waiting for something to happen. We *make* things happen; we *create* the difference, not in our old dysfunctional pattern of isolated control, but in choosing a partnership with our Higher Power. Then, by appreciating that we are powerful human beings, we ourselves become the 'somebody' who can fix us. This healing gives birth to a healthy spirituality and a rewarding relationship with God."

We are healed of our suffering only by experiencing it to the full.

MARCEL PROUST

Although a child is immature, he still has an organismic sense of wholeness, of I AMness. In other words, he feels connected and unified within himself. The feeling of unified wholeness and completeness is the true meaning of perfection, and in this sense every child is perfect.

JOHN BRADSHAW

Instead of heavy duty, try putting yourself on the gentle cycle.

ANONYMOUS

Recovery is possible. We can, indeed, be sober and fully alive. It may not always be easy and it may not always be fun, and it is always interesting. We often dwell on how difficult recovery is, yet in my experience and in what I know of others', it is a lot easier and better than living addictively.

ANNE WILSON SCHAEF

ness to assign blame (especially, in secret, to blame myself). I've uncovered my fear of intimacy and my lack of self-esteem. And I've seen how I've parented my kids in some of the same ugly ways I was parented."

Many report that self-disclosure among a community of fellow travelers yields rich rewards: the ability to feel life, rather than intellectualize about it; a reconnection with the lost self, with its capacity for delight and humor, for joy and sadness; and an increased sense of intimacy with lovers, children, and friends.

With its emphasis on the release of feelings of grief, sorrow, and rejection, Dr. Charles Whitfield, author of *Healing the Child Within*, calls the path of addiction and recovery the path of the heart. "The heart opens when we empty ourselves of old programming and return to the open, vulnerable, and authentic being we have always been. This True Self, the spark of divinity within us, is our link to God."

TWELVE STEPS TO A BETTER MARRIAGE

The Twelve Steps have a psychological validity that applies to people who are not in recovery as well, says Jacquelyn Small. To prove her point, she offers the following adaptation of the Twelve Step approach for settling marital conflicts:

When my husband and I have a fight and I become aware of a knot in my stomach, I first surrender my need to be "right," realizing the powerlessness of this tactic to heal the conflict. I then admit there's a higher meaning in our power struggle which, when acknowledged, could restore me to sanity. In the third step, I experience gratitude to the Higher Power for this opportunity to grow. I then make an inventory of myself, searching for the self-images and behavior patterns I may be rigidly defending, with an eye toward sacrificing them to end my self-defeating actions.

In the fifth step, I explore my "shadow" and begin to take responsibility for the wounded, vulnerable part of myself that may have precipitated the fight. In step six, I feel a readiness to release my manipulative behavior and to fulfill my emotional needs in more positive ways. Then, in the next three steps, I humbly embrace my totality (the light as well as the shadow), make a commitment to communicate more openly, then reach out to share myself at a deeper level in the here and now.

In the tenth step, as this emotional clearing process helps me open my heart, I relate to my partner with greater intimacy. In the next step, our defenseless communication, much like meditation, puts me in touch with the wisdom of my intuitive mind. In the final step, I express this expanded awareness in my professional life and personal relationships as an increased capacity for compassion and service.

I use this healing process whenever I wake up in a bad mood, when I'm feeling anxious or overwhelmed by my professional commitments, or when I'm struggling with a relationship. At first I had to memorize the Twelve Steps and make a conscious effort to apply them in my life. Now, after lots of practice, I automatically call on the steps whenever a problem arises, and I usually work through my feelings with relative ease.

It's never too late to have a happy childhood.

TOM ROBBINS

CO-DEPENDENCE: A SPIRITUAL PROBLEM

Drug and alcohol addiction damages more than the immediate abuser. According to recent psychological findings, people who grow up in alcoholic families develop the disorder of co-dependence, defined by Charles Whitfield as "the suffering and/or dysfunction that results from focusing on the needs and behavior of others." Psychologists originally coined the term to describe the unhealthy coping patterns of spouses and children involved with a chemically dependent family member. But they soon discovered that people raised in any type of dysfunctional family exhibit the same co-dependent symptoms as those raised in chemically addicted families.

To adapt to the intolerable stresses of living in a dysfunctional family, individuals abandon their authentic selves, suppress their feelings, and adopt rigid roles for self-protection and survival, writes best-selling author John Bradshaw in *Bradshaw On: The Family*. For example, if the mother of a family is a bedridden hypochondriac, one child may assume the role of Little Parent (the emotional caretaker), while another may become the family's Saint and Hero by becoming an honor student and class president. Other roles include the Scapegoat, Mascot, Lost Child, Perfect Child, and Rebel.

Be patient toward all that is unsolved in your heart and learn to love the questions themselves, like locked rooms and like books that are written in a very foreign tongue. Do not seek the answers, which cannot be given you because you would not be able to live them.

RAINER MARIA RILKE

ARE YOU ADDICTED TO RELATIONSHIPS?

"Some psychologists compare the intoxicating yet painful 'altered state' of an obsessive relationship to the 'high' produced by a drug," writes Jody Hayes in *Smart Love.* Many people become addicted to unfulfilling romances, with their strange mixture of bliss and despair, and mistake this form of excitement for authentic love. The following quiz can help you identify whether you are addicted to unhealthy relationships.

You often feel magnetically drawn to someone. You act on this feeling even when you suspect that this person or the relationship may not be good for you. | TRUE OR FALSE

When you are not in a relationship, you feel depressed. Meeting a new man or woman usually cures your feelings of depression and boosts your self-esteem. | TRUE OR FALSE

When you consider breaking up with a lover, you worry about what will happen to that person without you. | TRUE OR FALSE

To avoid being alone following a breakup, you immediately start to look for a new lover. | TRUE OR FALSE

Despite exerting intelligence and independence in other areas, you are distrustful and fearful of independence within a love relationship. | TRUE OR FALSE

To be happy, you need to have a mate in your life. | TRUE OR FALSE

Even when a relationship isn't good for you, you find it difficult to break up. | TRUE OR FALSE

In dysfunctional families, co-dependents sacrifice their identities to keep the family together, Bradshaw explains. They become outer-directed, adapting to the stress arising from chemical dependency, child abuse, work addiction, eating disorders, or unprovoked parental rage.

You have often been involved with people who are in some way unavailable. They may live far away, be married, already be deeply involved with someone else, or be emotionally distant.   TRUE OR FALSE

If a kind, available person likes you, you will probably find the person boring and ultimately reject him or her.   TRUE OR FALSE

You often "make over" your lover, trying to change him or her to meet your ideal.   TRUE OR FALSE

It is hard for you to say no to a person with whom you are involved, whether he or she wants time, money, sex, or something else.   TRUE OR FALSE

You do not really believe you deserve a good relationship.   TRUE OR FALSE

Sexually, you are more concerned with pleasing your partner than with pleasing yourself.   TRUE OR FALSE

You are unable to stop seeing a certain person even though you know that continuing to see him or her is destructive to you.   TRUE OR FALSE

You remain obsessed by the memories of a relationship for months or even years after it has ended.   TRUE OR FALSE

A clay pot sitting in the sun will always be a clay pot. It has to go though the white heat of the furnace to become porcelain.

MILDRED W. STRUVEN

If you answer "true" to most of these questions, you probably have a long-standing problem with addictive love. But do not lose hope: Recovery is possible, and with it, the opportunity for healthier, nonaddictive relationships in the future.

Having abdicated their personal power by allowing other people to define and control them, they grow dependent on others for a sense of identity and self-worth.

How can we recognize whether we have unwittingly become co-dependent? In *Codependent No More*, Melody Beattie, a former chemical-dependency counselor, lists some of the identifying characteristics. Codependents are caretakers, often perceived as selfless martyrs, who focus on others people's problems to avoid dealing with their own unmet needs. Suffering from low self-worth and an inordinate need for approval, they tend to be people pleasers. Overburdened and overresponsible, unable to defend their boundaries, they often try to control other people through manipulative behavior.

"Once we allow others to define our worth, then we must attempt to control what they think of us," write psychologists Erika Chopich and Margaret Paul in *Healing Your Aloneness: Finding Love and Wholeness Through Your Inner Child*. "All of our controlling behavior—our anger, blame, pouting, teaching, explaining, caretaking, compliance, and denial—comes from believing that we can control what others think of us and how they treat us, and that how they think of us and treat us defines us."

When two co-dependents enter a relationship, they often overtly or covertly try to manipulate the partner to provide the love and approval needed to fill what Bradshaw calls the "hole in the soul." Both partners attach themselves to the other for a sense of completeness, a strategy that stunts personal growth and development. By surrendering responsibility for our happiness to other people, we create power struggles, arguments, and ultimately broken promises, expectations, and hearts. We can break out of the co-dependent trap, says Bradshaw, by working through the pain of our unmet childhood needs and by cultivating an inner life.

"Co-dependence is a loss of one's inner reality and an addiction to outer reality," he writes. Ultimately, it is a spiritual disease, because its victims believe that their inner state depends on outer conditions. However, says Bradshaw, on the journey of spiritual transformation, we learn "there is nothing outside of self that can make one happy. Our happiness lies within the inner life."

RECOVERING FROM RECOVERY

While many proponents of the Twelve Step movement claim that recovery from substance abuse and co-dependence is an ongoing, lifelong process, psychotherapist Tina Tessina believes that people who have pursued their

Those who have the humility of a child may find again the key to reverence for, and kinship with, all of life.

J. ALLEN BOONE

inner work to completion can graduate to the Thirteenth Step, which is recovering from recovery itself.

"The Twelve Steps accomplish much for those trapped in addictive patterns, but they condemn participants to a life-sentence without parole," Tessina says. "Recovery programs replace dependency on substances and relationships with dependency on the programs themselves. While this is a necessary stage, I believe that people can outgrow it (and the perception of being 'adult children') and become healthy, autonomous adults who can manage their own lives."

Just as healthy parents discourage dependency in their children by urging them to leave the nest at the appropriate time, she argues, Twelve Step programs should encourage fully recovered members to take the Thirteenth Step. But how can we assess whether we are fully recovered or whether our flight from the nest is motivated by unresolved inner pain that we would rather avoid?

In *The Real Thirteenth Step: Recovering from Recovery,* Tessina gives the following checklist of questions to help people make that decision. Answering these questions affirmatively indicates that you are a candidate for full recovery.

- Have you completed each of the Twelve Steps at least once or followed another recovery program through completion?
- Do you devote some time each day to meditation, prayer, or solitary contemplation? Are you aware of the difference between your rational mind and your Higher Power, a higher wisdom within?
- Are you familiar with the triggers and mechanisms that underlie your compulsive, addictive behavior?
- Have you shared your story repeatedly with others and listened to their stories?
- Are you able to rely on others for support and ask for help when you need it?
- Have you had a successful relationship with a sponsor, buddy, or other support person for a significant length of time?
- If you are an adult child of an alcoholic or severely dysfunctional family, or a survivor of abuse or incest, have you had sufficient therapy to heal the damaging legacy of your childhood?
- Have you severed or limited all relationships with people who encourage your addictions and compulsions, unless they are also fully in recovery?
- Can you say "no" when necessary?
- Do you know the difference between instant and deferred gratifications, and can you choose intellectually between them? Can you make thought-out decisions and act instead of react?
- Are you enthusiastic and motivated about your life? Do you have a clear sense of who you are and what your purpose is?

To be surprised, to wonder, is to begin to understand.

JOSÉ ORTEGA Y GASSET

201

"If you can answer yes to most of these questions," says Tessina, "then you may be ready to relinquish a reliance on Twelve-Step meetings."

HEALING THE INNER CHILD

When we decide to heal our co-dependent behavior, says Charles Whitfield, we begin by reclaiming the child within, our spontaneous, loving, creative core that we abandoned in childhood for the inauthentic, co-dependent person we became to ensure our survival. The inner child connects us with our divine source, much as a wave is inseparable from the ocean. Yet under the influence of parents, teachers, clergy, and others, we disconnect from our ground of being by adopting co-dependent masks and behaviors that make us strangers to ourselves.

In *Healing the Child Within*, Whitfield describes the treasures associated with our divine child in the following manner:

> Our True Self accepts ourselves and others. It feels, whether the feelings may be joyful or painful. And it expresses those feelings. Our Real Self accepts our feelings without judgment and fear, and allows them to exist as a valid way of assessing and appreciating life's events. . . . It can be childlike in the highest, most mature, and evolved sense of the word. It needs to play and to have fun. And yet it is vulnerable, perhaps because it is so open and trusting. It surrenders to itself, to others and ultimately to the universe. . . . By being real, it is free to grow. And while our co-dependent self forgets, our Real Self remembers our Oneness with others and with the universe.

Like many in the recovery field, Whitfield does not believe that Twelve Step programs alone can restore addicted people and co-dependents to complete health. In his three-stage recovery model, people first break their addictions to substances and self-defeating behavior through Twelve Step programs. Then, either in individual or group therapy, they work on healing the inner child, a process that involves reexperiencing early-life traumas and grieving the nurturing support they never received. After completing this painful process, which usually takes three to five years, people grow into a state of greater autonomy, serenity, and authenticity.

"Since up to 95 percent of families are dysfunctional, we're all adult children either doing our work of recovery or in need of it," says Whitfield. "Even though our Child Within has gone into hiding, it never dies. When we rescue that frightened, wondrous inner being, we reclaim the power, creativity, and vitality to make life a spiritual adventure."

Except ye be converted and become as little children, ye shall not enter into the Kingdom of Heaven.

JESUS CHRIST

The way I treat my inner child is the way I am going to treat my outer child.

ROBERT M. STEIN

Reparenting the Inner Child

Although therapy plays an indispensable role in healing the inner child, psychologists stress the importance of maintaining an intimate relationship with our *wonder child* on a daily basis, in much the same way we work on relationships with our actual children. Once we have grieved our childhood losses, we need to reparent our inner child, whose growth was arrested in early stages of development. By loving, protecting, and comforting the inner child every day, we create the safe conditions that encourage him or her to come out and play without fear of reinjury.

"Since many of us were demeaned, ignored, ridiculed, judged, laughed at, or discounted as children by our parents and other caregivers, we learned to do that to ourselves," say Chopich and Paul. "By continuing to do that to ourselves, we perpetuate our low self-esteem through our unloving inner parenting. *Re-parenting ourselves means giving ourselves the love and approval we never received from others.*"

Although successful reparenting may require practicing a number of techniques, ultimately it rests on adopting an attitude of unconditional love toward our inner child, they explain. Regardless of how our inner child feels or behaves, we must extend love that is consistent and dependable. In our devotion to the child's welfare, this means tuning in on a daily basis and acting on behalf of its needs, wants, or desires without indulging or discounting them.

To maintain a trusting relationship with your inner child, psychologist Joan Borysenko recommends starting the day by communicating with him or her. While still underneath the covers, you simply visualize a safe place from childhood, greet your child, and solicit its feelings, concerns, and advice about the day ahead. Your listen respectfully, giving reassurance when needed, often in the form of hugs. Borysenko advises repeating the exercise before going to sleep, again listening to the child's feelings about the day's events and providing comfort and understanding when necessary.

In *Homecoming: Reclaiming and Championing Your Inner Child,* John Bradshaw presents a wealth of practical techniques for nurturing your inner child. One technique involves writing letters to the wounded child, asking forgiveness for years of abandonment and neglect. Another calls for establishing relationships with surrogate fathers and mothers, healthy adults whose presence tends to nourish the inner child, who is starved for positive parenting. A third technique involves acquainting the child with the power and protection of prayer.

"Your inner child needs to see that your adult has a source of protection beyond your finite human self," he writes. "And even though you are magical and godlike to your inner child, it is very important for him to know that you have a Higher Power available to you. I like to let my child know that I feel safe and protected in the belief that there is someone greater than myself. I call this someone God."

As we make the inner child an integral part of our lives, a new power and creativity begin to emerge, and we move naturally toward increased self-actualization. "The natural state of the wonder child is creativity," writes Bradshaw. "Getting in touch with your creativity is more than a homecoming: it is a discovery of your essence, your deepest, unique self."

A Rebirth of Spiritual Values

If the recovery movement is at root a spiritual phenomenon, then healing the inner child means more than just restoring us to psychological health. It may point to a collective yearning for the rebirth of spiritual values in a world that largely ignores them. As Jungian therapist Jeremiah Abrams

It is only with the heart that one can see rightly; what is essential is invisible to the eye.

ANTOINE DE SAINT-EXUPÉRY

writes in *Reclaiming the Inner Child,* "there is a great hunger for spirituality and meaning in our era, a longing for a second coming of a divine inner child whose appearance would announce the beginning of a new millennium of hope."

The inner child Abrams refers to lives in the depths of the unconscious as an archetypal image of divinity. When we consciously contact this divine source within ourselves, says Jungian analyst Edith Sullwold, we gain the courage and enthusiasm to break out of the prison doors of our limited way of living.

"We all need to heal the neglected, abused, unloved and vulnerable children we once were," Sullwold says. "But equally important, we need to befriend the child of our inner world whose innocence Zen Master Suzuki calls 'beginner's mind.' The child represents spontaneity and freshness, the deep urge of the human soul to explore its vast, unlimited territories. Our psyche always yearns to explore its fullness, and the child embodies that inner urge to break the boundaries of the known to explore the new, the fresh."

Abrams believes that the widespread emergence of the divine-child archetype presages a spiritual awakening both in the individual and in the culture. A spiritual renaissance based on reclaiming the inner child at first glance may appear unlikely. But researchers are beginning to gather evidence suggesting that spirituality is an innate condition of childhood, a discovery that lends credence to the notion of the inner child as a pathway to the Divine.

Psychologist Edward Hoffman, for example, has been investigating cross-cultural accounts of peak childhood experiences reported years later in adulthood. As children, his subjects typically experienced feelings of ego transcendence, ecstasy, and oneness with nature in the context of everyday life, he reports in his forthcoming book, *Visions of Innocence.* Driving through the countryside in the back seat of an automobile or gazing at the play of sunlight on fields of wildflowers can trigger ecstatic states of consciousness that supply spiritual nourishment to the young person for a lifetime.

"My findings validate the views of people in Twelve-Step programs: We do indeed come into the world with an inviolate core that is the essence of purity, spiritual sensitivity, and compassion for ourselves and others," asserts Hoffman. "If we can stay in touch with these joyous episodes from our childhood, they can provide us with the courage, strength, and direction we need to meet the vicissitudes of adult life."

Unfortunately, parents, religious educators, and other authority

Yea, though I walk through the valley of the shadow of death, I will fear no evil for thou art with me.

PSALMS 23:4

figures often unconsciously conspire to dishonor childhood spiritual experiences by denying, rejecting, or ridiculing them. For centuries, religious educators have systematically disregarded children's innate wisdom and have inculcated young minds with an obedience to authority and an unquestioning acceptance of dogmatic beliefs and practices. This approach breeds religious co-dependence, which quickly kills the inner child's sense of wonder and delight.

"Religious educators need to put aside their preconceived approaches, study children's spirituality with fresh, open minds, and develop curricula that draw forth children's wondrous inner resources," insists Hoffman. "A number of rabbis, priests, and ministers have expressed a willingness to test this new perspective. Obviously, many people within institutional religion will fear this innovative approach, but religious renewal in the coming years depends on it."

Institutional religions frequently tend to alienate people, he says, because they don't honor and nurture the inner child within the adult. When the inner child finds a place in our churches and synagogues, formulaic practices will give way to direct, intuitive experiences of the divine, ushering in an era of religious renewal based on the lived reality that "the child is the father of the man."

Parenting with Inner-Child Awareness

In an age of millennial expectations and cultural transition, spiritual renewal begins at home, according to psychologist Jeremiah Abrams. By befriending their own neglected childhood selves, parents can reach out to their flesh-and-blood children with compassion, putting an end to the inadvertent wounding passed on from generation to generation. Parenting of this nature has evolutionary significance, Abrams contends, because children raised with wholesome self-acceptance, self-esteem, and open communication will bring a higher human potential to the institutions of our ailing society.

"When we parent with inner-child awareness, we create a web of safety that encourages children to express themselves without fear of rejection or humiliation," Abrams says. "By seeing the open, vulnerable children that we are mirrored in our own children, we begin to relate more empathetically. This allows our children to be themselves and at the same time heals us of the wounds we received in childhood." Abrams offers the following suggestions for parenting with inner-child awareness:

It's not whether you get knocked down. It's whether you get up again.

VINCE LOMBARDI

206

*The world breaks everyone
and afterward many are
strong at the broken places.*

ERNEST HEMINGWAY

1. Recognize that how you treat your inner child is how you treat your outer child. Conscious parenting first and foremost requires having a healthy relationship with the child within.

2. Work on forgiving your parents and other significant adults for the un-enlightened behavior enacted on you during childhood. Forgiveness improves parenting, because we are no longer burdened by resentments that unconsciously get projected onto vulnerable children.

3. View both your inner and your outer child as teachers of love. The inner child knows what he needed to feel valued and loved. In consulting your inner child, you will find intuitive guidelines for practicing a loving form of parenting.

4. When a communication problem arises, try abandoning your reasonable adult position (with its assumptions and agendas) and with empathy enter into your child's emotional world. Give the child the understanding you wished you had received in childhood. Then, instead of imposing your solution on the problem, see whether you can discover an appropriate course of action that honors your need to be an effective problem-solver *and* the child's need for understanding.

5. Let your children know how grateful you are for their presence in your family and what a healing effect they have on your life. Children need to know that they can affect parents not just through manipulation, but through their natural, spontaneous being.

6. Approach parenting as a spiritual vocation rather than a social responsibility. As part of our creative generativity, parenting is a high and noble undertaking. When we sacralize the act of parenting, we realize that as important as our ambitions are, they cannot supersede the "people-making" task to which we are committed.

RESOURCES

Recommended Reading

The Recovery Resource Book: The Best Available Information on Addictions and Codependence, Barbara Yoder (Fireside/Simon & Schuster, 1990). A comprehensive guide to every type of self-help resource imaginable, including hundreds of book reviews, addresses for national Twelve Step programs, and a guide to publishers and treatment programs.

Homecoming: Reclaiming and Championing Your Inner Child, John Bradshaw (Bantam Books, 1990). A comprehensive guide with writing exercises, visualizations, affirmations, and interpersonal exercises to heal the wounded inner child.

Bradshaw On: The Family and *Bradshaw On: Healing the Shame That Binds You,* John Bradshaw (Health Communications, 1988). Highly readable books about the sources of dysfunctional family patterns.

Healing the Child Within, Charles Whitfield (Health Communications, 1987). Gives a detailed account of the recovery process for adult children of dysfunctional families.

Reclaiming the Inner Child, Jeremiah Abrams, editor (Jeremy P. Tarcher, 1990). A collection of articles drawn from depth psychology, literature, and the recovery movement about reclaiming the innocence and wonder of the child in adulthood.

Codependent No More, Melody Beattie (Harper & Row, 1987). Outlines in great depth the characteristics of the co-dependent personality and provides strategies for breaking these unhealthy traits.

The Inner Child Workbook, Cathryn Taylor (Jeremy P. Tarcher, 1991). A six-step program using ritual, writing, and visualization to heal childhood wounds.

Breaking Free of the Co-Dependency Trap, Barry and Janae Weinhold (Stillpoint Publishing, 1989). Looks at co-dependency as incomplete developmental tasks that can be completed in adulthood with therapy and group support.

Smart Love: A Codependence Recovery Program Based on Relationship Addiction Support Groups, Jody Hayes (Jeremy P. Tarcher, 1989). A workbook for recovery from relationship addiction, with first-person accounts of women who have moved through each stage of the process.

When God Becomes a Drug, Father Leo Booth (Jeremy P. Tarcher, 1991). Investigates religious addiction—using church membership, spiritual practices, or a belief system as a way of escaping from unresolved childhood pain and low self-esteem.

Twelve Step Groups at a Glance

The following organizations can refer you to local meetings, provide you with a packet of materials for starting a group in your area, or send you publications and books (available for a nominal cost). Please send a self-addressed, stamped envelope with requests.

Al-Anon and Alateen groups for relatives of and children of alcoholics. Al-Anon Family Group Headquarters, P.O. Box 862, Midtown Station, New York, NY 10018-0862; 212-302-7240. Twenty-four-hour hot line: 800-356-9996. In New York: 800-245-4656. In Canada: 613-722-1830.

Alcoholics Anonymous (AA), the original Twelve Step programs. AA World Services, Box 459, Grand Central Station, New York, NY 10163; 212-686-1100 or 212-686-5454 (TTD).

Adult Children of Alcoholics (ACA), P.O. Box 3216, Torrance, CA 90505; 213-534-1815. The *National Association for Children of Alcoholics (NACOA),* 31582 Coast Highway, Suite B, South Laguna, CA 92677; 714-499-3889.

Debtors Anonymous helps members get control of their finances. General Service Board, P.O. Box 20322, New York, NY 10025-9992; 212-642-8220.

Incest Survivors Anonymous, a national self-help program that helps members heal the pain of past abuse. P.O. Box 5613, Long Beach, CA 90805-0613; 213-428-5599. *Survivors of Incest Anonymous,* another national recovery group, runs a twenty-four-hour hot line: 301-282-3400. SIA World Service Office, P.O. Box 21817, Baltimore, MD 21222-6817.

Narcotics Anonymous, P.O. Box 9999, Van Nuys, CA 91409; 818-780-3951.

Overeaters Anonymous, World Service Office, P.O. Box 92870, Los Angeles, CA 90009; 213-542-8363.

Parents Anonymous runs support groups for potentially abusive parents and for abused children and operates a hot line: 800-421-0353. 6733 South Sepulveda Boulevard, Los Angeles, CA 90045; 213-410-9732.

Secular Organizations for Sobriety is a nonspiritual alternative to AA. Box 15781, North Hollywood, CA 91615-5781.

Catalogs

Hazelden's Educational Materials Catalog gives in-depth listings of recovery materials. Also available are catalogs of audio- and videotapes and a catalog for recovery professionals. Phone 800-328-9000; 800-257-0070 in Minnesota; and 612-257-4010 in Alaska and outside the United States.

Health Communications, Inc. (Enterprise Center, 3201 S.W. 15th Street, Deerfield Beach, FL 33442-8190; 305-360-0909). Publishes best-selling authors in the recovery field. Also available are collections of affirmations, audiotapes, pamphlets, and a directory of treatment programs.

The *Tools for Recovery* catalog (Recovery Publications, 1201 Knoxville Street, San Diego, CA 92110; 619-275-1350) offers books on adult children of alcoholics, co-dependence, spirituality, inner-child work, eating disorders, and sexual abuse.

New Dimensions in Healing
The Mind/Body Connection

Over the past several decades, researchers studying the subtle connections between mind and body have been laying the foundations for a revolutionary approach to the practice of medicine. These pioneers of mind/body medicine have gathered evidence suggesting that mental attitudes and emotional states have a profound effect on stimulating or depressing the immune system, which triggers the body's natural defense against illness. Consider some of their findings.

Medicine is not only a science, but also the art of letting our own individuality interact with the individuality of the patient.

Albert Schweitzer

- In one study, researchers at King's College Hospital in England tied the attitude of fifty-seven women treated with mastectomy for early-stage breast cancer to survival ten years later. Fifty-five percent of the women who faced the disease with a fighting spirit or who vehemently denied having it survived past the tenth year. By contrast, women who felt hopeless and who stoically accepted their fate had only a 22-percent survival rate.
- In another study, psychologist Janice Kiecolt-Glaser of Ohio State University had college students teach progressive muscle relaxation to nursing-home residents three times a week for a three-week period. At the end of the test period, those who practiced the stress-reduction technique showed more than a doubling of natural killer

213

cells, which patrol the body and destroy virus-infected cells and cancer cells. Residents who received either social visits or no intervention at all showed no change in immune function.

- Psychologist David McClelland of Harvard found that when students viewed a film on Mother Teresa designed to inspire feelings of compassion, they increased production of an antibody that provides protection against colds and upper respiratory infections. When these same students viewed a film on Attila the Hun, their antibody levels dropped.

These and other studies tend to confirm one of the basic tenets of holistic medicine: Because mind and body form an unbroken unity, positive mental states, such as hope and optimism, as well as negative ones, such as depression and despair, can have a direct bearing on the health or disease of our bodies. This notion comes as no surprise to students of spiritual life. For millennia, teachers East and West have stressed that a healthy spirit and positive emotions are intimately connected to physical health. Indeed, most spiritual teachings affirm that reliance on a higher power and the cultivation of cheerfulness, forgiveness, faith, and forbearance keep the mind in balance and protect the body from illness.

Now, modern scientists, with their sophisticated technology, are taking tentative first steps in confirming what mystics, yogis, and saints have discovered through intuition. Because of the emerging science of psychoneuroimmunology (PNI), many physicians are cautiously embracing the premise that illness is not purely a physical problem, but rather a problem of the whole person, including our psychological states and social habits.

Scientists in the burgeoning field of PNI study how the mind, the brain, and the immune system communicate by means of hormonal messengers, called neuropeptides. According to Joan Borysenko, a pioneer in the field of mind/body medicine, mental and emotional events in the brain trigger the release of these communication molecules. Because receptor sites for these substances exist not only in the brain, but in the immune system and nerve cells in various other organs, feelings originating in the brain/mind translate into chemical events in the body. For example, neuropeptide receptors in the limbic brain (the seat of emotions) also line the intestines, explaining why many people experience emotions as a gut feeling.

Since the entire body is interconnected at the level of neuropeptides, says Dr. Deepak Chopra, an endocrinologist and advocate of India's ayur-

The great majority of us are required to live a life of constant, systematic duplicity. Your health is bound to be affected if, day after day, you say the opposite of what you feel, if you grovel before what you dislike and rejoice at what brings you nothing but misfortune. Our nervous system isn't just a fiction, it's a part of our physical body, and our soul exists in space inside us, like the teeth in our mouth. It can't be forever violated with impunity.

BORIS PASTERNAK,
Doctor Zhivago

vedic medicine, we can no longer maintain a rigid distinction between mind and body. Every time we think, a neuropeptide magically appears as the point of transformation by which mental activities are converted into physical molecules. To think, Chopra says, is to practice brain chemistry.

"Sad or depressing thoughts . . . produce changes in brain chemistry that have a detrimental effect on the body's physiology," he writes in *Creating Health: Beyond Prevention, Toward Perfection.* "Likewise, happy thoughts of all kinds, loving thoughts, thoughts of peace and tranquility, of compassion, friendliness, kindness, generosity, affection, warmth and intimacy each produce a corresponding state of physiology via the flux of neurotransmitters and hormones in the central nervous system."

THE ROLE OF BELIEF IN HEALING

Medical science also has begrudgingly recognized the mind's role in healing through what is termed the placebo effect, which relies on belief alone to influence the outcome of disease. A placebo is a substance, such as a sugar pill, or a procedure, such as an unnecessary physical exercise, without any power to effect a change in the patient's condition. Yet many patients, when given inert substances to treat their illnesses, have such faith in what they believe is their medicine that the expectation of a cure causes them to release endorphins, the body's own natural pain-killers. In one study cited by Chopra, when patients suffering from bleeding ulcers were given placebos described as "the most potent current drug for treating ulcers," more than 70 percent of them stopped bleeding immediately. Another group, told that the drug they were given was experimental and therefore of unknown benefit, experienced only a 25-percent success rate. Chopra views the placebo effect as a "kind of permission that the mind gives the body so that healing can take place."

To Dr. Bernie Siegel, a Yale surgeon and best-selling author who has worked tirelessly to humanize the practice of medicine, placebos offer further support for a medicine of the future based on mind/body unity. "What the placebo effect suggests to us is that we may be able to change what takes place in our bodies by changing our state of mind," Siegel writes in *Peace, Love & Healing.* "Therefore, when we experience mind-altering processes—for example, meditation, hypnosis, visualization, psychotherapy, love and peace of mind—we open ourselves to the possibility of change and healing."

When we suffer from chronic depression, withhold the expression of

The fact that the mind rules the body is, in spite of its neglect by biology and medicine, the most fundamental fact which we know about the process of life.

FRANZ ALEXANDER, M.D.

Positive attitudes and emotions can enhance the environment of effective medical care. Patients who have confidence in themselves and their physicians may be better able to make use of medical treatment than those who go into treatment with attitudes of despair or defeat.

NORMAN COUSINS

215

our feelings, or reject ourselves because of low self-esteem, we send *die* messages to our immune systems, Siegel contends. But when we cultivate positive emotions, such as love, optimism, and hope, when we ventilate our feelings regularly and actively seek out support from others, we send what Siegel terms *live* messages to the immune system, which then works to keep us alive.

"I am convinced that unconditional love is the most powerful known stimulant of the immune system," he writes in *Love, Medicine and Miracles.* "If I told patients to raise their blood levels of immune globulins or killer T cells, no one would know how. But if I can teach them to love themselves and others fully, the same changes happen automatically. The truth is: love heals."

Although research in PNI is still in its infancy, mind/body medicine remains the treatment of choice for a number of illnesses, says Borysenko. This approach works well for stress-related disorders, such as hypertension, headache, irritable bowel syndrome, and digestive disorders. It also is playing an increasingly significant role in fighting major health problems, including heart disease, arthritis, cancer, and AIDS. Mind/body medicine especially benefits cancer and AIDS patients, who can learn to call on psychological and spiritual resources to mobilize the immune system.

"Until recently, Western medicine focused almost exclusively on the mechanisms of pathology," Borysenko explains. "But in the coming years, as we unravel the mysteries that govern mind/body interactions in the immune system, we'll change our focus and begin developing ways to stimulate our self-healing potential."

HEALTH AS HARMONY

Proponents of mind/body medicine interpret health and disease from a much broader perspective than those who subscribe to the biomedical or conventional model. The conventional view attributes illness to external agents such as viruses and bacteria that cause our health problems. But according to the emerging bio-psycho-social model of disease, our mind, body, and environment together determine whether we get sick. In this view, poor coping skills, high stress, and deficient social support may increase our susceptibility to illness.

"Disease is not so much the effect of noxious, external forces—the 'bugs,' both literal and figurative, in our lives—as it is the faulty effort of our minds and bodies to deal with them," writes psychologist Blair Justice

There is no difficulty that enough love will not conquer; no disease that enough love will not heal; no door that enough love will not open; no gulf that enough love will not bridge; no wall that enough love will not throw down; no sin that enough love will not redeem. . . . It makes no difference how deeply seated may be the trouble; how hopeless the outlook; how muddled the tangle; how great the mistake. A sufficient realization of love will dissolve it all. If only you could love enough you would be the happiest and most powerful being in the world.

EMMET FOX

in *Who Gets Sick*. "Most of the 'bugs,' the literal kind, already reside in our bodies. When our responses to problems in life are excessive or deficient, the central nervous system and hormones act on our immune defenses in such a way that the microbes aid and abet disease. The balance is upset between us and our resident pathogens."

Mind/body medicine relates this internal imbalance to psychosocial imbalances. If we view disease as a biofeedback system supplying us with essential information about our lives, then the upset balance within our bodies may represent an imbalanced relationship with our spouse, our work, our creative expression, or our spiritual orientation. Disease, then, sends us the message that we have fallen into a state of disharmony. As an occasion for course correction, it urges us to establish an essentially harmonious relationship with our purpose, our innate values, and an authentic way of being in the world.

In *Hands of Light: A Guide to Healing Through the Human Energy Field,* healer Barbara Ann Brennan describes the process by which disease can help restore us to wholeness: "Illness is the result of imbalance. Imbalance is a result of forgetting who you are. Forgetting who you are creates thoughts and actions that lead to an unhealthy lifestyle and

It doesn't matter what the disease is. There is always room for hope. I'm not going to die because of statistics. I hope you won't either.

BERNIE SIEGEL

Complete health and awakening are really the same.

TARTHANG TULKU

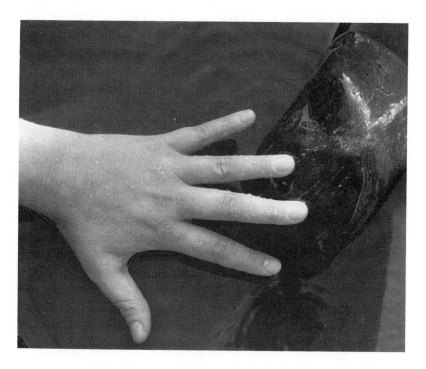

eventually to illness. . . . Illness can thus be understood as a lesson you have given yourself to help you remember who you are."

Seen from this perspective, disease presents us with the opportunity to investigate the attitudes, beliefs, and unresolved emotional issues that may be contributing to our physical discomfort. According to Stephen Levine, who has worked with hundreds of patients suffering from life-threatening illnesses, this investigation occurs not by treating the illness as an adversary, but by opening to it with nonresistance and exploring it with loving kindness and forgiveness. The patient who sends love into his illness and who releases the emotional holdings that armor his heart with fear and anger experiences genuine healing, which Levine defines as "the integration of body and mind into the heart." Healing may or may not lead to a physical cure, he says, but it always melts the prison cell of our self-made isolation and fear.

"The healing of the body for many [is] a by-product of a new balance of mind and heart," writes Levine in *Healing into Life and Death*. "It wasn't that these people felt better than ever because they had healed, but rather that they had healed because they had come upon a place of a bit more ease and peace within."

As Levine points out, some patients may heal into life, while others, their business finished, may heal into death. In either case, healing occurs as long as we embrace our wholeness with unconditional self-acceptance. "Real healing," he reminds us, "never stops. It cannot, for it is our birthright, our essential nature. The closer we come to our true nature, the closer we come to the healing for which we took birth."

Each of us seems to be born with a "blueprint" that not only turns us into a certain type of physical being, but also maps out the path of our psychological, intellectual, and spiritual development as well. When we deviate from that inner blueprint, it often takes a psychological or physical illness to get us back on course.

BERNIE SIEGEL

TEN WAYS TO HEAL YOUR LIFE

The following health guidelines appear in *Surviving and Thriving with AIDS: Hints for the Newly Diagnosed,* published by the New York People with AIDS Coalition. The advice, ostensibly for AIDS patients, contains wisdom applicable to everybody interested in healing his or her life.

1. Do things that bring you a sense of fulfillment, joy, and purpose, that validate your worth. See your life as your own creation, and strive to make it a positive one.
2. Pay close and loving attention to yourself, tuning in to your needs on all levels. Take care of yourself, nourishing, supporting, and encouraging yourself.

3. Release all negative emotions—resentment, envy, fear, sadness, anger. Express your feelings appropriately; don't hold on to them. Forgive yourself.

4. Hold positive images and goals in your mind, pictures of what you truly want in your life. When fearful images arise, refocus on images that evoke feelings of peace and joy.

5. Love yourself and love everyone else. Make loving the purpose and primary expression of your life.

6. Create fun, loving, honest relationships, allowing for the expression and fulfillment of needs for intimacy and security. Try to heal any wounds in past relationships, as with old lovers, and mother and father.

7. Make a positive contribution to your community, through some form of work or service that you value and enjoy.

8. Make a commitment to health and well-being, and develop belief in the possibility of total health. Develop your own healing program, drawing on the support and advice of experts without becoming enslaved to them.

9. Accept yourself and everything in your life as an opportunity for growth and learning. Be grateful. When you [mess] up, forgive yourself, learn what you can from the experience, and then move on.

10. Keep a sense of humor.

THE HEALING PARTNERSHIP

Perhaps more than any other single factor, the intimate alchemy between the healer and the patient helps to mobilize the body's natural resources. The mere presence of a healer often evokes hope in the patient and an expectation of recovery. When the two people create a partnership based on compassion, trust, and shared decision-making, and when the relationship nurtures the patient's hope for a positive outcome, even seemingly incurable diseases sometimes go into remission.

"Few things are more important than the way the physician communicates with the patient," says the late Norman Cousins in *Healers on Healing,* a collection of essays written by health specialists. "Attitudes about treatment can have an effect on the immune system. The patient's hopes are the physician's best ally. The physician who works with those hopes and bolsters them helps to create a climate in which the 'little black bag' can be put to optimal use."

Conversely, the physician who communicates a diagnosis with a sense of defeat and fatalism may actually promote a rapid advance of the

You can learn to follow the inner self, the inner physician that tells you where to go. Healing is simply attempting to do more of those things that bring joy and fewer of those things that bring pain.

O. Carl Simonton

A cheerful heart is good medicine, but a downcast spirit dries up the bones.

Proverbs 17:22

219

disease. "A truthful diagnosis must be given," he writes, "but the physician's artistry consists of an ability to communicate a diagnosis as a challenge rather than as a pronouncement of doom." The infusion of hope can help the patient dispel panic and depression, which compromise the immune system, and mount a spirited response to the challenge of the disease.

For the healing partnership to flourish, physicians must renounce the superhuman role foisted on them by the medical establishment and accept the wounded healer within themselves, argues Dr. Larry Dossey, a longtime advocate of holistic health.

Drawing on Jungian psychology, Dossey describes the doctor-patient relationship as a living archetype whose polarity exists within both members of the healing team. Psychologically, the patient has an inner physician who generally is suppressed in the traditional therapeutic relationship. Similarly, the healer has an inner patient whose woundedness is buried under a persona of medical infallibility.

"When a physician and a patient come together who have repressed, respectively, their woundedness and healthiness, a silent bargain is struck," Dossey writes in *The Heart of the Healer*. "The physician unconsciously agrees to de-emphasize the inner power of the patient in bringing about his own healing . . . and the patient silently agrees not to acknowledge his own power." When physicians give up their godlike detachment and admit to their vulnerability, he adds, a transformation in medicine will take place, enabling a new kind of healing to flower.

In *Healers on Healing,* Dr. Naomi Remen, who specializes in treating chronic and life-threatening illnesses, describes how honoring her own woundedness has a healing effect on her clients:

> My very presence facilitates something. I sit with you, and you don't have to be alone in this small, dark, fearful place in yourself. You sense that you can trust me. I, too, am wounded, so I can understand. I know how to find you and be there with you, not to "fix" anything—because nothing may be broken—but simply to be there with you in that place where you thought you could only be alone. If we do that, something happens. The woundedness in each of us connects us in trust. My woundedness evokes your healer, and your woundedness evokes my healer. Then the two healers can collaborate together. My presence with you allows things to change, to evolve toward wholeness.

By refusing to hide behind the white coat and lab report, physicians like Naomi Remen, Bernie Siegel, and many unheralded others are quietly but insistently restoring the human heart to the practice of medicine.

In the ultimate depth of being, we find ourselves no longer separate but, rather, part of the unity of the universe. That unity includes the sufferer and the suffering, and the healer and that which heals. Therefore, all acts of healing are ultimately our selves healing our Self.

RAM DASS

Rather than treating patients as disease processes, they risk bringing their full humanness to the therapeutic encounter. They not only call on their technological expertise, but on the inner qualities practiced by healers from time immemorial: patience, humility, compassion, and an ability to inspire and mobilize their patients' healing resources. In the words of Deepak Chopra, "If I had only one criterion for a good doctor, I would say he must love his patients. The doctor who makes a difference holds the patient in his heart and allows the flow of consciousness between himself and the patient."

IMAGERY IN HEALING

In yoking the ancient with the modern, the new healer not only employs X-rays, sophisticated lab tests, and medications to diagnose and treat illness. As a complement to these technological advances, the mind/body practitioner also uses imagery techniques discovered by ancient shamans

221

Life is like a tree, and its root is consciousness. Therefore, once we tend the root, the tree as a whole will be healthy. Nature controls healing from this deeper level already, for every cell participates in the body's inner intelligence, responding to the patient's thoughts, emotions, desires, beliefs, and self-image.

DEEPAK CHOPRA

millennia ago to help today's patients engage their innate healing resources. These techniques enable people to gain control of physiological processes usually considered inaccessible to conscious influence, such as heart rate, blood pressure, and immune function. By opening up communication channels with our deeper wisdom, imagery techniques also can reveal the attitudinal and lifestyle changes needed to restore our lives to a sense of balance.

Imagery, the thought process that invokes and uses the senses, serves as a language the body understands, says Dr. Jeanne Achterberg, author of *Imagery in Healing: Shamanism and Modern Medicine.* If the left hemisphere of the brain (which governs analytical thought) wants to tell the body to relax, it must convert its intention into an image, such as a sun-drenched afternoon at the beach. The right brain (which governs spatial relationships and feeling) then conveys this message to the autonomic nervous system, which controls involuntary functions, such as respiration and blood pressure. Because images relate to bodily states, tense muscles soon relax and habitual tension dissolves.

"Throughout the history of medicine, including the shamanic healing traditions, the Greek tradition of Asclepius, Aristotle and Hippocrates, and the folk and religious healers, the imagination has been used to diagnose disease," Achterberg writes. After being exiled from medical practice following the Renaissance, "imagery is once again being used as diagnosis. Because of their intimate contact with the physical body, images appear to express a body wisdom, an understanding of both the status and prognosis of health."

Achterberg and Dr. Frank Lawlis have developed an imagery technique that combines twentieth-century medical understanding with ancient shamanic practices. To practice body-mind imagery, patients enter a state of deep relaxation, then visualize the nature of their illness, the strength of their immune system, and the efficacy of the treatment they are receiving. After patients make drawings of each component of the imagery, physicians can then evaluate who is winning—the disease, treatment, or host defenses—and whether the patient's personal involvement in the healing process indicates a good outcome or not.

While diagnosis calls for receptive, spontaneous imagery to emerge, treatment of an illness generally involves the use of programmed imagery designed specifically for the physical condition. For example, cancer patients using the Simonton technique visualize the immune system as an ally that supports the body's defenses. Dr. Martin Rossman, author of

Healing Yourself: A Step-by-Step Program to Better Health Through Imagery, uses both forms of imagery in treating patients with bothersome symptoms. He recommends that once they are calmly focused, patients receive a spontaneous image of the problem, followed by another image that represents its healthy resolution. Focusing on this healthful image frequently produces dramatic results.

One of Rossman's patients, a woman with endometriosis, visualized her disease as tar encrusted to her pelvic organs and imagined cleaning it up with a potent cleaning solution, a scraper, and a mop. She persisted in her visualization for fifteen minutes several times a day, and three months later her gynecologist reported no visible symptoms of the disease. In another case, a businessman suffering from peptic ulcers visualized spraying the inside of his stomach and intestines with a cooling white foam three times a day between meals. Within a short time, his condition disappeared, allowing him to discontinue his ulcer medications.

"Imagery can help you whether you have simple tension headaches or a life-threatening illness," Rossman writes. "Imagery is a rich, symbolic, and highly personal language, and the more time you spend observing and interacting with your own image-making brain, the more quickly and effectively you will use it to improve your health."

Let yourself be healed
that you may be forgiving,
offering salvation to your
*   brother*
and yourself.

Your healing saves him pain
as well as you,
and you are healed
because you wished him well.

A Gift of Healing

Meeting Your Inner Advisor

Each of us has an inner physician, an embodiment of intuitive wisdom, that serves as a liaison between our conscious and unconscious minds, says Dr. Martin Rossman. This wise figure can provide insight into the nature of our illness, help us resolve inner conflicts that may be affecting our physical health, and offer support and comfort while we are healing. The exercise on page 232, "Meeting Your Inner Advisor," is adapted from *Healing Yourself.*

Social Intimacy and Health

Even with a collaborative doctor-patient relationship and the use of mind/body techniques, the healing equation remains incomplete without a crucial third element: social support. According to mounting evidence, a sense of social connection strengthens our resistance to disease, while a sense of isolation and alienation has an opposite effect.

"Stopping smoking, eliminating fat from the diet, regular exercise, and similar kinds of preventive health practices, though helpful, can't compare to the benefits of social connectedness," says Joan Borysenko. "Nothing bolsters the immune system and lowers the incidence of cardiovascular disease like feeling supported and loved by others and being able to extend nurturance and support in return."

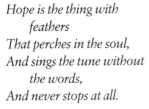

Hope is the thing with
feathers
That perches in the soul,
And sings the tune without
the words,
And never stops at all.

EMILY DICKINSON

Discovering the ways in
which you are exceptional,
the particular path you are
meant to follow, is your busi-
ness on this earth, whether
you are afflicted or not. It's
just that the search takes on a
special urgency when you
realize that you are mortal.

BERNIE SIEGEL

1. Relax physically by taking full, deep breaths and imagine yourself in a quiet place that is serene and secure.
2. Allow the image of a wise and compassionate figure to appear. Your advisor may be a wise old man or woman, a friendly animal or bird, a ball of light, a friend or relative, or a religious figure. Whatever the form, your inner advisor knows you well and cares for you with unconditional love.
3. Ask your inner advisor a question about your illness or symptom, and listen carefully to the response, as you would to a wise and respected teacher. Your advisor may communicate verbally or through symbolic forms of exchange. If you're uncertain about the advice you initially receive, continue the conversation until you feel you've learned all you can at this time.
4. Now imagine some specific action you can take in your daily life with the insights you have received. If you think you may encounter obstacles in carrying out your plan, ask your advisor for further help.
5. When it seems right, thank your advisor for meeting with you and ask for the easiest, surest method for getting back in touch. Realize that you can have another meeting with your advisor when you feel the need.
6. Say goodbye for now in whatever ways seems appropriate, and slowly allow yourself to return to waking consciousness refreshed, alert, ready to move to a higher level of wellness.

A word of caution: Whatever comes from this talk with your advisor should be considered carefully in the "clear light of day." Evaluate the risks and benefits of following the advice and make your own decision about whether or not to follow it. The choices and responsibility remain yours. Don't abandon your responsibility to your inner advisor, but do consider what it has to tell you.

Numerous studies demonstrate how a sense of community can enhance our health, our well-being, and even our survival. A study that tracked the health of residents in Alameda County, California, for more than nine years found that those with extensive social ties had significantly lower mortality rates. A widely quoted study of Roseto, Pennsylvania, a close-knit Italian-American community, uncovered one of the country's lowest fatality rates for heart disease, despite the fact that Rosetans consumed an unusually high-fat diet. What protected them, researchers discovered, was their strong sense of community and camaraderie.

Other recent studies have demonstrated that social support can increase the life span of patients with metastatic breast cancer and strengthen the immune function of elderly people in retirement homes. As impressive as these findings are, none can compare to Dr. Dean Ornish's landmark cardiac study, which sent shock waves through the medical community. Cardiac patients who made comprehensive lifestyle changes that included a low-fat diet, regular exercise, meditation, and group support not only halted—but in some cases actually reversed—the progress of coronary artery disease. While previous studies had demonstrated that a low-fat diet, exercise, and meditation could lower cholesterol levels, this study convinced Ornish that social intimacy can mitigate the stress that contributes to heart disease.

A pervasive sense of isolation disconnects people from their inner feelings, from other people, and from a transpersonal source of love and support, says Ornish. Operating on the premise that intimacy heals, he urges patients to use yoga and meditation not only to relieve stress, but to transform their sense of isolation. Members of his support groups learn to let go of their cultural masks, express their authentic selves, and eventually experience a sense of connectedness to a higher source of meaning and value.

"If you work at the level of intimacy within oneself, between people, and with a higher force, the physical heart begins to open," says Ornish in a *New Age Journal* interview. "'Open your heart' says it metaphorically, but the arteries also begin to open, which we can measure using arteriograms and PET scans. When you work with people at the emotional and spiritual levels, although it's difficult to measure, the arteries open much more than if you only treat people with drugs or invasive techniques."

In his work with patients, Ornish emphasizes the importance of compassion and altruism—"not as a way of getting a gold star or being a good boy or good girl," but because these community-building attitudes help people transcend their isolation. "The most selfish thing we can do," he says, "is to be unselfish, because it frees us."

From this perspective, spirituality, which Joan Borysenko defines as our deepest sense of belonging and connectedness, not only liberates us from our self-imposed sense of isolation, but from the physical suffering that inevitably accompanies it.

When you get to the end of your rope, tie a knot and hang on. And swing!

Leo Buscaglia

THE AIDS CRISIS AND HEALING

Many AIDS patients, recognizing that disease represents an imbalanced state of mind, body, and spirit, are turning to the integrated practices of holistic medicine to heal themselves. Refusing to see themselves as victims, they take responsibility for their health, look within themselves, and seek solutions that transcend the province of traditional medicine. Many view their diagnosis as a wake-up call to more conscious living, an invitation to spiritual growth and transformation.

In *Psychoimmunity & the Healing Process,* bodywork practitioner Jason Serinus describes the voyage of self-discovery undertaken by these courageous people:

> [They] have replaced medical pessimism, chemotherapy, and dangerous experimental drugs with affirmation, self-love, and a determination to achieve a new balance of mind, body, and spirit. Some of them consult nutritionists and psychic healers, while others combine Western and Eastern healing approaches. Some go to clinics in Mexico, others to yoga and meditation groups; still others choose to go dancing. Whatever their path, they refuse to succumb to the climate of fear and reaction. They listen to themselves. Some have stabilized their conditions or are in remission. Many are in the process of healing. And more than you will read about in the newspapers have journeyed deep within themselves, on pathways uncharted by medical science, and have found that they have healed themselves.

An AIDS diagnosis does not necessarily mean a death sentence, says Serinus, but healing demands a total commitment, "involving every thought, every cell, every habit and belief." Patients usually make lifestyle changes that include stress-reduction techniques, such as biofeedback, visualization, and meditation, a detoxifying natural-foods diet, vitamin supplementation, and therapeutic massage. They also work on replacing diseased mental attitudes with life-enhancing ones that protect their already compromised immune systems. As Serinus writes, "They must move radically inward, beyond any preestablished definitions of who they are and who they should be, to connect with the unconditional self-acceptance and love which are the essence of all healing."

But do psychosocial changes really make a difference? Dr. George Solomon and Dr. Lydia Temoshok of the UCLA School of Medicine, who have studied the psychological attitudes of long-term AIDS survivors, think they do. Among their findings:

- Long-term survivors refuse to accept their condition as a death sentence. As part of their "personalized means of active coping," they make lifestyle adjustments that include fitness and exercise programs.
- They work with their physicians as collaborators, without being either passively compliant or defiant.
- Passionately committed to working on their unfinished business, survivors have a sense of meaningfulness and purpose in life. They often involve themselves altruistically with other patients.
- Assertive and able to communicate openly, survivors frequently meet with other AIDS patients in a supportive environment.

The human spirit can't be diagrammed or dissected; it can't be seen by tomographic scanners and it can't be represented by numbers on a medical chart. Yet it is the single most identifiable feature of human uniqueness. Unless it is understood and respected, all other facts are secondary.

NORMAN COUSINS

227

The Center for Attitudinal Healing in Tiburon, California, founded by psychiatrist Gerald Jampolsky, provides such an environment. Practitioners of attitudinal healing define health as inner peace and healing as the process of letting go of fear. In the center's safe, nonjudgmental atmosphere, members of AIDS support groups are gently encouraged to release withheld fear and negativity, end their isolation by joining with others, and experience love unconfined by the body's physical condition. According to psychologist Jeff Seibert, the center's associate director, members focus not on getting rid of symptoms, but on establishing a state of emotional, mental, and spiritual harmony, from which healing of the body may occur.

"People with diseases like AIDS and cancer feel an urgency in straightening out their lives, examining their purpose, and confronting the reality of death," he explains. "Ironically, in spite of the physical and emo-

Again I am reminded of the words of the Twenty-Sixth Psalm, "Examine me, O Lord, and try me." Disease is surely one of the ways in which we are tried by life and offered the chance to be heroic. Though few of us will win Olympic gold medals or slay dragons, disease can be the spark or gift that allows many of us to live out our personal myths and become heroes.

BERNIE SIEGEL

PRESCRIPTIONS FROM A FORMER PATIENT

The following advice about illness comes from Evy McDonald, a coronary-care nurse and holistic medical researcher who is in remission from what is generally considered a terminal disease. It is reprinted with permission from a brochure available from the American Holistic Medical Association, 4101 Lake Boone Trail, Suite 201, Raleigh, NC 27607; 919-787-5146.

Don't get caught in the tangling web of Why. The search for the explanation and meaning of your illness can lead to frustration and desperation, paralyzing your ability to make decisions and take action.

Treat the critical symptoms first; look for insights later. Use whatever treatment is most appropriate for you and is in line with your own integrity—be it surgery or visualization or antibiotics. No one treatment is more "holistic" than another. Choose what works for you.

Release all expectations of how it will turn out. Your body may heal completely—or not at all. You may find that a wheelchair, cane, walker, or crutches becomes an integral part of your daily life. That does not determine whether or not you live in a state of wellness.

tional pain they experience, many of these patients express gratitude for this opportunity. The encounter with their own mortality changes their priorities in life, their values and aspirations. For many, it makes them truly cherish life and the ability to give and receive love."

Those of us whose current health status makes the encounter with death an event projected in the distant future could learn a lot from people who have no choice but to face impending death, says psychologist David Feinstein, co-author of *Rituals for Living & Dying*. People encountering death tend to drop the pervasive anxiety that makes them seek power, wealth, and fame. As their attention shifts to the immediate present, they recognize the preciousness of each moment and savor it. Opening to their deeper nature, they discover a deepened sense of purpose, a more profound sense of connection with other people and with the universe. They also contact the higher, universal values, such as love, beauty, truth, and justice, savoring them in a new way.

The more I can love everything—the trees, the land, the water, my fellow men, women, and children, and myself—the more health I am going to experience and the more of my real self I am going to be.

O. CARL SIMONTON

Let go of guilt and look inside. Getting ill is not a failure. Illness has a message that we need to understand and listen to. It is time to take a good, honest look at your life and evaluate. Your task is not to kill the messenger of illness by ignoring it, complaining about it, or simply suppressing the symptoms. Your task is to carefully examine your life, observing and searching for those discordant areas where harmony, fulfillment, or love are lacking. Which parts of your life are less than fulfilling? See yourself as clearly as you can—see who and what you are and how you are, in reality, living your life.

List those aspects of your life that you are willing to change. Your job—is it stressful? Relationships? Are you willing to make changes in these areas? Remember, it is all right to say no. The key is in being honest and not feeling guilty.

After (and only after) these steps comes the time to take action. This is the moment to begin, to stop sitting back and waiting for something to happen. You are the only one who can create a state of health and dynamic wellness.

In his book, Feinstein provides a step-by-step program of rituals to help create a more positive relationship with death. Using writing exercises, drawing, visualization, and physical movement, the program unearths the repressed fears and anxieties about death that may be draining our energy and clouding our outlook on life. The liberation of this normally unavailable energy enables us to live with greater awareness and vibrancy.

"We don't have to passively wait for the imminence of our physical death for permission to drop our surface attachments to life and to live from our depths," he says. "When we consciously confront our fear of death and accept its very real presence in our lives, we can start living with the vibrancy and immediacy similar to people facing death through catastrophic illness."

A patient who is mortally sick might yet recover from belief in the goodness of his physician.

HIPPOCRATES

The emotional environment we create within our bodies can activate mechanisms of destruction or repair.

BERNIE SIEGEL

NOT A GRAVE MATTER

Although our culture teaches us to view death as the enemy, we can use humor to embrace it as an inevitable part of the life process, states Allen Klein, author of *The Healing Power of Humor.* If we learn not to take anything in life too seriously, every experience—even death—is ripe for humor. In this spirit, we offer the following classic joke:

Mr. Pinsky persuaded his brother to take care of his Siamese cat while he was on an overseas business trip. Mr. Pinsky dearly loved this cat, but the brother did not. The very moment Pinsky returned from his trip, he called his brother to find out about the cat. The brother announced abruptly, "Your cat is dead," and hung up.

For days Pinsky was inconsolable. Finally, he was able to telephone his brother again. "It was needlessly cruel and uncaring of you to tell me so abruptly that my cat had passed away."

"What did you expect me to do?" blared the brother.

"You could have broken the news more gently," said Pinsky. "First, you could have said that the cat was playing on the roof. Later you could have told me he fell off. The next morning you could have called back and said that he broke his leg. Then, when I came to pick him up, you could have told me that he passed away during the night. But I guess you don't have it in you to be so civilized. Now, tell me, how's Mama?"

The brother waited a moment, then announced, "She's playing on the roof."

RESOURCES

Recommended Reading

Love, Medicine and Miracles, Bernie Siegel (Harper & Row, 1986). Shows how we can become "exceptional patients" by taking an active role in maintaining our own health.

Minding the Body, Mending the Mind, Joan Borysenko (Bantam Books, 1988). Demonstrates how illnesses, such as digestive disorders, PMS, and chronic pain, can be corrected without drugs or surgery by practicing relaxation and meditation and by adopting healthier attitudes.

Head First: The Biology of Hope, Norman Cousins (E.P. Dutton, 1989). Discusses how the mind/body connection is finding increasing acceptance in the medical community.

Healers on Healing, Richard Carlson and Benjamin Shield, editors (Jeremy P. Tarcher, 1989). A collection of essays on healing by physicians, psychologists, nurses, metaphysical healers, and shamans.

Quantum Healing: Exploring the Frontiers of Mind/Body Medicine, Deepak Chopra (Bantam Books, 1989). An exploration of psychoneuroimmunology drawing on Western medicine, neuroscience, and ayurveda, India's ancient healing tradition.

Who Gets Sick, Blaire Justice (Jeremy P. Tarcher, 1988). Explains how mental attitudes and emotions can affect physical health.

Hands of Light: A Guide to Healing Through the Human Energy Field, Barbara Ann Brennan (Bantam/New Age, 1988). An excllent resource on the theory and practice of the laying on of hands.

Healing into Life and Death, Stephen Levine (Doubleday, 1987). Offers meditations and exercises for working with pain and grief and shows how merciful awareness can act as a healing agent.

Imagery in Healing: Shamanism and Modern Medicine, Jeanne Achterberg (Shambhala Publications, 1985). A comprehensive study and guide for using imagery in the diagnosis and treatment of illness.

Spiritual Support Groups

ECaP (Exceptional Cancer Patients), 1302 Chapel Street, New Haven, CT 06511; 203-865-8392. Founded by Yale surgeon Bernie Siegel and Marcia Eager, ECaP holds weekly support groups for people who face cancer, AIDS, and other catastrophic illnesses. The *ECaP Directory of Information and Resources, 1990* ($5 donation plus $2 postage) lists holistic cancer-support groups, comprehensive healing programs, children's support organizations, and health information services.

The Center for Attitudinal Healing, 19 Main Street, Tiburon, CA 94920; 415-435-5022. Founded by psychiatrist Gerald Jampolsky, the center provides support groups worldwide for children with catastrophic illnesses and their families.

If you can't find a holistic support group in your area, consult *The Self-Help Sourcebook* (published by Self-Help Clearinghouse, St. Clare's–Riverside Medical Center, Denville, NJ 07834; 201-625-7101). The book ($9) features six hundred self-help groups that address a variety of issues from multiple sclerosis to anorexia to depression.

Death and Dying Workshops

Life, Death, and Transitions Workshops, with Elisabeth Kübler-Ross, are held at various locations nationwide for the terminally ill and for people suffering from traumatic events, such as rape, child abuse, and incest. Address: Elisabeth Kübler-Ross Center, South Route 616, Head Waters, VA 24442; 703-396-3441.

Conscious Living/Conscious Dying workshops, with Stephen and Ondrea Levine, offer a meditative approach to dealing with terminal illness. Address: c/o Daniel Barnes, The Access Group, 4 Cielo Lane, #4D, Novato, CA 94949; 415-883-6111.

Medical Associations and Healing Arts

Holistic Medicine: American Holistic Medical Association, 4104 Lake Boone Trail, Suite 201, Raleigh, NC 27607; 919-787-5146.

Holistic Nursing: American Holistic Nurses Association, 4101 Lake Boone Trail, Suite 201, Raleigh, NC 27607; 919-787-5146.

Acupuncture: American Association of Acupuncture and Oriental Medicine, 1424 16th Street NW, Suite 105, Washington, DC 20036; 202-265-2287.

Ayurvedic (Traditional Indian) Medicine: Maharishi Ayurveda Association of America, P.O. Box 282, Fairfield, IA 52556; 515-472-8477.

Chiropractic: American Chiropractic Association, 1701 Clarendon Boulevard, Arlington, VA 22209; 703-276-8800.

Therapeutic Touch: Nurse Healers Professional Associates, 234 Fifth Avenue, Suite 3399, New York, NY 10001; 718-726-3024.

AWAKENING CREATIVITY
Liberating the Inner Artist

Spiritual teachers emphasize that by abandoning our preconceived ideas and ordinary perceptual filters, we can experience high states of consciousness, inexpressible delight, and a sense of innocence and mystery about existence. A person familiar with this beatific state describes it this way:

There is one art, no more no less: to do all things with art-lessness.

PIET HEIN

"I sometimes wake up, become conscious, realize that I am surrounded by things and by people, and if I look closely at the sky or the wall or the earth . . . I have the impression that I'm seeing it all for the first time. Then, as if it were the first time, I wonder, or I ask, 'What's that?' I look all round me and I ask, 'What are all these things? where am I? who am I? what do these questions mean?' And then sometimes a sudden light, a great blinding light, floods over everything, obliterates all meaning, all our preoccupations, all those shadows, that's to say, all those walls that make us imagine limits, distinctions, separations, significances."

While this description sounds like the *satori* of a Zen master or the *samadhi* of a yogi or mystic, it actually happened to Eugene Ionesco, the Rumanian-born dramatist and proponent of the Theater of the Absurd. In a similar fashion, the diaries of many artists, sculptors, novelists, and musicians abound in accounts of mystical ecstasy, oneness with nature and humankind, and the transfiguration of life from a vale of tears into a celebration of truth and beauty.

THE CREATIVE LIFE AS A SPIRITUAL PATH

When we think of spiritual disciplines, we stereotypically imagine a meditator sitting cross-legged on a *zafu,* rather than a pianist rehearsing long hours for a recital or a painter executing a series of canvases in a relentless search for visual perfection. Yet in their passionate and single-minded devotion to mastering their disciplines, artists do, indeed, embark on a way, a yoga that leads to the attainment of truth, just as do meditation and prayer. If faithfully practiced, asserts painter Frederick Franck, the lifelong disciplines of art lead to the fulfillment of our specifically human potentials, bringing us in direct touch with the very structure of life.

In *Art as a Way,* Franck describes the nature of the artist's spiritual quest:

> The artist within must fight the battle for Meaning with pen on paper, or brush on canvas, or chisel in wood and stone. But his Way, as that of Everyman, leads from ignorance, delusion, folly, self-inflation and phoniness to truth and authenticity. . . . The point of practicing an art is less to discover who you are than to become your truth, to be able to shed all sham, imposture and bluff in relation to yourself and others. True art is not an indulgence of the little self, but a manifestation of the Self.

With its call to explore the inner world, the way of the artist requires cultivating many of the same virtues extolled by the world's spiritual traditions. Just as spiritual learning is often described as a deconditioning process that cleanses the doors of perception of our habitual mind-sets, so, too, artists must liberate themselves from the deadening influences of tradition-bound thought and opinion.

"Those who want to follow the Way of Beauty must break away from cultural dictatorship and move out into a no-man's land where everything is new and unknown," writes psychologist Piero Ferrucci in *Inevitable Grace.* "They must learn to live outside of stereotypes and worn-out attitudes, and free themselves from any bonds—roles, ties, ideologies, interests, or habits—that might hold them back. They must learn all over again, without fear or hesitation, to be themselves."

Just as spiritual seekers cultivate the capacity for universal compassion, so artists must break out of the citadel of the separate self by developing empathy for all life. As an inner discipline, says Ferrucci, empathy increases our sensitivity to other people so that we know their essence. Describing this practice, French writer Honoré de Balzac writes, "Listening to people talking I could enter into their lives, feel their tattered clothes on my back, walk with my feet in their shoes; their desires, their needs, all passed into my soul, or my soul passed into theirs."

Art is an antidote for violence. It gives the ecstasy, the self-transcendence that could otherwise take the form of drug addiction, terrorism, suicide, or warfare.

ROLLO MAY

The current cultural split lies not between scientists and everyone else but between those who innovate or create and those who do not. Innovators and the process of innovation must become the focus of study. Innovation is the lifeblood of cultural change.

ROBERT ROOT-BERNSTEIN

236

In the same way that meditators focus the mind to enter higher states of consciousness, artists in the heat of creation often become so concentrated that self and environment fuse, producing a state of absorption similar to the mystic rapture described in Hindu and Buddhist literature. The focused concentration of both artists and mystics serves to dissolve the ego. Unencumbered by the habit-bound mind and liberated from the tyranny of the ego, they then can penetrate the realm of awakened perception.

In *Free Play: Improvisation in Life and Art,* musician Stephen Nachmanovitch describes this state of egolessness as a "heartbreakthrough":

> A kind of *fana* [annihilation of individual selfhood] has taken place; we disappear and become a carrier wave, a vehicle for the music that plays us. The power of creative spontaneity develops into an explosion that liberates us from outmoded frames of reference and from memory that is clogged with old facts and old feelings. Addiction, procrastination, and fear are blown away by this carrier wave, and our music becomes a message about big Self.

To create works as an unobstructed channel, the artist must abandon expectations, goals, and self-images and surrender to the unknown with gratitude and trust. Through disciplined practice, Nachmanovitch says, the artist eventually arrives at this state of effortless effort by abandoning control and passing beyond hope and fear, with nothing to gain or lose. Empty of self and with nothing to hide, the artist gives birth to spiritual works stamped with the mark of divine revelation.

As gratifying as this experience may be, the heightened perception of poets, musicians, and dancers does more than beautify our lives. It has survival value in a world besieged by ecological, political, and economic problems that threaten global security. In Nachmanovitch's view, only an explosion of creativity in the arts, sciences, technology, and daily life can pull us through our present evolutionary challenge. Such an explosion calls for dropping outmoded thinking and adopting the fresh perceptions, the openness to explore possibilities, the imagination and playfulness that characterize the artistic response to life. For this reason, "art for art's sake" has become "art for life's sake" in our time.

"Creativity can replace conformity as the primary mode of social being," Nachmanovitch writes. "We can cling to that which is passing, or has already passed, or we can remain accessible to—even surrender to—the creative process, without insisting that we know in advance the ultimate outcome for us, our institutions, or our planet. To accept this challenge is to cherish freedom, to embrace life, and to find meaning."

Everywhere I go, I find a poet has been there before me.

SIGMUND FREUD

The artist must attune himself to that which wants to reveal itself and permit the process to happen through him.

MARTIN HEIDEGGER

Art is the method of levitation, in order to separate one's self from enslavement by the earth.

ANAÏS NIN

BREAKTHROUGH TO CREATIVITY

Throughout history, creative people searching for the right word, note, image, or theme have received sudden intuitive inspiration that appeared to come from another realm. In these ecstatic moments, they often describe themselves as mouthpieces or mediums for a divine power. According to John Milton, the Muse dictated to him the whole "unpremeditated poem" known as *Paradise Lost*. Johannes Brahms told one biographer, "Straightway the ideas flow in upon me, directly from God, and not only do I see distinct themes in my mind's eye, but they are clothed in the right forms, harmonies, and orchestration. Measure by measure the finished product is revealed to me when I am in those rare, inspired moods."

Inventors, philosophers, political leaders, and spiritual seekers, like artists, have tapped the intuitive mind to solve problems, make decisions, and find inspiration for their creative endeavors. Using intuition like a beacon light to explore the unknown, they have discovered what French mathematician Henri Poincaré called "divine hidden harmonies and relations." Because this thinking style operates in a seemingly illogical manner, many people tend to discount and mistrust this natural mental faculty. However, recent explorations in consciousness research have demonstrated that intuition is not just a gift of the gods, but an innate ability that can be trained as a guide in daily life.

Unlocking the Mysteries of Creativity

While the intimate relationship between intuition and creative breakthrough has long been recognized, the apparent unpredictability of the process has baffled those seeking to unlock its mysteries. The artist or scientist who experiences a luminous encounter with beauty or truth generally has as little understanding of the ineffable process as one who has not experienced it. Concerning the ecstatic creation of *Thus Spoke Zarathustra,* for example, philosopher Friedrich Nietzsche wrote:

> The notion of revelation described the condition quite simply; by which I mean that something profoundly convulsive and disturbing suddenly becomes visible and audible with indescribable definiteness and exactness. One hears—one does not seek; one takes—one does not ask who gives; a thought flashes out like lightning, inevitably without hesitation—I have never had any choice about it. . . . There is the feeling that one is utterly out of hand, with the most distinct consciousness of an infinitude of shuddering thrills that pass through one from head to foot.

Even though creative breakthroughs like Nietzsche's appear to be unpremeditated gifts of the Muse, the British author Graham Wallas, in his book *The Art of Thought,* discerned a predictable pattern to the process. He divided the breakthrough phenomenon into four steps, consisting of preparation, incubation, illumination, and verification.

In the preparation phase, write Willis Harman and Howard Rheingold in *Higher Creativity,* we formulate a question, wrestle with it using our conscious resources, then direct it to the unconscious mind for elaboration. During incubation, we may go for a walk by the beach, daydream, engage in fantasy, meditate, or sleep. These nondirected activities allow the question to percolate in our intuitive depths. In the illumination phase, the answer to our inquiry arrives like a flash of lightning, taking form as a literary image, the theme of a concerto, a scientific theory, or a business innovation. In the final stage, verification, we subject our intuitions to the rule of reason and labor to make our vision a practical reality.

If you can dream it, you can do it.

WALT DISNEY

I've always had this idea from the day I started to play music: that not only is it alive, but that it's endless and has no ego in it. There's something about creativity that every human being gets an equal share.

ORNETTE COLEMAN

Do not fear mistakes. There are none.

MILES DAVIS

239

Harman and Rheingold believe that by using certain techniques to access and program the unconscious mind, we can learn to enhance our chances for breakthroughs and increase the number of creative people in society. Their "tool kit for personal breakthrough" includes guided imagery, affirmation, alert relaxation, and dreamwork. By learning these fundamental skills, they claim, we can transform the creative enterprise from an inspirational phenomenon reserved only for creative geniuses to a learned skill available to people in all walks of life.

"Because the breakthrough experience is not limited to geniuses and visionaries, the utility of consciousness-related tools is not limited to art and invention," Harman and Rheingold write. "If we can indeed learn to harvest breakthroughs and increase our cultural creativity by tenfold or a hundredfold or a thousandfold, it would indisputably solve many of our most pressing problems."

Working under the assumption that creativity is indeed a learned skill, human potential pioneer Jean Houston has developed and tested techniques that have helped thousands of people create works of art, music, literature, and poetry. In one exercise, people rehearse creative skills in several minutes of clock-measured time that in an altered state of consciousness might feel like hours, days, or even weeks of subjective experience. For example, Houston may guide musicians with a knowledge of music history into the Realm of Music, where in two minutes of clock time they learn an original composition written in the style of Bach. When many of the musicians return to ordinary awareness, Houston claims, they frequently compose and play pieces that rank as decent second-rate Bach—and, in a few cases, even as first-rate simulations of the master.

"The news from the deeps is very good," Houston writes in *The Possible Human.* "It suggests that creative work and expression are the natural activities of the human being who is able to release, at least temporarily, the inhibitions of habituations and culture. As more knowledge is gained, and as techniques are refined, it ought to be possible to more effectively use those aspects of the creative process that, in the past, have tended to be random and uncontrolled."

THE INTUITIVE REALM

To enhance creativity, many researchers recommend using relaxation, visualization, guided imagery, and dreamwork—approaches associated with intuitive thought processes. In their view, investigating and harnessing the

I have spent my days stringing and unstringing my instrument while the song I came to sing remains unsung.

RABINDRANATH TAGORE

Everybody is talented, original, and has something important to say.

BRENDA UELAND

elusive nature of intuition promises to make the breakthrough experience available to a larger number of people.

"Intuition is a way of knowing that transcends reason and also bypasses the usual sensory channels," explains psychologist Frances Vaughan, author of *Awakening Intuition.* "We use reason to understand physical reality logically and empirically, and we use intuition to explore the non-physical realm, with its emphasis on inner knowing. Intuitive experiences include mystical insights into the nature of reality, inspiration in art, and discovery and invention in science, as well as extrasensory perception, hunches, and premonitions."

Philosophers and mystics regard intuition as a way of knowing in which the separation between subject and object is transcended, Vaughan says. Usually, we acquire knowledge by separating ourselves from objects to observe and analyze them objectively. This process of dualistic knowing yields knowledge about things. But intuition—which comes from the Latin *intuire,* or "inner knowing"—involves a fusion of the observer and

It took me four years to paint like Raphael, but a lifetime to paint like a child.

PICASSO

Imagination is more important than knowledge.

ALBERT EINSTEIN

All the arts we practice are apprenticeship. The big art is our life.

M. C. RICHARDS

If one is master of one thing and understands one thing well, one has at the same time, insight into and understanding of many things.

VINCENT VAN GOGH

the observed. When we identify with what we observe, subject/object boundaries begin to dissolve, and the inner nature of things stands revealed. For example, artists schooled in the Zen tradition may gaze at a cluster of bamboo for hours or even days in rapt attention before putting paint to canvas. Only when they know their subject from the inside do they attempt to give artistic form to their impressions.

According to Vaughan, intuitive experience falls into four categories: physical, emotional, mental, and spiritual. On the physical level, we experience intuition as bodily sensations, such as muscular relaxation or contraction, that help us evaluate whether our immediate environment is supportive or stressful. We experience intuition on an emotional level when we put aside our judging, observing mind, enter another person's inner world, and empathetically identify with his or her feelings. When the fusion of subject and object takes place on the mental level, we have the full-blown *eureka* experience of discovery that leads to artistic inspiration or the formulation of new theories in science, mathematics, or the business world. Intuition on the spiritual level expresses itself as mystical experience and the revelation of truth.

Our culture tends to discredit intuition, says author Philip Goldberg, because for the past three centuries the prevailing model for gaining knowledge in the West has been scientific. The followers of scientism hold that reliable knowledge is sensory-based and that reasoning is the royal road to truth. The scientific enterprise demands that all data should be quantifiable and devoid of contaminating personal biases, emotions, and opinions.

"The whole thrust of scientism has been to minimize the influence of the knower," writes Goldberg in *The Intuitive Edge*. "The institutions that teach us how to use our minds, as well as the organizations in which we use them, are so skewed toward the rational-empirical ideal that intuition is seldom discussed, much less honored and encouraged. From grade school to graduate school, and in most of our work settings, we are taught to emulate the idealized model of scientism in our thinking, problem solving, and decision making. As a result, intuition is subject to various forms of censure and constraint."

Yet the great pioneers of science, such as Newton and Einstein, uncovered nature's secrets through intuitive leaps that were later verified using rational, step-by-step methodology. Studies of corporate executives have revealed that top-level executives use both intuition and logic to guide major business decisions. We need to balance intuition and rationality in our lives, Goldberg contends, because "in a healthy mind and a healthy society, all faculties should develop harmoniously, each supplementing the other's strengths and shoring up its weaknesses."

To move intuition from a peripheral to a central position in our lives, Vaughan recommends three steps. The first requires stilling the mind of surface chatter that blocks intuition from reaching awareness. The single most powerful method to achieve this is meditation, which directs attention away from rational, analytical thinking. In the second step, we focus attention or concentrate on the aspect of reality we wish to contact. Then, after preparing the ground through voluntary practices, we cultivate a receptive, nonjudgmental attitude that allows intuition to penetrate conscious awareness without interference.

"When intuition is developed, it should lead the way into the unknown, with slower-moving reason following behind, evaluating the appropriateness of intuitive insights and inspirations along the way," Vaughan says. "Thus intuition might inspire us to embark on a new path through life, but rationality can help us with everyday decision-making as we struggle to manifest our vision.

"If we're only intuitive, we're likely to be dreamers. If we're only rational, we may find life to be disillusioning and dispiriting. But if we combine both faculties within ourselves, we can live as effective visionaries in the world."

CULTIVATING INTUITION IN EVERYDAY LIFE

In additional to inspiring creative geniuses such as Mozart, Goethe, and Einstein, intuition can elevate the performance of educators, scientists, and businesspeople in everyday settings in the workplace. For intuition to take root in our highly empirical culture, however, we need to reverse the prevailing attitude that considers the inner world of experience to be unreal and untrustworthy.

We start this reclamation project, says Goldberg, by ferreting out negative programs that are operating in our lives. For example, we may believe in intuition intellectually but harbor mistrust on an emotional level. If we suffer from low self-esteem, we may discredit any insight originating from within ourselves. If we cannot tolerate uncertainty and cling excessively to rigid rules and standardized procedures, we may close ourselves to the unpredictable, often surprising knowledge produced by intuitive leaps of mind.

Through diligent self-awareness, Goldberg asserts, we can program the intuitive mind with confident thoughts that express our faith in its ability to produce reliable, useful knowledge. Next, we can replace our

Creative choice is your birthright. Please own it.

JOHN BRADSHAW

The music of this opera (Madam Butterfly) *was dictated to me by God; I was merely instrumental in putting it on paper and communicating it to the public.*

GIACOMO PUCCINI

The essential function of art . . . is to become personally enlightened, wise, and whole. Then, as a consequence of the former function, the purpose of this wisdom, the purpose of art, is to make the community enlightened, wise, and whole.

PETER LONDON

Writing, like life itself, is a voyage of discovery. The adventure is a metaphysical one: it is a way of approaching life indirectly, of acquiring a total rather than a partial view of the universe. The writer lives between the upper and lower worlds: he takes the path in order eventually to become the path himself.

HENRY MILLER

need for security and predictability with what poet John Keats called "negative capability," a willingness to live in uncertainty, mystery, and doubt without anxiously forcing a logical conclusion to our dilemma. Finally, by relaxing the analytical mind's iron grip, we can give up our obsessive need for control, giving the intuitive mind more room to maneuver.

Once we have done this preliminary work, we can begin liberating our newfound abilities in the workplace. Even though intuition is stifled in overmanaged organizations that mandate decision-making from the top down, many executives use their nonlogical abilities to make decisions. However, they rarely admit to this questionable practice among their more skeptical colleagues. "While using facts and logic to provide the foundation for their decisions," writes management consultant William Miller in *The Creative Edge*, "they hide their actual decision-making process, dressing up their intuitive decisions in 'data clothes.'"

However surreptitious its role has been in corporate life, intuition is coming out of the closet, according to Michael Gelb, president of the High Performance Learning Center in Washington, D.C., a management consulting company that teaches people creative thinking skills. "As mounting waves of information assault executives and as competitive pressures continue to grow, the business community must turn to a faculty other than step-by-step logic and analysis to keep afloat," he says. "For this reason, intuition is beginning to play an increasingly essential role in corporate life. Ten years ago business people found intuition training entertaining. Today they're seeking it out with a sense of real urgency."

In his work, Gelb teaches corporate clients to set up creativity rooms that give people what he terms "brain breaks" from their normally focused, goal-driven, stress-related mind styles. During these ten-minute breaks, people may practice stretching exercises or inner focusing techniques, listen to classical music, doodle with colored pencils, or even practice juggling, a nonlinear activity that induces a relaxed, creative mental state. When they return to their desks and computers, their deadlines and staff meetings, they frequently have contacted the intuitive wellsprings from which creative solutions to previously insoluble problems can flow.

PROBLEM-SOLVING THROUGH SCUBA DIVING

Imagery serves as the language of intuition, and the process of learning it is twofold: First we invoke imagery; then we interpret it. It is better to postpone interpreting imagery while we are visualizing, because personal hopes and preconceptions could lead to self-deception rather than intuitive self-knowledge.

With this advice in mind, here is an imagery exercise adapted from *The Creative Edge* by William Miller.

1. Think of a situation at work that needs improvement or special creative insight. Write this down in a sentence or two as if you were a newspaper reporter giving a completely objective overview of the situation. Then close your eyes and lead yourself into a state of deep relaxation.

2. Imagine yourself on a warm, sunny beach in the Bahamas or in Hawaii. Feel the warm breeze blowing across your face, and hear the waves rolling gently onto the shore.

3. Feeling confident, put on your scuba-diving gear, wade into the water up to your chest, then dive underwater and begin swimming about ten feet below the surface. Among the beautiful tropical fish, breathe easily, dive a little deeper, and feel how safe you are.

4. As you gaze down to the ocean floor about fifteen feet below, something captures your attention. Swim toward it and if it's alive, feel a relationship of trust between you. No danger exists for you . . . or it. Then ask it to speak to you about how it represents a solution to your situation. Have a dialogue with it, and ask it to clarify anything you want to know. Then thank it and swim on.

5. As you swim farther, you notice a small, sealed chest nestled in the sand, surrounded by dark green seaweed. Swim down to the chest and open it. Inside you find a piece of paper folded in half on which is written a message in response to your inquiry.

6. After reading the message, return to the beach, take off your scuba gear, and lie on the warm sand. As the warm sun and breeze caress your skin, reflect on the solutions you have found, noting to what degree they solve your situation.

LIBERATING THE INNER ARTIST

Whether arrived at spontaneously or through structured exercises, creativity involves more than producing finely crafted objects that please our aesthetic sense or solving work-related problems with ingenuity. It serves as a vehicle for journeying within ourselves to uncover hidden patterns of

Art is prayer—not the vulgarized notations handed down to us in the scriptures, but a fresh vital discovery of one's own special presence in the world. Marc Chagall was once asked if he attended a synagogue; he answered that his work is prayer.

JOSEPH ZINKER

meaning normally unavailable to the everyday mind. At home in the depths, the creative person encounters the hidden blueprint, the unheard melody of one's life, that exists in a potential state, waiting to be unfolded in the world of space and time. As a citizen of two realms—the inner and outer worlds, the conscious and unconscious minds—he or she expresses the psyche's natural urge for wholeness in works that embody in a tangible way the process of self-discovery.

If creativity serves as such a healing force in the psyche, why do so few people embrace it as a lifestyle?

"Many of us feel frustrated when it comes to being creative," writes psychologist Sandra Shuman, author of *Source Imagery: Releasing the Power of Your Creativity*. "Something obstructs us, whether it's a feeling of inferiority, fear of failure or another anxiety. Or, our beliefs may get in the way: we think that only certain people are born 'creative,' that we need special training or don't have enough talent."

Most of us view art as an activity reserved for a highly trained elite because of a historical tradition that elevates art and artists to the realm of the special, the more-than-human, according to visionary historian José Arguelles. This belief system creates little enclaves of artists sprinkled here and there among large masses of non-artists who seek to be entertained by those who are genuinely creative.

"We can trace this attitude of widespread creative impotence to the rise of industralism, which values efficiency, routine, and specialization, while depreciating creativity and imaginativeness," Arguelles explains. "Because most people have creativity ground out of them by factory-like schools, only a few specialists remain unscathed and manage to keep their aesthetic sensibilities alive. These people become artists. Originally we all have the capacity to create art, but having disowned our inherent powers, we seek them secondhand through specialists called 'artists.'"

When we attempt to reown our inherent creativity, we face a chorus of critical inner voices, rooted in our childhoods, that often paralyze us with performance anxiety. The most tyrannical of these is the Critical Parent, a composite of the disciplining side of parents and teachers that is oppressive and overly harsh. Whenever we risk expressing ourselves creatively, says Shuman, the self-invalidating voice of our Critical Parent whispers to our frightened Inner Child, "You're no good" or "You have no talent." To rescue the Inner Child, who is the source of our spontaneity, imagination, and expressiveness, we need to activate the Nurturing Parent, the internalized voice that gives us positive strokes through words of encouragement and appreciation.

Learn to write about the ordinary. Give homage to old coffee cups, sparrows, city buses, thin ham sandwiches. Make a list of everything ordinary you can think of. Keep adding to it. Promise yourself, before you leave the earth, to mention everything on your list at least once in a poem, short story, newspaper article.

NATALIE GOLDBERG

"To free the creative child once and for all, we've got to retrieve him from the restrictions imposed on him in the past," Shuman writes. "We have the ability to treat him differently now; we can create a loving environment for him to live in—one in which he can be free to express himself without embarrassment, without fear, without restraint, in all his betwitching grace."

Once we have liberated ourselves from the childhood demons that keep our creativity in chains, we still need to overcome our obsessive veneration of great artists whose works dictate standards of what is artistic and what isn't. According to Peter London, a practicing art therapist and painter, we need to disabuse ourselves of the notion that what worked for Rembrandt, Monet, and Picasso will work for us—or ought to. To release our inner artist, we need to stop comparing our work with external standards of excellence (and the feelings of ineptitude that invariably result from such comparisons). We then can embark on a journey of creative discovery in which each painting, poem, or sculpture issues forth with the awe and exhilaration of a new beginning.

Inside my empty bottle I was constructing a lighthouse while all the others were making ships.

C. S. LEWIS

"Do not set stock in correct responses, in familiar ways, or in the ways of others," counsels London in *No More Secondhand Art: Awakening the Artist Within*. "The solution to the problems posed in art do not lie outside in the realms of technique and formula; they reside in the realm of fresh thinking about perennial issues, in honest feelings and awakened spirit."

When practiced in this spirit, London concludes, art transcends the decorative functions it has assumed in contemporary life. Returning to its ancient and sacred role of affirming the covenant between humankind and nature, art becomes a powerful vehicle of personal and collective transformation.

GUIDELINES FOR ENHANCING CREATIVITY

According to art educator Mona Brookes, the founder of the Monart Drawing Schools and author of the best-selling book *Drawing With Children,* creative expression feeds our souls and alleviates stress. Because it nurtures an appreciation for beauty in the natural world, it also is intimately connected with ecological awareness. The following guidelines, culled from years of teaching experience, have helped thousands of children and adults make breakthroughs to new levels of creative expression and fulfillment:

1. Create a nonjudgmental environment that encourages people to risk artistic exploration without having to like everything they create. No artist, inventor, or creative thinker likes everything he or she produces. This liberating insight helps beginning artists explore new avenues of creative expression without having to live up to false standards of excellence.

2. Do away with the words *good, bad, better, best,* and *mistake.* These words kill creativity. Once we think in terms of good or great, we automatically set up a dichotomous system of thinking in which the thought "Maybe it's bad" lurks around the corner. Such thoughts stifle our ability to explore new lines of thinking and experimentation.

3. Cultivate an appreciation of bizarre questions. In seeking innovative forms of self-expression or problem-solving, allow yourself to entertain thoughts and questions without labeling them "crazy" or "weird." We owe many of our greatest scientific and artistic breakthroughs to people who dared to ask unusual questions.

4. Model an appreciation and respect for differences. Do away with the concept that one kind of art is Real Art in opposition to another. Apply the Golden Rule to creativity: Extend the same generosity and respect for the artistic productions of others that you wish them to extend to yours.

5. Produce a noncompetitive atmosphere. When competition rises, creativity plummets, because in our zeal to outstrip imagined adversaries, we focus excessively on our performance, rather than on the process of creative discovery. By contrast, a cooperative spirit encourages people to learn from each other and to take delight in others' success.

6. Don't be afraid to use a little structure. An environment that encourages "Anything goes" doesn't provide enough direction to direct our creative energies. Reasonable, organic discipline goes a long way in bringing out the musician, dancer, poet, or sculptor in us.

7. Have fun. In developing their creativity, some people become so inflated with self-importance and bogged down in seriousness that they lose the capacity for spontaneous play, which is an important ingredient in the artistic equation. To make sure your Inner Child shows up when you're ready to paint or write poetry, drop your expectations and performance goals, and get carried away by the sheer fun of making something.

The Zen ways and arts draw a bridge from real artistic creation (in painting, architecture, poetry) to artistic skills like flower arrangement and gardening, and ultimately to all of everyday life. The religious is found in the everyday, the sacred in the profane; indeed the everyday is religious, the profane is sacred.

HEINRICH DUMOULIN

PRACTICE: CORNERSTONE OF A CREATIVE LIFE

While the literature of creativity abounds with ecstatic descriptions of breakthrough moments, the day-to-day discipline leading to these inspired states hardly gets the same press. Yet according to author and writing enthusiast Natalie Goldberg, the heart and soul of writing—indeed, of any creative endeavor—involves the patient, often unexciting, rather unglamorous practice of doing it on a regular basis, whether we produce "the worst junk in the world" or inspired masterpieces.

"Don't worry about your talent or capability," she advises in her eminently helpful book, *Writing Down the Bones.* "Katagiri Roshi [her Zen teacher] said, 'Capability is like a water table below the surface of earth.' No one owns it, but you can tap it. You tap it with your effort and it will come through you. So just practice writing, and when you learn to trust your voice, direct it. If you want to write a novel, write a novel. If it's essays you want or short stories, write them. In the process of writing them, you will learn how. You can have the confidence that you will gradually acquire the technique and craft you need."

The discipline of writing practice, Goldberg says, helps us cut through what she terms "monkey mind," the surface mind beguiled by the distractions of modern life, to "wild mind," a vast, rich resource similar to the unconscious in Western psychology. In this process, we burn through to first thoughts, which are unencumbered by ego and unobstructed by social politeness or the internal censor.

Practice consists of timed exercises of at least ten minutes and up to an hour or more undertaken with an unwavering commitment to write— no matter what. Goldberg's rules are simple and straightforward:

1. Keep your hand moving. (Don't pause to reread the line you have just written. That's stalling and trying to get control of what you're saying.)
2. Don't cross out. (That is editing as you write. Even if you write something you didn't mean to write, leave it.)
3. Don't worry about spelling, punctuation, grammar. (Don't even care about staying within the margins and lines on the page.)
4. Lose control.
5. Don't think. Don't get logical.
6. Go for the jugular. (If something comes up in your writing that is scary or naked, dive right into it. It probably has lots of energy.)

As Goldberg teaches, we need to accept ourselves in our full humanness when writing in this manner:

> Let go of everything when you write, and try at a simple beginning with simple words to express what you have inside. It won't begin smoothly. Allow yourself to be awkward. You are stripping yourself. You are exposing your life, not how your ego would like to see you represented, but how you are as a human being. And it is because of this that I think writing is religious. It splits you open and softens your heart toward the homely world.

Poetry is just the evidence of life. If your life is burning well, poetry is just the ash.

Leonard Cohen

How I Spent My Summer Vacation

"Our task [in writing]," say Natalie Goldberg, "is to say a holy yes to the real things of our life as they exist—the real truth of who we are." With this guiding principle in mind, here is a writing exercise from her recent book, *Wild Mind: Living the Writer's Life.*

OK, let's finally put that old black dog to rest. Write about your summer vacation, that composition you wrote every fall for a 100 years. Only this time, tell the truth: What did you really do that summer? Go back to the summer before eighth grade and write about what went on. What do you remember clearly? Of the whole summer, it might be just one day when you found out that when a girl kisses she sometimes sticks her tongue in your mouth. It was old Sally. You were in the junior-high parking lot, 4 p.m. under the elm tree. It knocked out the memory of every other day that summer, not to mention that it almost knocked out the braces on your teeth.

What did you do the summer you were 40 years old, 28 years old? The first summer after your divorce, the last summer before you were married?

Remember to be specific. Tell the original details. Once and for all, let it rip. Let's tell our English teachers what really went on. Believe me, as a former English teacher, I think they would probably be relieved.

When training your intuition, try to remain indifferent to the "thought brigade" that arrives in full force, convincing you with impeccable logic, critical judgment, and habitual doubt that your intuitions are baseless fabrications. Put the judging, doubting mind aside when seeking information, but engage your discriminating mind when verifying the results of your impressions.

Helen Palmer

Resources

Recommended Reading

Awakening Intuition, Frances Vaughan (Doubleday, 1979). A well-known book on the nature of intuition, with numerous exercises for developing it.

Art as a Way: A Return to the Spiritual Roots, Frederick Franck (Crossroad Publishing, 1981). Demonstrates how to use the discipline of art as a path of awakening.

Higher Creativity: Liberating the Unconscious for Breakthrough Insights, Willis Harman and Howard Rheingold (Jeremy P. Tarcher, 1984). Argues that creativity consciously can be triggered to produce breakthroughs in business, science, and the arts.

Writing Down the Bones: Freeing the Writer Within, Natalie Goldberg (Shambhala Publications, 1986). Gives techniques, based on the author's experience in Zen meditation, to become a better writer and to gain self-knowledge in the process.

Source Imagery: Releasing the Power of Your Creativity, Sandra Shuman (Doubleday, 1989). A guide to liberating the inner child from critical attitudes that stifle creativity. Contains numerous exercises to free the artist's eye and the writer's hand.

No More Secondhand Art: Awakening the Artist Within, Peter London (Shambhala Publications, 1989). Gives innovative techniques for liberating one's inner artist to fulfill individual potentials and to awaken higher levels of consciousness.

Pain and Possibility: Writing Your Way Through Personal Crisis, Gabriele Rico (Jeremy P. Tarcher, 1991). Discusses how to use creativity to achieve deep psychological healing and growth.

Drawing for Older Children and Teens, Mona Brookes (Jeremy P. Tarcher, 1991). A course in drawing using a successful method that also works for adult beginners.

Would the Buddha Wear a Walkman? A Catalogue of Revolutionary Tools for Higher Consciousness, Judith Hooper and Dick Teresi (Simon & Schuster, 1990). Lists hundreds of products and services to expand your mind.

Free Play: Improvisation in Life and Art, Stephen Nachmanovitch (Jeremy P. Tarcher, 1990). Explores the origins of art, what blocks creativity, and what facilitates it.

The Creative Journal for Children, Lucia Capacchione (Shambhala Publications, 1982). Gives seventy-two exercises in writing and drawing to foster children's creativity, self-esteem, and learning skills.

Spinning Inward, Maureen Murdock (Shambhala Publications, 1987). A handbook of guided imagery for children that has exercises for learning, creativity, and relaxation.

The New Sense Bulletin (formerly *Brain/Mind Bulletin*), Marilyn Ferguson, executive editor (Box 42211, Los Angeles, CA 90042, $45/year). A newsletter on creativity and consciousness.

Music to Create By

Michael Gelb, president of the High Performance Learning Center in Washington, D.C., recommends the following music to enhance our creative endeavors. For the receptive, idea-generating phase of the creative process:

Silk Road (Gramavision), an album of synthesizer music by Kitaro.

Golden Voyage (Awakening), the classic inspirational album by Dexter & Bearns.

Music for a Brain-Nourishing Environment, which Gelb commissioned from composer John Ramo.

Works by various Windham Hill artists (almost anything by George Winston or Alex De Grassi).

For the active, implementation phase of the creative process:

Chariots of Fire (Polygram) by Vangelis

Equinox or *Oxygene* (Dreyfus) by Jean Michele Jarré

The Four Seasons by Antonio Vivaldi

In the Mood by Glenn Miller

The Brandenburg Concertos by Johann Sebastian Bach

For the climactic finale to the creative process:

The *Messiah* by Georg Friedrich Handel

THE EVERYDAY GAIAN

Living in Harmony with the Earth

In an old-grove forest in the Pacific Northwest, a group of women and men kneels in front of an advancing bulldozer on a road under construction by the U.S. Forest Service. After pleading with government officials to abandon the logging project, the group is engaging in a nonviolent protest to protect this pristine forest from encroachment in the name of progress.

In a cathedral in San Francisco, poets, musicians, spiritual teachers, government officials, and ecologists take part in a service that celebrates the grandeur of the natural world. After reciting Earth poetry by Gary Snyder and Robinson Jeffers, participants pour water from the rivers of California into the baptismal font. To strengthen their solidarity with what Native Americans call their animal relatives, they also express appreciation for the region's migratory birds, willow trees, blue herons, burrowing owls, striped bass, and baby possum.

In a supermarket in St. Louis, members of a neighborhood environmental group meet with the shop manager to discuss how the store can conserve energy, purchase organic produce, and stock items that come in recyclable packaging. They also propose setting up a newspaper recycling operation outside the supermarket.

More than any other time in history, mankind faces the crossroads. One path leads to despair and utter hopelessness, the other to total extinction. I pray we have the wisdom to choose wisely.

WOODY ALLEN

255

In a large corporation in Atlanta, environmentally conscious office workers set up in-house paper, glass, and aluminum recycling programs. They also substitute biodegradable paper cups for the polluting styrofoam variety and lobby for faucet aerators and toilet-water displacement gadgets that substantially reduce water consumption.

Responding to environmental degradation that staggers the imagination, consumers, scientists, educators, and politicians across the country and around the world have begun mobilizing in defense of our long-suffering, assaulted planet Earth. We face problems of such interlocking complexity–global warming, the deterioration of the ozone layer, acid rain, deforestation, toxic waste, urban smog, and water pollution–that our survival is at stake.

"The 1990s is the decade of the environment . . . because of events almost beyond our control," says physicist Fritjof Capra, president of the Elmwood Institute, an international ecological think tank in Berkeley, California. "Concern with the environment is no longer one of many 'single issues'; it is the context of everything else–our lives, our business, our politics."

DEEP ECOLOGY

As environmental protection moves from the background to the foreground of our lives, many ecologists are espousing a new vision that goes far beyond our immediate concerns with conserving the planet's dwindling resources. Proponents of this emerging school, called deep ecology, believe that all sentient beings and ecosystems have the inherent right to exist free from excessive human interference. While so-called shallow or reform ecologists focus on efficient control and management of the environment to benefit humanity, deep ecologists see beyond utilitarianism to the underlying matrix that unites all life forms in an unbroken community of species. In its breadth of vision, this new perspective represents a profound détente between the above and the below.

"Deep ecology is supported by modern science . . . but it is rooted in a perception of reality that goes beyond the scientific framework to an intuitive awareness of the oneness of all life, the interdependence of its multiple manifestations and its cycles of change and transformation," writes Capra in *The Turning Point*. "When the concept of the human spirit is understood in this sense, as the mode of consciousness in which the individual feels connected to the cosmos as a whole, it becomes clear that ecological awareness is truly spiritual."

The expansion of human power has hardly begun, and what we are going to do with our power may either save or destroy our planet.

The earth may be of small significance within the infinite universe. But if it is of some significance, we hold the key to it.

In our own age we have been forced into the realization that there will be either one world, or no world.

ABRAHAM JOSHUA HESCHEL

The world is charged with the grandeur of God.

GERARD MANLEY HOPKINS

In keeping with the Gaia Hypothesis, formulated by English scientist James Lovelock, deep ecologists view the world as a living organism whose many species make up a single breathing entity. When we consider ourselves as a species among species, we live in harmony with the natural world, experiencing it as the life-giving source of our physical, emotional, aesthetic, moral, and spiritual nourishment. However, when we sunder this intrinsic bond and exploit natural resources regardless of the long-term consequences, we lose intimacy with the Earth community, fall prey to alienation, and ultimately brutalize ourselves spiritually.

"Reenchantment with the Earth as a living reality is the condition for our rescue of the Earth from the impending destruction we are imposing on it," writes Father Thomas Berry in *The Dream of the Earth*. "To carry this out effectively, we must now, in a sense, reinvent the human as a species within the community of life species. Our sense of reality and of value must consciously shift from an anthropocentric to a biocentric norm of reference."

Simply stated, anthropocentrism places humanity center stage in creation, while biocentrism, in the words of environmentalist Aldo Leopold, sees it as a "plain member of the biotic community." According to environmentalist John Seed, the notion of humanity as the crown of creation, the ultimate measure of value, runs deep in the Western psyche. Rather than viewing the world as a web of interconnected strands, for example, the Judeo-Christian and humanist traditions see it as a pyramid with one species—ours—at the apex. This fundamental orientation, expressed in the biblical injunction that humankind has dominion over all the Earth's creatures, has led to human arrogance, he says, which threatens not only ourselves, but all of life.

To stop the unprecedented destruction of species and habitats, argue deep ecologists, we not only need to change our consumption and lifestyle patterns, but to abandon the deeper anthropocentric assumptions that give rise to this unconscious behavior. In the view of Jim Nollman, author of *Spiritual Ecology: A Guide to Reconnecting with Nature,* "There can be no great healing of the planet until the humans adopt and adapt to a biocentric standard."

Deep ecologists do not underestimate the challenges posed by this fundamental shift in perception. After all, Nollman admits with candor, because we live in an advanced industrial society, even the most environmentally sensitive among us inadvertently inflict some measure of damage on the Earth. We can mitigate that damage, he counsels, by becoming what he terms "cross-generational Bodhisattvas," Earth stewards

The earth has enough for every man's need, but not for every man's greed.

MAHATMA GANDHI

When I say that the fate of the sea turtle or the tiger or the gibbon is mine, I mean it. All that is in my universe is not merely mine; it is me. And I shall defend myself. I shall defend myself not only against overt aggression but also against gratuitous insult.

JOHN LIVINGSTON

who, like Iroquois tribal council members, consider the impact of our decisions on the next seven generations. In this respect, deep ecologists bring a transformational perspective to environmental issues. They can work on urgent, short-term problems in the political arena while holding a long-term vision of planetary interdependence that broadens the context of environmental planning and action.

Acting on behalf of the Earth, writes deep ecologist Bill Devall in *Simple in Means, Rich in Ends,* some of these "new warriors" practice the spiritual discipline of reading and commenting on environmental impact statements. They manifest spiritual courage by protecting the integrity and well-being of the land from shortsighted business interests. Passionate, aroused, sometimes angry, they identify deeply with a territory,

CELEBRATING THE SPRING EQUINOX

"Ancient people recognized not only their connection with nature, but also the effect that the rhythms of nature had on their bodies and lives," write Danaan Parry and Lila Forest in *The Earthsteward's Handbook.* One way to tune into the Earth is through seasonal celebrations that align us with nature's cycles. Parry and Forest offer the following suggestions for celebrating the spring equinox, the day when the sun enters Aries (between March 19 and 23). During this time, days and nights are of equal length, the sun grows in strength and intensity, and the rebirth of vegetation fills us with a sense of inner renewal.

In planning a ritual or ceremony, consider these elements:

Choose a location. Your celebration can be on private property or in a park. Rituals performed outdoors strengthen our connection with nature; those performed indoors tend to be more introspective, fostering the connection with each other and with the intangible and spiritual.

Salute the four directions. The east is traditionally associated with sunrise, wisdom, and the dawning of the light; the south with warmth and fertility; the west with sunset and reflection; and the north with cold, illumination, and purification.

Bless the four elements. Earth is associated with the body; water with the emotions; air with the mind; and fire with the spirit.

To the extent that most of us are users and consumers of energy and of a certain style of life, we are covertly giving the go-ahead to our government to protect those things for us. We must realize that inherent in every time you turn on the ignition of your car or climb into a jet plane, you are in some way part of the chain reinforcing six percent of the world that's using about fifty percent of the natural resources. And that's not fair. We can't play "King of the Mountain" much longer.

RAM DASS

a river, a mountain, or another species and defend it with a sense of responsibility that transcends limited self-interest.

Eco-warriors have two weapons: the insight that everything is connected and the exercise of compassion in daily life. Calling on these ineluctable weapons, says Devall, we can begin taking appropriate action in creating a healthy, sustainable world.

THE BASIC PRINCIPLES OF DEEP ECOLOGY

Deep ecology, which seeks to harmonize humans with the will of the land, owes its existence to Arne Naess, a contemporary Norwegian philosopher. Dissatisfied with what he terms shallow ecology, which in his view

---

Personalize the celebration. Give each person a chance to reflect on and share how the event being celebrated affects his or her life. To evoke personal feelings, consider using music, dance, and the ritual sharing of food or drink (which might include decorated boiled eggs, light breads flavored with anise or cardamon, and Rhine wine). For your equinox celebration, consider

- choosing a budding girl/woman to represent spring. Crown her and sing to her.
- having children give flowers to everyone or showering them with petals.
- singing spring songs.
- dancing line and circle dances.
- reflecting on the colorful flowers you give the world.

"A celebration can be as simple as one person singing a song to the full moon or taking a walk in its light, or as elaborate as a large group of people performing a well-planned ritual followed by feasting and merriment," Parry and Forest write. "Whether done individually, in small groups, or in large groups of up to 100 people, ritual celebrations encourage us to use our creative energies to link more consciously with the natural order."

Let my hidden weeping arise and blossom.

RAINER MARIA RILKE

Protecting something as wide as this planet is still an abstraction for many. Yet I see the day in our own lifetimes that reverence for the natural systems—the oceans, the rainforests, the soil, the grasslands, and all other living beings—will be so strong that no narrow ideology based upon politics or economics will overcome it.

JERRY BROWN

lacks a guiding philosophy or religious foundation, Naess saw the need for an ecology movement that asks deeper questions and challenges our ready-made assumptions about economic and political public policy. "We are not outside the rest of nature and therefore cannot do with it as we please without changing ourselves," he writes in *Ecology, Community and Lifestyle.* By deepening our identification with all life forms in the ecosystem, he suggests, we can help heal Gaia, "the fabulous, old planet of ours."

Here is the eight-point platform of deep ecology proposed by Naess and environmental philosopher George Sessions:

1. The well-being and flourishing of human and nonhuman life on Earth have value in themselves. . . . These values are independent of the usefulness of the nonhuman world for human purposes.
2. Richness and diversity of life forms contribute to the realization of these values and are also values in themselves.
3. Humans have no right to reduce this richness and diversity except to satisfy vital needs.
4. The flourishing of human life and cultures is compatible with a substantial decrease of the human population. The flourishing of nonhuman life requires such a decrease.
5. Present human interference with the nonhuman world is excessive, and the situation is rapidly worsening.

The whole earth is in jail and we're plotting this incredible jailbreak.

HUGH ROMNEY
aka WAVY GRAVY

Look about you. The environment is burning up in a hundred, a thousand places, worldwide. But there is no fire escape here, no "out," no other solution than a shift in knowing who we are.

JIM NOLLMAN

6. Policies must therefore be changed. The changes in policies affect basic economic, technological, and ideological structures. The resulting state of affairs will be deeply different from the present.

7. The ideological change is mainly that of appreciating life quality (dwelling in situations of inherent worth) rather than adhering to an increasingly higher standard of living. There will be a profound awareness of the difference between big and great.

8. Those who subscribe to the foregoing points have an obligation directly or indirectly to participate in the attempt to implement the necessary changes.

THE ECOLOGICAL SELF

Becoming what Jim Nollman calls a cross-generational Bodhisattva on behalf of the Earth requires more than a head-nodding assent to the ideas of deep ecology. It calls for something far more revolutionary: a perceptual shift that extends our sense of identity beyond the human family to include the nonhuman world. On this biospiritual journey, what we call our self broadens to include woodlands in danger of deforestation, marine animals threatened with slaughter, and farmland infested with pesticides and herbicides. According to deep ecologists, when we extend awareness and identify with other animals, mountains, and rivers, we are realizing the *ecological self,* the transpersonal mode of being that interconnects us with all of life.

"The ecological crisis that threatens our planet derives from a dysfunctional notion of the self," says Buddhist scholar Joanna Macy. "Mainstream culture has conditioned us to identify with what Alan Watts called the 'skin-encapsulated ego,' a personal self that is separate and distinct from the web of life. Based on an essentially pathological sense of individualism, we've exploited nature, overconsumed nonrenewable resources, and degraded the biosphere. Fortunately, we're beginning to replace this dysfunctional identity with the ecological self, which is co-extensive with other beings and the life of our planet. This process, which I call the greening of the self, serves as the basis for adequate and effective environmental action."

How can such a patently spiritual notion mobilize political and economic action? Naess argues that when we identify with the entire biosphere, self-defense and the defense of nature become synonymous. In his view, people generally do not respond well to moral exhortations to sacrifice self-interest on behalf of the environment. However, when we experience the genuine self-love of our widened and deepened ecological

Deep ecology . . . requires openness to the black bear, becoming truly intimate with the black bear, so that honey dribbles down your fur as you catch the bus to work.

ROBERT AITKEN

Instead of production, primarily, we have to think of sustainability. Instead of dominating nature, we have to acknowledge that nature is our source and best teacher. Instead of understanding the world in parts, we need to think about the whole.

WES JACKSON

self, our behavior naturally follows norms of strict environmental ethics, without any moral pressure to do so.

In *Thinking Like a Mountain*, environmentalist John Seed describes the differences between acting with *ego*centricity and acting with *eco*centricity:

> "I am protecting the rainforest" develops to "I am part of the rainforest protecting myself. I am that part of the rainforest recently emerged into thinking." . . . When our strategies are formed and informed by a larger context than our narrow ego selves, when we realize we are acting not just from our own opinions or beliefs, but on behalf of a larger Self—the Earth—with the authority of more than four billion years of our planet's evolution behind us, then we are filled with new determination, courage and perseverance, less limited by self-doubt, narrow self-interest and discouragement. The apathy from which many of us suffer, the sense of paralysis, is a product of our shriveled sense of self.

The Eco-Self in Buddhism and Shamanism

While the eco-self may strike Western philosophers as an innovative notion, Buddhism and shamanism have long traditions that honor the Earth as a living being, according to anthropologist Joan Halifax. Buddhism teaches that the self with which we normally identify exists only in a conventional sense as a separate social entity. Meditative insight reveals that this personal self is co-extensive with everything else in creation—the atmosphere we breathe, the trees that oxygenate the atmosphere, and the sun that fuels the Earth's energy processes. Similarly, members of tribal cultures view the Earth as a living organism, with their identities inextricably linked to the worlds of minerals, plants, animals, and the spirit that animates all of creation.

"Buddhists recognize that because suffering pervades the entire material world, we need to extend compassion to all sentient beings," explains Halifax, author of the forthcoming book *True Nature: Views of Earth from Buddhism and Shamanism.* "But we fail to identify with the suffering of the plant and animal world, partly because its untamed power threatens our sense of egoic control. When we accept that nature dwells in our psyches as well as in the outer world, we'll look at the natural world through the eyes of compassion, greeting the cedar tree, the wolf, a river, or a mountain as family members worthy of our love and protection."

Macy and Seed have developed a workshop, the Council of All Beings, in which participants express their compassion for nature through

The world is too much with us; late and soon,
Getting and spending, we lay waste our powers:
Little we see in nature that is ours.
We have given our hearts away.

WILLIAM WORDSWORTH

If we lived a life that valued and protected trees, it would be a life that also valued and protected us—and gave us great joy. A way of life that kills trees, our present way of life, kills us too, body and soul.

WANGARI MAATHAI

We do not like to harm the trees Whenever we can, we always make an offering of tobacco to the trees before we cut them down. We never waste the wood, but use all we cut down. If we did not think of their feelings and did not offer them tobacco before cutting them down, all the other trees in the forest would weep, and that would make our hearts sad, too.

A FOX INDIAN

ritualized processes usually performed outdoors. Drawing on Macy's Despair and Empowerment workshops, the council first gets people in touch with feelings of despair, hopelessness, anger, and rage about the Earth, feelings normally repressed through everyday busyness. After going through a series of exercises (including guided visualizations) that assist people in remembering their rootedness in nature, they shed their human identities and speak from the perspective of other life forms in defense of the Earth.

These ritual processes awaken us from our normally anesthetized state of apathy, which protects us from the deep pain lying just below the surface, Macy says. When we stop repressing the pain and yield to its life-transforming message, a deep caring and compassion arise that empower us to act with newfound energy and mental clarity.

"Don't ever apologize for crying for the trees burning in the Amazon or for the water polluted from mines in the Rockies," Macy writes in the anthology *Dharma Gaia*. "Don't apologize for the sorrow, grief and rage you feel. It's a measure of your humanity and your maturity. It is a measure of your open heart, and as your heart breaks open, there will be room for the world to heal."

A Sense of Place

We can best realize the ecological self by establishing a close rapport with our immediate environment, says deep ecologist Bill Devall. This means exploring our bio-region, the unique terrain, climate, life forms, and culture of the land we inhabit. In an era of rootlessness and obsessive mobility, bio-regionalists sustain and celebrate connections with the land and its ecosystems, as well as with local history and community aspirations. In this way, they seek to contribute to planetary health by living in harmony with the distinctive geological formations and life forms in their own backyard. As Devall writes in *Simple in Means, Rich in Ends,* "The more we know a place intimately, the more we can increase our identification with it. The more we know a mountain or a watershed, for example, and feel it as our self, the more we can feel its suffering."

To establish a sense of place, Devall offers the following questions as an exercise in self-awareness. Answering them, he says, may require a few moments' reflection or a lifetime of intimate experience with your place.

- What are the native plants of your region? What species have become extinct due to human intervention? What is the most endearing feature of the landscape for you? What do you fear most in your region? Where are the headwaters of the river upon which you live? What is the history of human modification of the landscape in your region?
- What is the nighttime like in your region? Can you see the stars on a clear night, or are they obscured by smog or city lights? How much time to do you spend outdoors rather than indoors?
- Have you visited the toxic waste dumps in your city or region? Can you name the chemical compounds which have been deposited in the dumps?
- Does the law of your region guarantee water rights for fish and wildlife, or is all the water appropriated for human use?
- How much fossil fuel is used and how is it distributed in your bio-region?
- Climb the highest hill or mountain in your region. What do you find?
- Were there massacres of native peoples in your region? If so, visit the sites, trying to visualize the killing. Try to re-create how these people lived.
- Where are remnant primeval forests or native grasslands or deserts in your bio-region? Visit them in every season and mood. Discaover their qualities of light and shadow.
- Do you attempt to see undomesticated birds and animals every day? Do you listen to the noise of the city or to sounds of rain, wind, and bird calls?

The meaning of "true" in "the entire Earth is the true human body" is the actual body. You should know that the entire Earth is not our temporary appearance, but our genuine human body.

DOGEN

Perception . . . is a constant communion between ourselves and the living world that encompasses us.

DAVID ABRAM

Dreaming a New Earth

The widespread emergence of the ecological self as a cultural force is coming none too soon, according to geologian Thomas Berry. A long, creative chapter in the Earth's history is drawing to a wrenching, sorrowful conclusion, while an ecological epoch, promising a renewed relationship between humanity and nature, looms on the horizon. Whether the sun of this new epoch rises over a regenerated or an increasingly alienated humanity depends on the urgency with which we take action to preserve the world from eco-destruction.

During the past 65 million years, called the Cenozoic Era by geologists, wave upon wave of life graced the Earth with a rich profusion of flowers, birds, and mammals, Berry explains. Even with the advent of human civilization, the development of agriculture and the domestication of nature, the Earth's creative efflorescence continued without significant interruption. But as we gained increasing control over the natural world through industrialism, our perceived mastery disrupted the planet's biosystems on the scale of hundreds of millions of years of geological and biological change.

"In our enchantment with technological growth, we have extinguished so many species that by all reckoning the Cenozoic Age is over," Berry says. "Yet in its ashes, the Ecozoic Age is struggling to be born, guided by a vision we can no longer call utopian, since our survival depends on it. Recognizing human life as derivative and the natural world as primary, we'll grant all species their habitats and freedom of life expression. As we cease assaulting the planet in a frenzied attempt to find salvation through technology and consumerism, we'll learn to treat the Earth as a self-organizing community deserving of our respect and courtesy."

During the Ecozoic Age, the Earth will become the primary concern of every human institution, profession, program, and activity, Berry asserts. Economists, for example, will operate according to geo-economic principles and practices that meet the genuine needs of all people without damaging the fragile biosphere. Putting the Earth Economy first, they will not pursue the shortsighted goal of increasing the gross national product if their actions cause a declining gross earth product. In the same way, the medical profession, recognizing that we cannot have healthy people on an ailing planet, will marshal its expertise to maintain and enhance the well-being of the Earth.

In terms of governance, we will move from a limited democracy to a more comprehensive biocracy that protects the rights of all endangered

When the Copernican Revolution superseded the ancient Ptolemaic worldview, the earth took its rightful place as one planet among many. Man was no longer the center of the universe and though his self-image was deflated, he grew in maturity. In the same way, we must take our rightful place in nature—not as its self-centered and profligate "master" with the divine right of kings of exploit and despoil, but as one species living in harmony with the whole.

R. D. Laing

My father considered a walk among the mountains as the equivalent of churchgoing.

ALDOUS HUXLEY

Here is calm so deep, grasses cease waving . . . wonderful how completely everything in wild nature fits into us, as if truly part and parent of us. The sun shines not on us, but in us. The rivers flow not past, but through us, thrilling, tingling, vibrating every fiber and cell of the substance of our bodies, making them glide and sing.

JOHN MUIR

species. "In the not too distant future, we can envisage a constitution not simply for humans on this continent, but for the entire North American community of species," Berry predicts. "Legislators have already begun moving in this direction by requiring environmental impact statements on major projects that might compromise the safety of ecoystems."

Because our industrial practices already have extinguished so many life forms, nurturing the world back to health—admittedly a long-term project—will require a new spirituality that celebrates the sacred within the natural world. Recognizing divine presence in all of nature's myriad expressions will not only reinstate us as guardians of the Earth community. The new spirituality also will facilitate the readjustment of values needed during the transitional period, when conspicuous consumption is supplanted by a more sustainable lifestyle that balances inner needs with outer resources.

"The human family is going through a collective initiation process, passing from childhood into a state of adult responsibility for the planet," Barry says. "If we diminish consumption, recycle, and support waste disposal programs only to preserve our present industrial system, then we'll fail the test. But if we undertake these measures as midwives of the incoming Ecozoic Age, we'll begin healing the past and shaping the future as Earthlings, inextricably linked to the planet whose destiny we share."

THE EARTHWISE CONSUMER

If we are to become effective Earth stewards, the visionary ideas of deep ecologists such as Berry and Devall need to hit home in our lives. Indeed, says consumer advocate Debra Dadd, the best place to begin an environmental clean-up is in our own homes. We unwittingly stock them with products made from inadequately tested synthetic substances that cause cancer and weaken our immune systems. As Dadd points out, our everyday living environments contain more chemicals than were found in chemistry laboratories at the turn of the century. Whereas professionals in industrial settings abide by strict health and safety codes, we use these same chemicals without guidance or restriction.

Even if we reduce exposure to toxic household cleaning products, eliminate the use of pesticides, purify our tap water, and switch to safe personal-care products, we still face a bigger issue: how our consumer decisions affect other people, other species, and the entire planet.

"Every time we make a purchase to fulfill our individual needs, we also make a choice that affects the environmental quality of the world we

WHY EAT LESS MEAT?

It takes between 22 and 44 times less fossil fuel to produce beans and grains rather than meat.

It takes 16 pounds of feed and 2,500 gallons of water to produce one pound of beef.

Half of the world's grain harvest is fed to livestock.

An estimated 85 percent of our topsoil erosion is associated with raising livestock.

About half of the 25 million pounds of antibiotics produced in the United States annually is fed to livestock.

Calorie for calorie, you can get an equivalent amount of protein from vegetables such as broccoli and cauliflower as you can from meat.

In a study of 24,000 Seventh Day Adventists, meat eaters had a three times greater incidence of heart disease than did vegetarians.

FROM *Diet for a Small Planet*
BY FRANCES MOORE LAPPÉ

The clearest way into the universe is through a forest wilderness.

JOHN MUIR

Earth, with her thousand voices, praises God.

SAMUEL TAYLOR COLERIDGE

live in," writes Dadd in *Nontoxic, Natural, & Earthwise.* "Even if a product is relatively safe for us to use, its manufacture and disposal may harm the Earth. And this then affects our own health as the soil, air and water that provide our sustenance become polluted."

To assess the environmental impact of our purchases, Dadd suggests visualizing a product's span of existence from cradle to grave. We can begin by tracing the manufacturing process back to either planting and harvesting crops, raising livestock, or processing natural resources from the Earth. Constructing a mental flow chart, we can follow the product from the factory to the warehouse, from the store to our home, and finally from the garbage can to the landfill. As we survey the process, we can assess whether the product damages the ecosystem in its manufacture, use, or disposal. With our own environmental impact statement in mind, we then can make earthwise decisions at the supermarket, hardware store, or gardening center.

If all this sounds complicated, Dadd says, one fundamental insight can simplify the process: What we call consumer goods are really pieces of nature several times removed from the Earth and dressed up in attractive

There is really no such creature as a single individual; he has no more life of his own than a cast-off cell marooned from the surface of your skin.

LEWIS THOMAS

packaging designed to stimulate nondiscriminating purchases. "We make the Earth connection at the supermarket by calling things by their real names," she explains. "In this awareness exercise, we see beyond the consumer label 'lettuce,' recognizing it as a living plant harvested from the ground for our health. We see beyond the name of a sugar-coated cereal, realizing it's imported from a tropical island where agricultural workers sprayed large quantities of pesticides on the sugar cane. When we realize that the product we're contemplating buying is no longer natural, a desire arises from within to buy and consume products closer to their natural state."

In her book, Dadd provides consumers with criteria for evaluating purchases based on product ingredients, packaging, energy use, compassion for animals, and social responsibility. She calls products *earthwise* if they are made from recycled materials or renewable natural resources produced by sustainable methods, are biodegradable, have not been tested on animals, and are manufactured by companies that do not exploit local workers or Third World economies; she calls products *natural* if they are manufactured from renewable resources but in ways that pollute local ecosystems. *Nontoxic* products, made from nonrenewable petrochemicals, do not actually threaten human health, although their manufacture and disposal may produce toxic wastes.

Switching to a healthier lifestyle, a process undertaken in incremental steps, is not always easy given current limitations in the marketplace. To help us on this journey, Dadd offers the following general guidelines:

Reduce your level of consumption by buying simpler products. Instead of eating an apple pie, eat an apple. Instead of buying a loaf of bread shipped cross-country at a great expenditure of natural resources, select one baked locally.

Begin phasing out toxic products that rely heavily on petrochemicals. Avoid cleaning products made from synthetic chemicals, scented beauty and hygiene products, synthetic fibers and fabric finishes, office supplies with volatile chemicals, and building materials made from formaldehyde.

Stock your home with safe, alternative products that don't pollute the environment. For example, choose cotton over polyester fabrics. Instead of plastic products made from petrochemicals, choose wooden alternatives (manufactured ideally through the practice of sustainable forestry). Rather than use ammonia or some all-purpose cleaner, try homemade alternatives using baking soda, distilled white vinegar, lemon juice, Borax, or liquid soap.

"Each of us must decide what steps we're willing to make and then take them at our own pace," Dadd cautions. "Without being overwhelmed by the magnitude of change required to live in an earthwise fashion, we need to remind ourselves that each small step we take benefits not only ourselves, but the Earth."

PLANET SURVIVAL KIT

Guidebooks on ecologically sane living such as Debra Dadd's are proliferating in bookstores across the country—and for good reason. Living in the last decade of the twentieth century, we feel a mounting urgency to act quickly and skillfully so that our children can inherit a viable world. In the words of Lester Brown, president of the Washington-based think tank Worldwatch Institute, "We do not have generations, we only have years, in which to attempt to turn things around."

Many guidebooks suggest from dozens to hundreds of health-giving ways to modify our living habits. To prevent information overload, the following Planet Survival Kit offers a modest number of strategies that can make a difference in healing the Earth:

Plant trees around your home or in your community. Because trees absorb carbon dioxide emissions caused by burning fossil fuels, they help combat global warming (the so-called Greenhouse Effect). Trees also conserve energy by shading and cooling homes, reducing the need for air conditioning. In addition, they absorb air pollution and beautify the often harsh urban environment. "Tree planting takes the simple act of an individual and elevates it, revealing the truth about where true power rests in the world," write Andy and Katie Lipkis in *The Simple Act of Planting a Tree.* "The result of a single person's planting can be monumental, and when individual acts are added up, the result is powerful evidence of what one can do for the world."

Cut down on driving. To help curb our automotive wanderlust, Vietnamese Buddhist monk Thich Nhat Hanh has composed a simple verse to recite before turning the ignition key: Before starting the car,/I know where I am going./The car and I are one./If the car goes fast, I go fast.

In *Peace Is Every Step: The Path of Mindfulness in Everyday Life,* he comments on the meaning of this verse:

All truly wise thoughts have been thought already thousands of times; but to make them truly ours, we must think them over again honestly, till they take root in our personal experience.

JOHANN WOLFGANG VON GOETHE

In the last several years, two million square miles of forest land have been destroyed by acid rain, partly because of our cars. "Before starting the car, I know where I am going" is a very deep consideration. Where shall we go? To our own destruction? If the trees die, we humans are going to die also. If the journey you are making is necessary, please do not hesitate to go. But if you see that it is not really important, you can remove the key from the ignition and go instead for a walk along the river bank or through the park. You will return to yourself and make friends with the trees again.

Recycle paper, glass, and aluminum cans. Besides mitigating the garbage glut that threatens to close many of our landfills, recycling saves natural resources and helps conserve energy. It also combats the Greenhouse Effect, water pollution, ozone depletion, soil erosion, and acid rain. "Citizens new to recycling quickly learn that the best way to cut down on trash is to buy less in the first place," write Peggy Taylor and Laura Danylin Duprez in *New Age Journal*'s "Earth Day 1990 Action Guide." "Recycling leads to a new, healthier way of living."

Eat low on the food chain. The higher we eat on the food chain, the more natural resources and pesticides we consume, according to the "Personal Action Guide" published by the United Nations Environmental Program. The pamphlet lists a sobering statistic: If Americans reduced meat eating by only 10 percent, the savings in grain could feed the 60 million people who starve to death each year. Among its strategies, the guide suggests cutting down on meat consumption, buying organic food, growing food gardens rather than lawns, and supporting laws that ban harmful pesticides.

Become more energy efficient at home. There are two ways to reduce home energy use, says Debra Dadd in *Nontoxic, Natural & Earthwise:* We can practice conservation (turning off lights when we aren't in the room) or energy efficiency (using energy-efficient light bulbs, which provide the same amount of light for less energy). "By taking already known energy-conservation and efficiency measures," she writes, "we can cut our total energy use in half or better (some estimates go as high as 80 percent) without affecting our quality of life."

Invest in the environment. We can put our money to work for the environment by making donations to our favorite organizations, according to the "Earth Day 1990 Action Guide." We also can invest in funds that screen their companies according to strict social and ecological criteria, while still yielding excellent returns. Finally, we can use credit cards issued by environmental organizations, such as American Rivers, Defenders of Wildlife, Environmental Defense Fund, and the National Wildlife Federation.

*Come forth
into the light of things.
Let Nature be your
teacher.*

WILLIAM WORDSWORTH

Become an environmental activist. Positive change doesn't just depend on individual effort, Joanna Macy points out. She advises people to join or start local support groups united by a common concern, such as recycling, tree planting, hazardous-waste disposal, or energy conservation.

"Don't approach environmental action in a dutiful, moralistic way, but as a gift to the Earth, a wonderful doorway through which courage and companionship enter your life," she says. "Because we're interconnected in a deep ecological sense, working on a single-issue project, such as recycling, has a direct bearing on saving the Amazon rainforests, reducing global warming, and conserving energy. This insight keeps us from feeling overwhelmed by the enormity of the global crisis."

The care of rivers is not a question of rivers, but of the human heart.

TANAKA SHOZO

LIVING MORE SIMPLY

When we, as individuals, decide to modify our diet, recycle, and lower our level of comsumption, we might wonder how small, seemingly insignificant actions can have an impact on the global environment. Yet no matter how small our personal actions may appear, observes social scientist Duane Elgin, we should never underestimate their importance.

"The character of a whole society is the cumulative result of countless small actions, day in and day out, of millions of persons," he writes in *Voluntary Simplicity.* "Who we are, as a society, is the synergistic accumulation of who we are as individuals. . . . Small changes that seem insignificant in isolation can be great contributions when they are simultaneously undertaken by many others."

In his book, Elgin popularized the notion of voluntary simplicity, a manner of living that is "outwardly more simple and inwardly more rich." People who adopt this lifestyle reduce their reliance on material possessions to explore the deeper psychological and spiritual dimensions of life. No longer equating standard of living with quality of living, they refuse to be misled by advertisers whose assumptions about the supposed good life ignore the damage inflicted on the environment in the name of material prosperity.

Yet advocates of simple living do not suffer from material privation. Having found the balance between frugality and extravagance, they live in a way that is life-affirming, rather than life-denying. Debra Dadd describes how we find the golden mean between poverty and excess:

> It requires learning the differences between our needs and wants, the necessary and superfluous, the useful and the wasteful; it requires preserving what is vital and eliminating the extraneous. It means choosing what is deeply

satisfying over passing whims. It necessitates considering what is good for the rest of humanity and the Earth as well as what is good for ourselves. When we identify what our true needs are and how we can satisfy those needs, we can begin to pare away the excess.

Deep ecologists insist that living in this manner does not imply self-sacrifice. "There are no ration cards or policemen watching us to see how much gasoline we consume or how loudly we play our stereo tape decks," observes Bill Devall in *Simple in Means, Rich in Ends.* However, when we awaken to a life beyond the barbed-wire fence of the conditioned self, we discover a basis for appropriate action arising from within, not based on abstract moralism but on contact with the living currents of the Earth.

For those who find guidelines useful, the Simple Living Collective of San Francisco in 1977 proposed four consumption criteria for simple living:

1. Does what I own or buy promote activity, self-reliance, and involvement, or does it induce passivity and dependence?
2. Are my consumption patterns basically satisfying, or do I buy much that serves no real need?
3. How tied is my present job and lifestyle to installment payments, maintenance and repair costs, and the expectations of others?
4. Do I consider the impact of my consumption patterns on other people and on the Earth?

If collectively we begin to reappraise our consumption habits based on these criteria, we may begin to set in motion the social, economic, and spiritual forces to create a more sustainable society. In *Seeing Green: The Politics of Ecology Explained,* Jonathon Porritt, a founder of Britain's Green Party, gives a foretaste of how our concept of wealth will change in such a society:

> In a sustainable, ecological future, the wealthy will be those who have the independence and the education to enhance the real quality of their lives; the poor will be those who look back to an age where money might, but never quite did, buy happiness. . . . The wealthy will be re-using and recycling and taking pride in how long things last and how easy they are to repair; the poor will be wondering when the novelty went out of novelty. The wealthy will be fully involved in their parish or neighborhood council, getting things done for themselves and their community; the poor will still be blaming the Government. Wealth, in both its physical and its spiritual dimension, will have regained its meaning.

In a world in which one billion people live on the edge of physical survival and wasteful consumption of nonrenewable resources threatens an already compromised planet, voluntary simplicity may be an idea whose time has come. As Elgin points out, simple living is in the springtime of growth, and its contemporary expression represents only its initial blossoming. Perhaps when the flower is in full bloom, the Earth's anguish will become a painful but instructive memory and we will embark on a course of cultural renewal.

The world is not to be put in order, the world is order incarnate. It is for us to put ourselves in unison with this order.

HENRY MILLER

No snowflake falls in an inappropriate place.

ZEN SAYING

RESOURCES

Recommended Reading

The Dream of the Earth, Thomas Berry (Sierra Club Books, 1988). A collection of visionary essays that urges us to live in harmony with the natural world as a sacred community rather than as resources for economic exploitation.

Dharma Gaia, Allan Badiner, editor (Parallax Press, 1990). A collection of essays by Buddhist scholars and practitioners showing the link between Buddhist teachings and ecological awareness.

Voluntary Simplicity, Duane Elgin (William Morrow and Company, 1981). Calls for a lifestyle that stresses decreased consumption and increased cultivation of the inner life to help combat the world's ecological crisis.

Nontoxic, Natural, & Earthwise, Debra Lynn Dadd (Jeremy P. Tarcher, 1990). A buyer's guide by a noted consumer advocate that helps us assess the health hazards and environmental impact of our purchases.

Thinking Like a Mountain: Toward a Council of All Beings, John Seed, Joanna Macy, Pat Fleming, and Arne Naess (New Society Publishers, 1988). A collection of readings, meditations, poems, guided fantasies, and workshop notes designed to induce a sense of empathy for the Earth.

Simple in Means, Rich in Ends: Practicing Deep Ecology, Bill Devall (Peregrine Smith Books, 1988). Shows how to adapt our lifestyles and take part in political activism based on an awareness of the ecological self.

Toward a Transpersonal Ecology: Developing New Foundations for Environmentalism, Warwick Fox (Shambhala Publications, 1990). A scholarly study showing the connection between ecology and spirituality.

50 Simple Things You Can Do to Save the Earth, The Earthworks Group (The Earthworks Press, 1989). Gives a wealth of practical strategies to help make a difference in saving the world from ecological destruction.

The Simple Act of Planting a Tree: Healing Your Neighborhood, Your City, and Your World, TreePeople with Andy and Katie Lipkis (Jeremy P. Tarcher, 1990). Gives practical instructions for organizing neighbors and local businesspeople to plant trees to beautify and protect urban ecosystems.

The Spiritual Dimension of Green Politics, Charlene Spretnak (Bear & Company, 1986). Examines the link between spiritual values and Green principles of ecological wisdom, social responsibility, grass-roots democracy, nonviolence, and sexual equality.

Gaia: An Atlas of Planet Management, Norman Myers, editor (Doubleday, 1984). The definitive source book that outlines the extent of the environmental crisis and gives guidelines for restoring the biosphere.

Publications and Organizations

In Context: A Quarterly of Humane Sustainable Culture, (P.O. Box 11470, Bainbridge Island, WA 98110, $18/year). Features articles on the spiritual aspects of ecology, designing healthy cities, lifestyles for a small planet, and earth stewardship by Earth-minded folks such as Hazel Henderson, Lester Brown, Amory and Hunter Lovings, and John and Nancy Todd.

The Cathedral of St. John the Divine (1047 Amsterdam Avenue, New York, NY 10025; 212-316-7400) has developed spiritually based ecology programs, which are covered in the newsletter *Cathedral.*

Chinook Learning Center (P.O. Box 57, Clinton, WA 98236; 206-321-1884). This workshop and retreat center runs programs year-round that explore a comprehensive vision of the future from an ecological, ecumenical spiritual perspective.

Council of All Beings Workshops (contact Gateway, 6134 Chinquapin Parkway, Baltimore, MD 21239; 301-433-7873). Led by Buddhist scholar and activist Joanna Macy, these gatherings help participants develop imagination as an essential tool in approaching environmental challenges.

Greenhouse Crisis Foundation (1130 17th Street NW, Suite 630, Washington, DC 20036; 202-466-2823). Headed by Jeremy Rifkin, this organization provides information to churches and schools about global warming. The foundation publishes the *Green Lifestyle Handbook: 1,001 Ways You Can Heal the Earth* ($10.95).

Planet Drum Foundation (Box 31251, San Francisco, CA 94131; 415-285-6556). Promotes bioregional education through conferences, the twice-yearly publication *Raise the Stakes,* and other publications, such as *A Green City Program: For the San Francisco Bay Area and Beyond.*

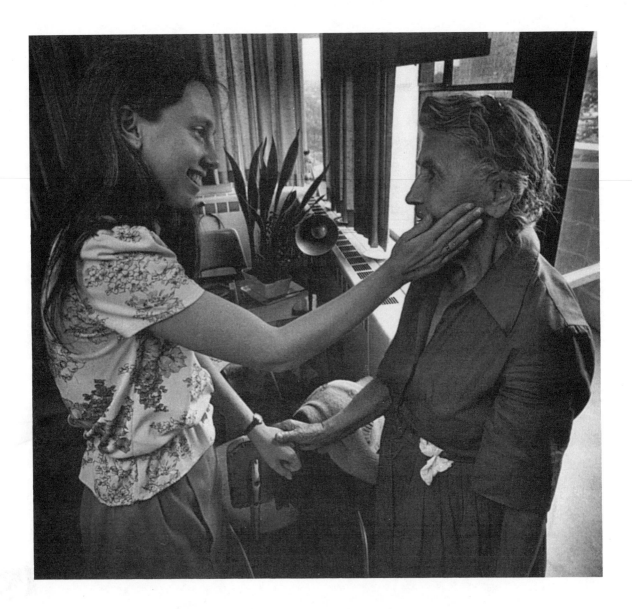

COMPASSIONATE ACTION

Making a Difference Through Spiritual Activism

When we deeply consider the vast human suffering in the world, many of us experience a struggle between our heart's natural desire to reach out to others and our mind's self-protective strategy of remaining separate and disengaged. An incident that happened in one of Ram Dass's workshops on service illustrates this predicament, which we all share.

In 1989 he was teaching a course on compassionate action at the Cathedral of St. John the Divine in New York City. As part of the curriculum, each of the several hundred participants, including Ram Dass, agreed to take part in service activity focused around homelessness, such as working in a shelter or a soup kitchen. One evening, speaking before an open microphone to the participants, a woman confessed to an ongoing moral conflict she was suffering over a beggar on her local street corner for whom she budgeted around two dollars and fifty cents per week in spare change. Before the course, she had merely deposited quarters in his paper cup and went on her way essentially unchanged. Now she wondered why she could no longer perform this act in a perfunctory manner.

"I realized that although I had passed by this man for more than a year, I had never actually acknowledged his existence as a fellow human being," she said. "When I asked myself why, I discovered I was afraid—not of rape or theft—but of caring so much that this man would wind up living

I don't know what your destiny will be, but one thing I do know: the only ones among you who will be really happy are those who have sought and found how to serve.

ALBERT SCHWEITZER

277

with me in my apartment. If I opened my heart to him, he'd be like family. Would I say to my uncle, 'Well, I'll give you $2.50 a week, but you have to stand on the corner?'"

"This incident burned itself into my memory," Ram Dass says. "Like this woman, many of us close our hearts in the presence of suffering. Fear is the mind's reaction against the heart's inherent generosity. The mind protects you as a separate entity, while the heart connects you directly to the joy and suffering of others. In our imbalanced culture, in which the mind tends to suffocate our compassion and direct engagement with life, we need heart-to-heart resuscitation."

AWAKENING TO SERVICE

For inspiration in this endeavor, we turn naturally to the world's spiritual traditions, which emphasize compassionate action to alleviate suffering. Over the millennia, spiritual seekers in ashrams and monasteries worldwide have investigated how selfless service fulfills the dual purpose of relieving the suffering of others and purging the server of self-centeredness.

Traditionally, spiritual seekers have practiced their disciplines as part of the solitary quest for enlightenment. Today, the distinctions between spirituality and social activism are blurring, and engaged forms of spiritual practice are cropping up everywhere, based on the notion that genuine wisdom and compassionate action are not incompatible. Indeed, given the gravity of the environmental crisis and the extent of political and social injustice around the globe, they are of necessity joining forces. In this enterprise, spirituality completes itself in political action, and activism acquires a soul.

"The call is clear: 'Activists, Look Within!'" write spiritual activists Vicki Robin and Joe Dominguez in *In Context: A Quarterly of Humane Sustainable Culture.* "Discover that spirit which is the spirit of the Earth and work from there. The sacredness of all life must undergird our agendas and policies and technologies and initiatives—but we *must* act. Therefore, the call is equally clear: 'Meditators, Arise (from your benches and cushions) and Make a Difference!'"

To live the life of a spiritual activist, we need to integrate all levels of our being, says Mirabai Bush, director of the Project Action Group on Guatemala for the Seva Foundation, a service organization working to alleviate suffering around the world. In her view, since the human potential explosion of the 1960s we have explored spiritual, psychological, and so-

You've got to serve somebody.

BOB DYLAN

If you help others, you will be helped, perhaps tomorrow, perhaps in one hundred years, but you will be helped. Nature must pay off the debt. . . . It is a mathematical law and all life is mathematics.

G. I. GURDJIEFF

cial aspects of the self, all of which are required for conscious, caring responses to the accelerated changes we face in the '90s and beyond.

Over the past three decades, some people have pursued the path of political activism hoping to change institutions in largely structural ways, Bush observes. Others, believing political change to be discouraging, if not impractical, work, withdrew from social activism to pursue the path of self-reflective, inner-directed change. Still others focused their work on the psychological level, seeking clarity about their personal histories and motivations in an effort to increase their openness with others.

"To establish healing relationships with each other, other cultures, other species, and the Earth, we need to balance and express all these sides of our nature," Bush says. "Social institutions change slowly, and without a spiritual dimension to political work, we can easily experience anger, impatience, despair, and cynicism, the precursors to burnout. When our social and political action is inspired by spiritual practice, we have both the vision and inner strength needed for the long haul."

Apart from a few exemplary figures such as Mother Teresa, Dorothy Day, Mahatma Gandhi, Martin Luther King, Jr., Cesar Chavez, and Thich Nhat Hanh, we have few models of compassionate action to guide us in this undertaking. Because our culture emphasizes individualism to an almost obsessive degree, we identify with entrepreneurial heroes who excel at amassing personal fortunes, athletes skillful at defeating their opponents, or movie stars who bask in a cult of individuality. The conspicuous absence of compassionate heroes in our lives does more than desensitize us to the world's suffering; it contributes to the nameless pain we feel from not being able to connect with people on a deep level because our psychological defenses make reaching out a fearful prospect.

While withdrawal into the insulated self keeps us seemingly safe, the growing realization of global interrelatedness is conspiring to tear down our sense of separateness, says Shams Kairys, who has served as a Seva Foundation regional director. "As the world grows smaller through electronic communications and we're increasingly saturated with television images of suffering in Sub-Sahel Africa, Central America, and the streets of our cities at home, our boundaries are shattering under the compression of many social, political, and spiritual forces," he says. "This process calls forth a more extended concept of who our family members really are and what our abiding concern should be. No one has to stand over us, cracking a whip and shouting, 'Serve!' Compassionate action arises naturally from the awareness of our non-separateness and the desire to relieve suffering wherever we can."

We can refuse the call to dissolve our boundaries by resorting to a number of less-than-skillful strategies, write Ram Dass and Paul Gorman in *How Can I Help?*. We may deny that a problem concerns us, keep suffering at arm's length by pitying others, or assume an aura of professional warmth when dealing with those who seek our services. If, however, we can drop our cherished model of helper and helped and discover the extended self that lies beyond the prison cell of the ego, we can begin practicing what Ram Dass and Gorman call Helpful Being. Motivated by a sense of unity, we break through the boundaries of the separate self, reaching out to others with greater trust and patience.

Describing the challenges involved in serving others, Ram Dass and Gorman write:

> On this path we will stumble, fall, and often look and feel a little foolish. We are confronting long-standing patterns of thought and action. Compassion for ourselves, perspective, humor . . . these are our allies. With their help, we can come to see, in the words of the Bhagavad Gita, that "no step is lost on this path . . . and even a little progress is freedom from fear." The reward, the real grace, of conscious service, then, is the opportunity not only to help relieve suffering but to grow in wisdom, experience greater unity, and have a good time while we're doing it.

There is hunger for ordinary bread, and there is hunger for love, for kindness, for thoughtfulness; and this is the great poverty that makes people suffer so much.

MOTHER TERESA

Put your heart, mind, intellect and soul even to your smallest acts. This is the secret of success.

SWAMI SIVANANDA

What Can We Do?

All talk of service remains theoretical until we get our feet wet. In *Gandhi's Seven Steps to Global Change,* Guy de Mallac, who teaches a course on nonviolence at UC-Irvine, offers dozens of practical suggestions in response to the question "What can we do?" The following answers represent a sampler of the riches to be found in this little volume:

> Actively search for action groups and institutions in your area which are involved in some form of selfless service (i.e., unpaid, non-self-seeking service), community work, or social work (providing shelter for the homeless, job training, emergency meals, etc.) . . . Contact at least one or two local branches of such organizations and find out more about their programs. Then get involved in your preferred choice, giving half a day or an evening a week to some form of selfless service, either through an organization or directly to a needy party. . . .
>
> In the light of Gandhian principles, review your current bread-winning occupation. Maybe you'll wish to consider some other form of activity, perhaps changing to a means of livelihood which serves a more useful purpose in society. . . .
>
> Make some commitment of your time and energies to work for a group which is pursuing peace. . . . Get involved in political activity sustained by non-violent values. . . .

Nothing in this world can take the place of persistence.
Talent will not; nothing is more common than unsuccessful men with great talent.
Genius will not; unrewarded genius is almost a proverb.
Education will not; the world is full of educated derelicts.
Persistence, determination alone are omnipotent.

RAY KROC

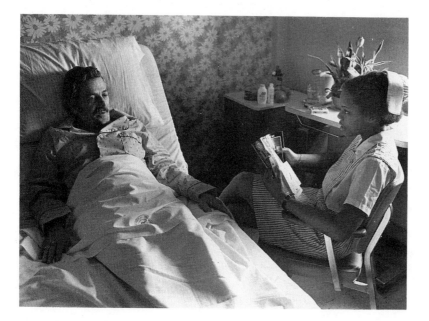

Do not let a single day go by without practicing some form of giving. . . . In some cases, give money, hot meals, clothes—certainly. But preferably, give the opportunity to work; give training that will enable the recipient to earn a living. Give basics: presence, time, attention. Give peace, strength, acceptance and joy to others.

Practice hospitality. Open up your home. Invite people who are not likely to be invited into a home. On occasion, allow [immigrants], travelers, etc. to use your home as a place of rest and refreshment.

Investigate carefully the human needs within your own family and your circle of friends and acquaintances, and decide what form of service or commitment you can make to meet some of those needs.

Consider the human needs within your immediate neighborhood: Those people who just moved next door, who may appreciate a few welcoming words. The family in your apartment building who can't afford a babysitter. The old lady whose eyesight is failing and who needs someone to read to her or to just sit and talk. The "latch-key kids" down the block whom you could befriend. A sick person for whom you might pick up groceries. Children with academic needs, whom you could tutor.

THE PATH OF SERVICE

The question "What can we do to alleviate suffering in the world?" evokes the almost instinctive response "Help others." Yet spiritual teachers for millennia have insisted that social and global transformation must start in one place: within. In the words of Sri Nisargadatta, a teacher of Advaita Vedanta, "If you are serious about the sufferings of mankind, you must perfect the only source of help you have—yourself."

If the marriage between spirituality and activism is to honor both the personal and the political, we need forms of work that enable us to relieve suffering while awakening to our true identity in the process. Fortunately, we can balance both sides of this human equation through the Eastern tradition of karma yoga, the practice of nonattached work performed for the purpose of service. In this ancient approach to growth, as we dedicate the fruits of our actions to the well-being of humanity, work becomes a vehicle to free ourselves of self-centeredness. Rather than withdrawing from the world to seek self-knowledge, practitioners of this path use work as a form of meditation, using their impeccable contribution to others to reduce egocentric motives within themselves.

"The practice of karma yoga allows a synergism between personal and transpersonal aims," says psychiatrist Roger Walsh. "To the extent that I relieve someone else's suffering, I grow also. The more I awaken in

If the building of the bridge does not enrich the awareness of those who work on it, then the bridge ought not to be built.

FRANTZ FANON

She had been so wicked that in all her life she had done only one good deed—given an onion to a beggar. So she went to hell. As she lay in torment she saw the onion, lowered down from heaven by an angel. She caught hold of it. He began to pull her up. The other damned saw what was happening and caught hold of it too. She was indignant and cried, "Let go—it's my onion," and as soon as she said, "My onion," the stalk broke and she fell back into the flames.

E. M. FORSTER

the process, the more I can effectively help others. Thus karma yoga takes us out into the world so we can go more deeply into ourselves. That encounter with ourselves, then, allows us to go into the world as a more effective agent of transformation. The necessity for this process continues as long as 'inside' and 'outside' are thought of as separate."

Serving others in the spirit of karma yoga essentially overturns our habitual distinction between helper and helped. Normally, we think that as helping agents we are bestowing benefits on disempowered others, when in fact we may be doing ourselves a favor. Because we are the prime beneficiary of our acts, says Swami Vivekananda, we owe a debt of gratitude to the people we help. In his classic text *Karma-Yoga,* he explains this apparent paradox:

> We must remember that it is a privilege to help others. Do not stand on a high pedestal and take five cents in your hand and say, "Here, my poor man!" But be grateful that the poor man is there, so that by making a gift to him you are able to help yourself. It is not the receiver who is blessed, but it is the giver. Be thankful that you are allowed to exercise your power of benevolence and mercy in the world.

In theory this sounds appealing—working with a higher motivation, freeing ourselves from addictions to status and recognition, finding a higher source of fulfillment from within. In practice, however, we may discover that lurking beneath our humanitarian persona are motives of a more adulterated nature. One of our subpersonalities may feel puffed up with self-righteousness. Another may crave recognition for deeds of valor performed under trying circumstances. Still another hidden self may judge the helped through a screen of middle-class prejudices or compare its spiritual progress with that of other people engaged in similar service activities.

"Compassionate action is a fierce, demanding, and revealing form of inner work, because we get to witness all our conditioning," says Mirabai Bush. "Just as sitting meditation gives insights into our mental processes, so does service reveal the many forms of desire, impatience, anger, and greed that usually operate on a subconscious level. When we come face to face with our inner motivations, we need to extend compassion to ourselves for the full humanity we discover—the high and the low. As our awareness deepens through service, we eventually drop our self-serving motivations and experience more frequent contact with the source of deep compassion."

Action should culminate in wisdom.

BHAGAVAD GITA

What we need is more people who specialize in the impossible.

THEODORE ROETHKE

In the process, says Roger Walsh, we also learn to drop our attachment to the successful outcome of our contributions. Focusing on work in the present moment, rather than the imagined achievement of a goal in the future, we give up tension, the fear of failure, and resentment at those who block us. "The result," Walsh writes in *Staying Alive: The Psychology of Human Survival*, "is greater equanimity, clarity and effectiveness, since our vision is now less distorted by egocentric desires and fears. Last, but hardly least, we also feel happier."

There must be more to life than having everything!

MAURICE SENDAK

We make a living by what we get,
but we make a life by what we give.

NORMAN MACESWAN

The topic of unselfish love has been placed on the agenda of history and is about to become its main business.

PITIRIM SOROKIN

GUIDELINES FOR GETTING STARTED

The path of compassionate action extends the natural caring acts we perform each day to a broader social arena. Mirabai Bush, co-author with Ram Dass of *Compassion in Action: Setting Out on the Path of Service*, offers the following guidelines, gleaned from years of experience, to those starting out on the path.

1. Reflect on what is calling you to action. Of all the suffering that surrounds us, what causes your heart to tremble? What wakes you in the middle of the night? What leaps off the newspaper page?

2. Think about what you would really love to do—not what you feel obligated to do—and find out whether you can relieve suffering in that way.

3. Look at your resources, skills, and talents and see what you have that could help. Include time, money, friends—and your imagination.

4. Investigate your motives. Don't judge them; just look at them dispassionately. Even though your motives are likely to be mixed, sorting through them will help you choose the most appropriate action.

5. Start small and learn as you go. Human-scale endeavors are more likely to teach us the basic lessons we need as we continue on our journey of awakening.

6. Start right where you are. If you look around, you'll find a perfect match for your talents. Don't overlook the obvious. Ask everyone you know.

7. Don't be sidetracked by fear, which is common at the beginning of any new venture, especially one that may reveal our vulnerability and limitations. The treasure guarded by the dragon called fear contains both the challenge of our so-called weaknesses and the reward of being more human-hearted. Slay the dragon.

Those who go through the purifying fires of compassionate action may serve as role models of a more mature human development in a society desperately in need of moral and spiritual guidance, Walsh points out. They also may help rebalance our current cultural models, which tout self-serving activity and self-gratification as the *summum bonum.* "Whether karma yoga ever becomes a significant force for cultural transformation and for the alleviation of world suffering might be one of the most important questions of our time," Walsh says. "Our very survival may well depend on how widespread that lifestyle and philosophy become."

8. Stay awake to suffering; become sensitive to others' pressing needs. If you can't find an opportunity to serve in your immediate environment, go to where the need is—inner cities, AIDS hospices, the Third World, a polluted beach in your area. Ask questions and listen with openness.

9. Decide whether you're drawn by community or whether you want to work alone or with a few friends. Most long-lasting change comes through people working together for a common cause, but some of that work—reflection, study, artistic expression—takes place alone. Whatever your choice, there is a need for your contribution.

10. When you commit to a course of action, allow for an unfolding process that will present you with surprises and mistakes. Accept it all as part of learning about ourselves, others, and our interconnectedness with the world.

11. Remember the deep and abiding truth that because we are all interconnected, when one of us suffers, we all suffer. Develop and deepen practices, such as meditation, prayer, walks in nature, or martial arts, that remind you of this truth.

12. Take care of yourself. Although the process of compassionate action is often enriching and joyful, simply being in the presence of suffering also can be stressful. Whatever you do to regenerate yourself—taking warm baths, playing volleyball, or listening to good music—will give you endurance.

13. Take the leap. Once you have reflected on who you are, what is calling you, and how you might best respond—then just do it. The first step may be the hardest, but guidance and direction will be revealed as you continue on your journey.

Every man must decide whether he will walk in the light of creative altruism or the darkness of destructive selfishness. This is the judgment. Life's most persistent and urgent question is, What are you doing for others?

MARTIN LUTHER KING, JR.

I slept and dreamt that life was joy.
I awoke and saw that life was service.
I acted and behold, service was joy.

RABINDRANATH TAGORE

CREATIVE ALTRUISM

The idea that unselfish love might contribute to the regeneration of society sounds a bit utopian, like the idealistic utterance of someone untested in the marketplace of life. Yet that hard-boiled marketplace, supposedly governed by inexorable laws of economic self-interest, recently has witnessed the emergence of a new breed of social entrepreneurs. Inspired by the spirit of creative altruism—service rooted in a vision of social transformation—these people create grass-roots, often volunteer-based solutions to community problems, such as homelessness, hunger, teenage pregnancy, or drug and alcohol addiction.

"Creative altruists apply caring, imagination, and enterprise to unmet needs in their communities," says Tom Hurley, director of the Altruistic Spirit Program at the Institute of Noetic Sciences in Sausalito, California. "Sometimes facing significant opposition or inertia, they translate their visions of a more human society into practical projects that empower people to experience dignity, initiative, and increased self-esteem."

Established in 1987, the Altruistic Spirit Program sponsors research and educational projects that explore the nature of creative altruism. The program was inspired by Harvard sociologist Pitirim Sorokin, who considered the cultivation of unselfish love as the one antidote to the materialistic trends of Western civilization. Each year the Altruistic Spirit Program honors outstanding altruists whose contributions to humanity demonstrate the transformative power of compassion.

For example, while distributing meal tickets at a soup kitchen in New York City, Guy Polhemus discovered that the homeless support themselves by collecting empty cans and bottles and redeeming them for nickel deposits. Perceiving a social need and mobilizing the power of creative imagination, he used his own money to found WE CAN, a recycling and redemption center staffed entirely by homeless men and women. The center not only contributes to a sustainable economy through recycling but also provides the homeless with a sense of dignity and esteem.

Celeste Tate of Las Vegas started Gleaners, a food bank that collects unsold food from grocery stores and distributes it in Gleaners' own supermarkets. Customers do not have their self-worth assaulted by receiving handouts; they either pay two dollars a bag for groceries or donate their time to the supermarket. The concept has proved so successful that it has spawned a network of 192 stores across the country.

According to Hurley, these and numerous other examples illustrate that creative altruism is not an aberration of human nature, but a spon-

The desire to serve others is the highest impulse of the human heart and the rewards of such service are beyond measure. If you wish to taste this joy, then just do it. Just take one step. . . . You will see that the tyranny of self-concern, worry, and trivial pursuits can be released from your life with that single step. It doesn't really matter what you do, it only matters that you do it.

GANGA STONE

A man's true wealth is the good he does in this world.

MOHAMMED

taneous and natural expression of our fundamental relatedness. "Our society misunderstands the altruistic impulse, equating it with a tight-lipped attitude of self-sacrifice," he says. "If we subscribe to a model that sees human beings as essentially self-interested, then altruism clearly calls for self-denial. But if we revision human nature to include our innate capacity for empathy, then acting on behalf of others leads to self-fulfillment, rather than personal privation."

As the altruistic spirit awakens in the collective psyche, more and more people are volunteering their services to nonprofit community organizations that focus on needs not met by government or the business sector. These people, experiencing the poverty of abundance, are redefining success as the expression of inner-directed values in the service of their communities, write John and Eleanor Raynolds in *Beyond Success*. Working on hot lines in mental health clinics, visiting residents in nursing homes, or helping prisoners study for high school degrees, they are looking for a calling in life, rather than conventional career satisfaction.

The altruistic spirit benefits people of all ages, the Raynoldses point out. Service work helps young people eager to harness their idealistic energy through involvement in the affairs of the world. Volunteer work can help middle-aged people rejuvenate stale careers, explore untried aspects of themselves, push themselves to new levels of achievement, and ultimately find new direction in their lives. For older people, service work provides a sense of belonging and usefulness to others that infuses life with vitality and robust health.

"Helping others and helping ourselves are just different ways of doing the same thing," they write. "Modern life has become so fragmented and compartmentalized that it is sometimes hard to see the connectedness, but when we can get past the trees to a broad view of the forest, we understand that when we help someone learn to read, enjoy an afternoon outing, experience the comfort of a hot meal and a safe place to sleep, we are also helping ourselves."

THE BENEFITS OF CARING

In his insightful and helpful book *On Caring,* philosopher Milton Mayeroff describes how caring for others leads to self-actualization. While others make this claim—often rhapsodizing about this potential of the human spirit—Mayeroff shows with remarkable simplicity and directness how we become more ourselves through tending to the needs of others. Here, then, are some of the benefits of caring as adapted from his book:

And now abideth faith, hope, charity, these three; but the greatest of these is charity.

CORINTHIANS 13:13

It is high time the ideal of success should be replaced with the ideal of service.

ALBERT EINSTEIN

In a value-driven economy, the human spirit knows no limits.

ANITA RODDICK
FOUNDER OF THE BODY
SHOP INTERNATIONAL

Blessed is he who has found his work. Let him ask no other blessedness.

THOMAS CARLYLE

The awakening of our essential humanity. Caring requires human-hearted qualities, such as patience, honesty, trust, humility, and courage. In caring for others, we actualize these qualities that otherwise might remain in latency.

Basic certainty. When caring becomes the primary commitment of our lives, our habitual state of rootlessness comes to an end, and we find ourselves in place in the world, steadied and centered in daily living. From this position of basic certainty, we can withstand the discordant experiences of day-to-day living with strength and equanimity.

A sense of purpose. "Through finding and helping to develop my appropriate others, I discover and create the meaning of my life. And in caring for my appropriate others, in being in-place, I live the meaning of my life."

The feeling of "enoughness" in life. We no longer project our fulfillment into the future, because we find a richness of meaning in the present moment. "And when present living is enough, I experience myself as being enough."

Autonomy. Caring frees us from certain ways of living, widespread in our society, that are hostile to growth. "I am free of experiencing life as a race in which I am concerned with how I compare with others: whether they are ahead of me; whether I am catching up to them, maintaining my distance from them, or falling behind them. . . . Also I am free of experiencing life as a *market place* in which I see myself and others as commodities to be sold, and try to make myself into the package that happens to be in demand at a particular time."

Faith. As a basic trust in life, faith enables us to walk with confidence into the unknown, secure in the knowledge of life's essentially intelligible nature.

Gratitude. "I am thankful for the opportunity and the capacity to give of myself. Caring becomes my way of thanking for what I have received; I thank by caring all the more for my appropriate others and the conditions of their existence."

THE COMPASSIONATE CORPORATION

Imagine a time in the future in which people go into business to express their altruistic impulses through the vehicle of socially responsible work. In this scenario, companies provide humane workplaces in which people can actualize themselves. Inspired by a vision of social transformation, corporations and their employees work not only to profit themselves but also their immediate communities, the nation, developing nations in the Third World, and ultimately the Earth itself. If this vision contradicts sound business thinking, consider these companies as harbingers of the *possible company*:

- The Body Shop, a chain of more than three hundred franchised outlets that sells natural cosmetics in thirty-four countries, has a strong commitment to community service and nonexploitative trade with Third World countries. The Body Shop often purchases ingredients for products from local communities in developing countries and pays First World prices for these resources, often four times the rate offered by other purchasers. According to founder Anita Roddick, franchisees are expected to participate in community projects, such as AIDS programs or battered women's shelters—on company time.
- Ben & Jerry's Homemade (Ice Cream), Inc., often touted as the prototype of a humanely run, socially responsible business, contributes

Almost anything you do will seem insignificant, but it is very important that you do it.

MAHATMA GANDHI

The center of human nature is rooted in ten thousand ordinary acts of kindness that define our days.

STEPHEN JAY GOULD

7.5 percent of its pre-tax profits to projects dedicated to social change. For example, the company supports 1% For Peace, an organization working to redirect 1 percent of the U.S. military budget to peace-promoting activities. It also invests in South Shore Bank, which finances small minority-owned businesses and low-income housing in Chicago's poorest neighborhoods. On the home front, Ben & Jerry's keeps employees happy by fostering an open, participatory workplace, providing free counseling to employees on a confidential basis and limiting the wage spread to a fixed ratio between the lowest and highest salaries.

The emerging new paradigm, then, views businesspeople not as greedy, self-interested despoilers of the Earth but as planetary citizens with responsibilities that transcend the traditional, more narrow concerns of commerce.

"The business of business is changing," according to Willis Harman, a founding member of the World Business Academy, an international network of business executives and entrepreneurs who use their skills and resources to create a positive future for the planet. "As a new corporate ethic emerges, companies will not promote conspicuous consumption, economic growth for its own sake, and profitability divorced from its social consequences. Assuming responsibility for the well-being of the whole, they will make decisions based on ecological sensitivity, the sustainability of natural resources, and the welfare of the world's citizens."

With its transnational influence, business has become the dominant institution on the planet, Harman says. Increased power brings responsibility, yet until recently business has lacked a guiding ethic equal to the task of planetary stewardship, in part because the assumptions under which it operates are proving inadequate in the world marketplace.

"The modern economic system and its component parts, such as the corporation, are constructed on the basis of a picture of reality which emphasizes the separateness of things and the competitive struggle for existence," write Harman and John Hormann in *Creative Work: The Constructive Role of Business in a Transforming Society*. "Yet . . . the culture appears to be shifting to a picture emphasizing wholeness and relationship." Operating from this whole-systems perspective, in which the planet becomes the context of business decisions, the new corporation has three goals: to provide fulfilling work for its personnel; to conduct activities in the best interest of the planet; and to achieve the first two goals so well that profit automatically follows.

It was all done by Christ and Gandhi and St. Francis of Assisi and Dr. King. They did it all. We don't have to think about new ideas; we just have to implement what they said, just get the work done.

CESAR CHAVEZ

When I do not know who I am, I serve you.
When I know who I am, I am you.

INDIAN PROVERB

Given this orientation, philanthropy plays an important but secondary role in the overall contribution business makes to society, says Ben Cohen, co-founder of Ben and Jerry's. "Our major impact in transforming society comes from integrating a concern for the community into as many of our day-to-day business decisions and transactions as possible," he argues. "This means buying from suppliers with a social mission, using ingredients that contribute to a sustainable world, and investing funds and human resources in ways that benefit the community. Today we're able to integrate our two 'bottom lines'—profit and social service—in an increasing percentage of our activities, but our long-term goal is to do this 100 percent of the time."

In the past, people motivated by the service ethic have steered clear of corporate life because of its less-than-altruistic mindset, Cohen observes. But in the future, as the concerns of business and human services merge in the compassionate corporation, more people will choose the path of business to manifest their altruistic impulses. Evolving into a force for social transformation, business will support measures that protect the environment, empower the disadvantaged segments of society, and make the workplace more humane.

"In today's world, despite conventional thinking, it's possible to pursue your business dreams without sacrificing your inmost values," Cohen asserts. "It's also necessary. This calls for doing business in non-traditional ways, taking risks not just to increase profit, but to increase your business's contribution to the community."

ENGAGED BUDDHISM

Just as businesspeople are becoming engaged in contemporary social affairs typically considered outside their bailiwick, so are Buddhists allying themselves with organizations that fight hunger, poverty, and oppression in the world. To these modern peace workers, a sense of life's interconnectedness awakens a sense of social responsibility.

Such notions as engaged Buddhism initially may strike us as contradictory, given the religion's otherworldly or escapist reputation in the West. But according to Fred Eppsteiner, editor of *The Path of Compassion*, the principles and even some of the techniques of an engaged Buddhism have remained latent in the tradition since its inception. "Qualities that were inhibited in pre-modern Asian settings can now be actualized through Buddhism's exposure to the West, where ethical sensitivity, social activism, and egalitarianism are emphasized."

Rabbi Moshe Leib of Sassov said: How to love men is something I learned from a peasant. He was sitting in an inn along with other peasants, drinking. For a long time he was silent as all the rest, but when he was moved by the wine, he asked one of the men seated beside him: "Tell me, do you love me or don't you love me?" The other replied: "I love you very much." But the first peasant replied: "You say that you love me, but you do not know what I need. If you really loved me you would know." The other had not a word to say to this, and the peasant who had put the question fell silent again. But I understood. To know the needs of men and to bear the burden of their sorrow—that is the true love of men.

MARTIN BUBER

291

The purpose of life is a life of purpose.

Robert Byrne

There's a way to oppose and still be beyond opposition. There's a way to express viewpoints but remain outside the destructive clash of opinion. There's a way to call for justice but not get lost in constantly judging. And there is harmony beneath discord. From such a perspective we're more able to recognize what's appropriate. When an action is appropriate, when it's in the Way of Things, it has great power, the power inherent in the Way.

Ram Dass and
Paul Gorman

The Order of Interbeing, developed by Vietnamese Buddhist monks during the Vietnam War, exemplifies this new religious sensibility. Members of the order vow to observe its fourteen precepts, which apply the contemplative concerns of Buddhism—the cultivation of mindfulness, ethical behavior, and equanimity—to what are considered worldly problems, such as political repression, social injustice, and widespread physical misery.

The following precepts, with their explicit call for an activist spirituality, appear to extend the awareness of suffering from the spiritual and psychological realms to the social and economic arenas:

- Do not avoid contact with suffering or close your eyes before suffering. Do not lose awareness of the existence of suffering in the life of the world. Find ways to be with those who are suffering by all means, including personal contact and visits, images, sound. By such means, awaken yourself and others to the reality of suffering in the world.
- Do not accumulate wealth while millions are hungry. Do not take as the aim of your life fame, profit, or sensual pleasure. Live simply and share time, energy, and material resources with those who are in need.
- Always speak truthfully and constructively. Have the courage to speak out about situations of injustice, even when doing so may threaten your own safety.
- Do not live with a vocation that is harmful to humans and nature. Do not invest in companies that deprive others of their chance to life. Select a vocation which helps realize your ideal of compassion.
- Do not kill. Do not let others kill. Find whatever means possible to protect life and to prevent war.
- Possess nothing that should belong to others. Respect the property of others but prevent others from enriching themselves from human suffering or the suffering of other beings.

When integrated into Western life, says Buddhist teacher Thich Nhat Hanh, these principles have the potential of healing our Earth, which is like a small boat in danger of sinking. Who among its passengers will inspire us to act with confidence and equanimity? In *The Path of Compassion,* he gives this answer:

The Mahayana Buddhist sutras tell us that you are that person. If you are yourself, if you are your best, then you are that person. Only with such a person—calm, lucid, aware—will our situation improve. I wish you good luck. Please be yourself. Please be that person.

RESOURCES

Recommended Reading

How Can I Help?, Ram Dass and Paul Gorman (Alfred A. Knopf, 1985). Gives guidance and inspiration in how to practice compassionate action in everyday life.

The Path of Compassion, Fred Eppsteiner, editor (Parallax Press, 1985). A collection of writings on socially engaged Buddhism by teachers and commentators, such as the Dalai Lama, Joanna Macy, Thich Nhat Hanh, Gary Snyder, Robert Aiken, and Charlene Spretnak.

Staying Alive: The Psychology of Human Survival, Roger Walsh (New Science Library, 1984). Discusses karma yoga as a strategy to fight planetary problems, such as pollution, nuclear weaponry, and ecological imbalance.

Despair and Personal Power in the Nuclear Age, Joanna Macy (New Society Publishers, 1983). Shows how to overcome apathy, fear, and powerlessness to become an effective agent of planetary healing.

In the Footsteps of Gandhi, Catherine Ingram (Parallax Press, 1990). Conversations with spiritual social activists, such as Joan Baez, Ram Dass, Cesar Chavez, Gary Snyder, and Joanna Macy.

Gandhi's Seven Steps to Global Change, Guy de Mallac (Ocean Tree Books, 1989). A little book that is full of practical suggestions for making the world more equitable and peaceful.

Karma-Yoga, Swami Vivekananda (Ramakrishna-Vivekananda Center, 1955). A spiritual classic that explains theoretical and practical aspects of a life of service.

The Healthy Company, Robert Rosen (Jeremy P. Tarcher, 1991). Offers a fresh vision of the steps that managers and their companies can take to become more vibrant, healthy, and profitable.

Creative Work: The Constructive Role of Business in a Transforming Society, Willis Harman and John Hormann (Knowledge Systems, 1990). Explores how social responsibility is becoming a central concern of modern corporations.

Beyond Success, John Raynolds and Eleanor Raynolds (MasterMedia Limited, 1988). Shows how volunteer service can make life more meaningful.

How to Make the World a Better Place: A Guide to Doing Good, Jeffrey Hollender (William Morrow, 1990). Gives more than one hundred quick and easy actions to effect positive social change.

Compassion in Action: Setting Out on the Path of Service, Ram Dass and Mirabai Bush (Bell Tower, 1991). The authors give autobiographical reflections and practical suggestions for spiritual social activism.

Publications

Volunteer! A guidebook to international projects from the Commission on Voluntary Service and Action, Box 347, Newton, KS 67114.

Sojourners: Faith, Politics and Culture (Box 29272, Washington, DC 20017; 202-636-3637, $27/year, 10 issues). This magazine of Christian social action covers spiritually based environmentalism, recovery and addiction, violence in South Africa, responses to AIDS, and community organizing among Native Americans.

Friends Journal: Quaker Thought and Life Today (1501 Cherry Street, Philadelphia, PA 19102-1497; 215-241-7277, $18/year). Reports on global peace, human rights, environmental awareness, faith-based action, and news of projects needing volunteers.

Buddhist Peace Fellowship (P.O. Box 4650, Berkeley, CA 94704; 415-525-8596, $25/year). This newsletter covers the peace movement from a Buddhist perspective.

Peace Review (2439 Birch Street, Suite 8, Palo Alto, CA 94306; 415-328-5477, $24/year, quarterly). This international publication covers such topics as the threat of nuclear war, human rights, peace education, and feminism as a force for peace in conflict-ridden nations.

Tapes and Workshops

The *Hanuman Foundation Tape Library catalog* (P.O. Box 2320, Delray Beach, FL 33447; 407-272-9165) lists audio- and videotapes of Ram Dass's talks on spirituality and compassionate action, along with his workshop and retreat schedules.

New Generation Press (48 North Third Street, Emmaus, PA 18049; 215-967-6656), runs regeneration workshops for community and church groups that teach innovative approaches to agriculture, local sustainability, and health care. The newsletter *New Generation News* ($12/ year) profiles many inspiring projects.

The *Snow Lion Publications Newsletter and Catalog* (P.O. Box 6483, Ithaca, NY 14851; 800-950-0313) keeps readers posted on appearances and books by the Dalai Lama and other leading Tibetan Buddhists.

Reaching Out, hosted by Ram Dass. An innovative television course that motivates participants to practice compassionate service in their own lives and communities. Information: Choice Point, 6116 Merced, #165, Oakland, CA 94611.

CHAPTER 15

THE SHADOW
Embracing Our Totality

In the famous story *The Strange Case of Dr. Jekyll and Mr. Hyde,* Robert Louis Stevenson dramatically depicts how the forces of light and darkness struggle for supremacy on the battlefield of the human heart. This cautionary tale, which illustrates how the unacknowledged dark side of human nature can barbarize and eventually destroy the civilized side, serves as a warning to those who believe we can have pleasure without pain, good without evil, and light without shadow. Such naive dualism, the story suggests, only serves to contaminate our personal relationships, our work life, and, ultimately, our spiritual endeavors.

In the story, Dr. Henry Jekyll, a distinguished scientist, becomes increasingly aware of powerful desires and impulses that run counter to his respectable public image. Concluding that he has a dual nature, Jekyll produces a drug that enables him to separate the antagonistic personalities. By taking the drug, he transforms into Edward Hyde, a small, hateful, and deformed man incapable of human feeling. As Hyde, "I knew myself to be more wicked, tenfold more wicked, sold a slave to my original evil; and the thought, in that moment, braced and delighted me like wine."

At first Hyde pursues "undignified pleasures," but as his influence over the Jekyll personality grows, the scientist's veneer of civilized behavior cracks under an onslaught of monstrous impulses he is impotent to

A cover of darkness, separation, and confusion are necessary prerequisites for the eventual rebirth of a lost and wandering soul.

NOR HALL

fight. When Hyde murders one of Jekyll's colleagues "with a transport of glee," the scientist lives in such horror of his other self that he eventually takes his own life.

This story, written more than a century ago, still mesmerizes readers because in its portrayal of the archetypal struggle between light and darkness, we glimpse intimations of a similar process at work in our own lives. "Each of us contains both a Dr. Jekyll and a Mr. Hyde, a more pleasant persona for everyday wear and a hiding, nighttime self that remains hushed up much of the time," write Connie Zweig and Jeremiah Abrams in *Meeting the Shadow: The Hidden Power of the Dark Side of Human Nature.* "Negative emotions and behaviors—rage, jealousy, shame, lying, resentment, lust, greed, suicidal and murderous tendencies—lie concealed just beneath the surface, masked by our more proper selves. Known together in psychology as the personal shadow, it remains untamed, unexplored territory to most of us."

ENCOUNTERING THE SHADOW

The shadow refers to the dark, feared, unwanted side of our personality that does not fit with the ideal image we hold of ourselves, explains John A. Sanford, an Episcopal priest and Jungian analyst, in *Evil: The Shadow Side of Reality.* Conditioned by parents, religious teachers, educators, and peers, we identify with ideal personality traits, such as politeness, kindness, generosity, and forgiveness. At the same time, we banish into the unconscious those qualities that contradict the mask of civility we have adopted. Thus in attempting to conform to our ideal, we disown selfishness, anger, vindictiveness, and uncontrolled sexual urges.

"The rejected qualities do not cease to exist simply because they have been denied direct expression," Sanford writes. "Instead, they form the secondary personality that psychology calls the Shadow." We can recognize this alter ego in our dreams as a same-sex figure who embodies qualities the conscious ego deems inferior, much as Hyde carries Jekyll's aggressive, mean-spirited impulses. We also can recognize the shadow through the excessive anger, loathing, or judgmentalness we heap on people because of behavior that strikes us as distasteful or morally reprehensible.

For example, a woman raised in a puritanical home in which her natural sensuality was denied expression may witness another woman's provocative behavior at a dinner party and self-righteously proclaim, "How disgusting! I could never imagine acting in such an obviously lewd,

If a pickpocket meets a Holy Man, he will see only his pockets.

HARI DASS

If a man has beheld evil, he may know that it was shown to him in order that he learn his own guilt and repent; for what is shown to him is also within him.

BAAL SHEM TOV

immoral fashion." In this case, the sexually repressed woman experiences her forbidden, inferior "other" through a mirroring process psychologists call projection. Inwardly split and denied access to her own desires, she unconsciously projects this unacceptable part of herself into the outer world, where it is snagged by someone who then carries her disowned energies. Both attracted and repelled at the same time, the woman judges her supposed adversary with the same repugnance she inflicts on her rejected self.

We blame, criticize, or revenge ourselves on someone when the shadow carries a rejected, negative attribute, writes Jungian analyst M. Esther Harding. But when the projected quality is positive, we may admire, love, envy, or even hate the person for positive attributes we have not developed. In *The 'I' and the 'Not-I'* Harding describes how we also disown parts of our light-bearing nature:

> If we do not live up to our own potential, the positive qualities will be repressed into the shadow, and we will have . . . a bright shadow instead of a dark one. When we project this bright shadow onto someone else, the person who carries the projection will seem to us to be "always right," able to do easily and well things that are difficult for us, and so on. We burden him with our expectations of his abilities instead of acquiring for ourselves the possibilities of achievement which are potentially present in us. A person who is content to take an inferior position, who prefers to have an easy job rather than to buckle down and develop himself and his work, and who then admires, and overadmires, someone else who does things well, has projected his bright shadow onto his neighbor.

The Collective Shadow

Besides projecting the shadow onto individuals, we also project it on a collective level, transforming minority groups, religious groups, cultures, and nations into scapegoats and enemies. Thus through the agency of projection, the Nazis with their ego ideal of Aryan superiority slaughtered Jews, gypsies, homosexuals, and other minority groups that lived out the so-called master race's socially disowned parts. In a similar fashion, Moslems project the figure of Satan onto the United States; white supremacists project it onto peoples of color; and middle-class Americans find its rejected, despised image in the hordes of homeless people who wander our cities.

Seen from this perspective, war involves projecting the shadow onto a group, dehumanizing the perceived enemy, then systematically venting destructive impulses in an attempt to find an *ultimate solution* to our own

If a man wishes to be sure of the road he treads on, he must close his eyes and walk in the dark.

St. John of the Cross

Who never ate his bread with tears,
Who never sat weeping on his bed
During care-ridden nights
Knows you not, your heavenly powers.

Johann Wolfgang von Goethe

A Poison Tree

I was angry with my friend;
I told my wrath, my wrath
did end.
I was angry with my foe;
I told it not, my wrath did
grow.
And I watered it in fears,
Night and morning with my
tears.
And I sunned it with smiles,
And with soft deceitful wiles.
And it grew both day and
night,
Till it bore an apple bright.
And my foe beheld it shine,
And he knew that it was
mine.
And into my garden stole,
When the night had veil'd the
pole.
In the morning glad I see;
My foe outstretched beneath
the tree.

WILLIAM BLAKE

inferior elements. To find peace in the outer world, psychologists argue, we must reverse this process by re-owning our shadow and reconciling ourselves with the inner adversary we have so unmercifully reviled.

"The heroes and leaders toward peace in our time will be those men and women who have the courage to plunge into the darkness at the bottom of the personal and the corporate psyche and face the enemy within," writes philosopher Sam Keen in *Faces of the Enemy: Reflections of the Hostile Imagination*. "Depth psychology has presented us with the undeniable wisdom that the enemy is constructed from denied aspects of the self. Therefore, the radical commandment 'Love your enemy as yourself' points the way toward both self-knowledge and peace."

Turning the mirror around and grappling with our shadow reduces the distance between our idealized and real selves. The encounter also can empower us in our personal relationships, our careers, and our creative lives. As Sanford points out, re-owned anger can make us stronger and more resolute in our actions. Re-owning the inner thief can help protect us from being duped by Machiavellian people in the business world. By re-owning our feeling, power, and sexuality in midlife, we add renewed creative vitality to our lives.

Ultimately, embracing the dark side helps us move toward wholeness on the path Carl Jung called individuation. "There is no light without shadow and no psychic wholeness without imperfection," he writes in *Psychology and Alchemy*. "To round itself out, life calls not for perfection but for completeness; and for this the 'thorn in the flesh' is needed, the suffering of defects without which there is no progress and no ascent."

In *The Way of Transformation*, Jungian analyst Jolande Jacobi comments on the necessity of befriending the weak and despised elements within us: "For everything repressed, inferior, immoral, even pathological can, God willing, become the matrix for a renewal, for a rebirth on a higher level. In the negative and evil may be hidden the germs of a transformation into the positive and good; they can be the starting point for a reversal and purification."

HOW TO RECOGNIZE YOUR SHADOW

"Every disowned aspect of ourselves represents a piece of God, no matter how primitive or heinous it may look to our rational minds," says psychologist Hal Stone, co-author of *Embracing Ourselves*. "Whenever we meet someone who carries our shadow energies and regard that person as our teacher rather than our adversary, we can begin the work of reclaiming our repressed wholeness."

Stone offers the following guidelines for recognizing and working with the shadow:

1. Examine who in your immediate environment "pushes your buttons." Whom do you judge or hate? Whom do you overvalue? For instance, do you put someone on a pedestal because of financial success, wisdom, or authority that you consider unattainable in your own life?

2. Recognizing these people as your teachers, ask, "What qualities within these people either excessively repel or attract me?" Identifying these traits opens the door to your disowned selves.

3. Next, investigate what caused you to reject these qualities. Was your father an aggressive, overbearing tyrant who caused you to become a passive people-pleaser who disowns negative energies? Was your mother impersonal and cold, requiring you to become personal and caring all the time? Were your parents money-driven and highly competitive, causing you to develop a loving, spiritual identity that rejects money altogether?

4. Pay attention to the images that emerge in your dreams and fantasy life. For example, disowned selves in dreams may appear as thieves or criminals trying to break into your house or ferocious animals chasing you. Once you begin embracing these alien selves on a conscious level, the unconscious will cooperate with your efforts by presenting friendlier, less menacing images to work with.

5. Discover where in your life you're being victimized. If you disown aggression, for example, inevitably you'll attract mean, aggressive people who direct hostile energy your way. Once you re-own this shadow energy and you no longer block the expression of your natural self-protective impulses, you'll stop being victimized by projected energy returning in harmful ways.

6. Examine whether you're carrying long-standing, unconscious negative feelings for family members that somehow feel "normal" after a lifetime of familiarity. Look unflinchingly at your relationships with parents, children, brothers, and sisters—any intimate family members you take for granted who may carry a disowned self.

7. Once you uncover a disowned self, you can open up lines of communication with it by doing journal work. Let's say that you want to enter into a dialogue with your vulnerable self. Use your dominant hand to take the part of your aware ego and the nondominant hand to express your weaker, disowned self. You also can use movement work and artwork to contact the shadow aspects of your personality.

Like the moon, life surely has a side permanently turned away from us which is not its counterpart but its complement toward perfection, toward consummation, toward the really sound and full sphere and orb of being.

RAINER MARIA RILKE

Nothing burns in hell but the self.

THEOLOGIA GERMANICA

OWNING THE SHADOW

If thou has not seen the devil, look at thine own self.

RUMI

Every individual existence is brought into rhythm by a pendulum to which the heart gives type and name. There is a time for expanding and a time for contraction; one provokes the other and the other calls for the return of the first. . . . Never are we nearer the Light than when the darkness is deepest.

SWAMI VIVEKANANDA

As *The Strange Case of Dr. Jekyll and Mr. Hyde* makes abundantly clear, neither repressing nor living out the shadow solves the problem of dealing with our dark side, for in both cases the personality remains unintegrated. To heal our inner divisions, Carl Jung counsels that we consciously bear the tension of the opposites, embracing the light and dark, the saint and sinner, the good citizen and criminal within our own hearts. This complex, ongoing struggle, he says, requires that we accept the shadow, familiarize ourselves with its qualities and intentions, and then enter into unavoidably long and difficult negotiations with it. This process, called shadow-work by Zweig and Abrams, calls for great commitment, vigilance, and honesty.

"The aim of meeting the shadow is to develop an ongoing relationship with it, to expand our sense of self by balancing the one-sidedness of our conscious attitudes with our unconscious depths," they write in *Meeting the Shadow*. "A right relationship with the shadow offers us a great gift: to lead us back to our buried potentials."

Besides leading to more genuine self-acceptance, Zweig and Abrams say, shadow-work helps defuse the negative emotions that erupt unexpectedly in our daily encounters. It liberates us from the paralyzing guilt we inflict on ourselves for harboring weak, shameful thoughts and feelings. By recognizing the projections that shape our opinions of others, we can heal our relationships through honest self-examination and direct communication. And because, in this way, we add less of our personal darkness to the collective shadow, we contribute in some small but significant way to world peace.

What Zweig and Abrams call "shadow-work" poet Robert Bly calls "eating the shadow," a slow process by which we repossess the energy and power that rightfully belong to us. In *A Little Book on the Human Shadow*, he outlines the five stages involved in exiling, hunting, and eventually retrieving the shadow.

For example, in growing up a young boy may project his interior witch, the destructive, negative side of the unconscious, onto his mother. When he matures and marries, he transfers this projection onto his wife, where it may remain in this first stage for a number of years. In the next stage, called rattling by Jungian analyst Marie-Louise von Franz, the man notices an inconsistency between what he perceives as his wife's witchy persona and other, more generous and loving qualities that don't fit the projection. In the third stage, sensing that his projection is coming unglued, the husband attempts to repair the mask, unconsciously hoping to avoid responsibility for creating his wife's unpalatable behavior.

In the next stage the mask slips, and the husband experiences a sensation of diminishment in his life. Having projected his strong warrior energies onto an external woman who carries them for him, he may be overly empathic and gentle but unable to act with decisiveness in the world. In the final stage, the husband consciously begins what Bly calls eating the shadow, a process that doesn't happen once but hundreds of times. Here are some of Bly's suggestions for retrieving a projection:

> In daily life one might suggest making the sense of smell, taste, touch, and hearing more acute, . . . visiting primitive tribes, playing music, creating frightening figures in clay, playing the drum, being alone for a month, regarding yourself as a genial criminal. A woman might try being a patriarch at odd times of the day, to see how she likes it, but it has to be playful. A man might try being a witch at odd times of the day, and see how it feels, but it has to be done playfully. He might develop a witch laugh and tell fairy stories, as the woman might develop a giant laugh and tell fairy stories.

While techniques abound in retrieving our darker energies, Jungian analyst James Hillman suggests that curing the shadow is essentially a problem of love. "How far can our love extend to the broken and ruined parts of ourselves, the disgusting and perverse?" he asks in *Insearch: Psychology and Religion.* "How much charity and compassion have we for our own weakness and sickness? How far can we build an inner society on the principle of love, allowing a place for everyone?"

To build this inner society, he concludes, we must learn to laugh at our folly, which is Everyman's. When we yoke the moral recognition of our need to change to a "loving, laughing acceptance" of our inferior parts, we decrease the resistance between the conscious and unconscious minds, aiding in the redemption of our darker energies.

DRAWING THE SHADOW

We can use guided visualization to contact our hidden selves, then make these images conscious through drawing, according to Los Angeles artist Linda Jacobson. These images may include imaginary characters, dream personalities, or people from daily life who symbolize the uncomfortable, unattractive parts of ourselves we generally prefer not to see. The following exercise, adapted from Jacobson's essay in *Meeting the Shadow: The Hidden Power of the Dark Side of Human Nature,* provides a safe way of recognizing and incorporating some of our hidden qualities.

Every part of our personality that we do not love will become hostile to us.

ROBERT BLY

Jung said the truth of the matter is that the shadow is ninety percent gold. Whatever has been repressed holds a tremendous amount of energy, with a great positive potential. So the shadow, no matter how troublesome it may be, is not intrinsically evil. The ego, in its refusal of insight and its refusal to accept the entire personality, contributes much more to evil than the shadow.

JOHN A. SANFORD

---☆---

I would rather be whole than good.

    C. G. JUNG

If we could read the secret history of our enemies, we should find in each man's life sorrow and suffering enough to disarm all hostility.

    HENRY WADSWORTH LONGFELLOW

1. Visualize yourself in a beautiful garden, filled with brightly colored flowers and plants. In this sacred garden, which evokes feelings of safety and power, you feel fulfilled, full of a radiant light.

2. In the midst of your reverie, a shadow figure appears in the garden. Opposite to you in every way, this person pushes all your buttons and upsets you terribly. Is he or she a dream figure, someone you know, or a composite of different characters? Study this figure's features carefully. What colors and moods surround him or her? Do you feel anger, fear, awe, hatred, respect, love, or disgust?

3. Looking more deeply, ask yourself, "Why is this person so offensive to me?" What does the person's voice sound like? Is this person critical, selfish, cruel, timid, sexy, or arrogant?

4. Take a moment to fully experience this shadow figure. Let your feelings permeate every cell of your body so that this being is clear in your mind. Then, with your eyes closed, begin to draw your feelings. When you are ready, slowly open your eyes and continue your drawing for fifteen minutes.

5. Using materials that are quick and easy to use, such as oil or chalk pastels, spontaneously allow images to surface without critical editing of your inner vision. As you draw either abstractly or representationally, focus more on emotional expression than on the formal concerns of art. The simple act of drawing is healing, because now you have a conscious image of your shadow to work with.

6. If a frightening image appears, such as an abused victim or an angry tyrant, try to keep drawing. Painful feelings may offer the greatest opportunity for renewal and can be used as raw creative energy.

7. From your initial drawings, you may want to develop a series of images of your shadow. The images and colors may change, taking many forms, as they reflect the healing process.

---☆---

Other exercises for working with the shadow include:

- making a drawing that integrates your shadow into the rest of your persona.
- entering into a written dialogue with your shadow drawing to find out what it needs.
- drawing yourself from the shadow's point of view.

THE SHADOW IN SPIRITUAL LIFE

While navigating the turbulent waters of midlife, W. Brugh Joy, a physician turned healer, had a life-transforming nightmare that shattered forever his understanding of spiritual life. In the dream, he drove into a well-lighted service station to get some gasoline for his car. After a friendly old man pumped the gas, he looked into his rear-view mirror and discovered that a member of a Hell's Angels motorcycle gang was sitting in the back seat. Recognizing the intruder as Evil Incarnate, he recoiled in horror and awakened screaming.

Until this dream, Joy had been pursuing the traditional spiritual path, with its insistence that by cleaving to God as light, love, and compassion, the seeker can avoid the problem of evil simply by transcending what sages and saints call the world. Following this dream and other experiences, he expanded his vision to include both poles of existence—the positive, light-giving side and the negative, chaotic side—as divine elements operating within his psyche.

"Whatever spiritual forces are, they have a dark side," Joy writes in *Avalanche: Heretical Reflections on the Dark and the Light.* "While there may be only one God, God has many faces. Christ and Lucifer are twin rays. . . . Cain and Abel are two aspects of the same energy . . . and I had very dark aspects that were not yet in my conscious awareness."

Through painful exploration, Joy discovered that his shadow contained aggressive and sexual energies at odds with his persona of spiritual teacher and healer. As he began befriending these unrefined aspects of himself, he came to view them as casualties of the war traditional spirituality wages against embodied existence. The age-old approach urges seekers to denigrate physical and emotional life, to impose ideal codes of behavior on themselves, and to strive through discipline to achieve a state of illumination that transcends the physical world. The emerging approach, Joy contends, honors our physical and emotional needs, soft-

The son of a Rabbi went to worship on the Sabbath in a nearby town. On his return, his family asked, "Well, did they do anything different from what we do here?" "Yes, of course," said the son. "Then what was the lesson?" "Love thy enemy as thyself." "So, it's the same as we say. And how is it you learned something else?" "They taught me to love the enemy within myself."

HASIDIC STORY

Instead of hating the people you think are war-makers, hate the appetites and the disorder in your own soul, which are the causes of war.

THOMAS MERTON

To try to be good, and disregard one's darkness, is to fall victim to the evil in ourselves whose existence we have denied.

JOHN A. SANFORD

The awakened path is to realize that the unseen, unconscious aspects of self are real and form part of the Whole. A Saint is not Holy without the Sinner. A Male cannot be whole without the Female. A Female is not complete without the Male. The Virgin is not complete without the Whore.

W. BRUGH JOY

pedals spiritual ideals imposed from the outside, and urges seekers to penetrate more deeply into who they are, not who they feel they should be.

Practicing such an inclusive spirituality is easier said than done. In theory, spiritual seekers easily grasp the necessity of embracing their darker sides. In practice, says Hal Stone, they experience tremendous resistance in reclaiming demonic energies, the natural, instinctive forces associated with aggression, sexuality, and power that have been repressed in the unconscious. To honor both the heavenly and earthly dimensions of life, we must redeem these demonic energies disowned over the centuries in the name of higher growth. But on this unmarked trail, as we face the monsters and dragons viewed as antagonists for the past five thousand years, we balk at the enormity and unfamiliarity of the task and often repress rather than integrate these energies—with disastrous results.

"For many people, the consciousness movement has become a gigantic defense against living," Stone says. "Under the guise of transmuting their instinctual energy, many people try mightily to become more 'spiritual,' more loving, more pure, instead of embracing their psychic wholeness and becoming what they are."

In most cases, he observes, the attempt to transmute lower energies into higher ones leads to repression, because the lower forces simply don't transform. Instead, they go into the unconscious, creating a psychic split between the spiritual energies people strive toward and the earth energies that live within them in a disowned state. Because it requires an immense expenditure of energy to clamp down on their instinctual nature, many well-meaning spiritual people pay the price with tension, illness, and lack of vitality.

Such people often fall prey to their shadows in the form of unscrupulous spiritual teachers who take advantage of their gullibility. According to yoga scholar Georg Feuerstein, many spiritual seekers, unaware of hidden emotional wounds from childhood, project godlike qualities onto gurus, transforming ordinary mortals into idealized parental substitutes and authority figures. Unaware of their own shadows, these people fail to observe the shadow side of the so-called masters they follow with undiscriminating adoration. The darker side of these teachers contains hidden power drives, repressed sexuality, a contempt for vulnerability, and an inordinate desire for personal wealth. The recent spate of scandals in spiritual communities, involving sexual exploitation, abuses of power, and financial chicanery, reveals the depth of repressed shadow material in these teachers.

"Disciples create gurus in their own image, and gurus then treat them according to the image they have created," Feuerstein says. "In this mutual conspiracy of shadows, any statement issued by the guru, no matter how absurd or arbitrary, gets translated into a divine commandment, a process that easily can lead to authoritarian doublethink and cultish behavior. To break this cycle of mutual victimization, both gurus and disciples need to own their shadow qualities."

When this happens, spiritual seekers will cease projecting unresolved childhood needs onto teachers and will assume greater responsibility for their own growth. Likewise, gurus will step down from their pedestals, give up their exclusive identification with the persona of enlightened master, and enter into genuine dialogues with students that will include a mutual and respectful criticism of each other's personal weaknesses. Having re-owned the projection of disciple, gurus will not view themselves as finished products but as travelers on a path with limitless possibilities for learning.

"Recognizing that the shadow operates in both teachers and students can protect us from the distortions of spiritual life," Feuerstein says. "At the same time, it can help lay the foundations for a partnership model of growth in which the mutual respect and love between teacher and student will set both free."

SPIRITUAL EMERGENCY

At times during the journey of spiritual transformation, we may delve into dark areas so remote from the world of ordinary reality that to the untrained eye these experiences appear pathological in nature. During critical stages of inner growth, we may see dazzling visions of deities and distant lands, feel jolts of energy surging through our bodies, or go through archetypal battles with mythological beings involving themes of death, dismemberment, and rebirth. With the gates to the unconscious mind torn wide open, we frequently undergo a "dark night of the soul" that dredges up repressed emotions of fear, loneliness, and alienation that make us question our fundamental sanity. While mainstream psychiatry judges these experiences as psychotic, consciousness researchers Christina and Stansilav Grof view them as spiritual emergencies, dramatic and difficult episodes of inner transformation that have a great healing potential for the psyche.

During spiritual emergencies, we are bombarded with puzzling, often

Sickness, jail, poverty, getting drunk—I had to experience all that myself. Sinning makes the world go round. You can't be so stuck up, so inhuman that you want to be pure, your soul wrapped up in a plastic bag, all the time. You have to be God and the devil, both of them. Being a good medicine man means being right in the midst of the turmoil, not shielding yourself from it. It means experiencing life in all its phases. It means not being afraid of cutting up and playing the fool now and then. That's sacred too.

LAME DEER

Evil may be not seeing enough. So perhaps to become less evil we need only to see more.

CORITA

I cannot understand my own behavior. I fail to carry out the things I want to do, and I find myself doing the very things I hate. When I act against my own will, that means I have a self that acknowledges that the law is good, and so the thing behaving in that way is not myself but sin living in me . . . with the result that instead of doing the good things I want to do, I carry out the sinful things I do not want.

SAINT PAUL

terrifying phenomena that challenge our familiar beliefs about reality, the Grofs point out. As we descend into the unconscious and encounter repressed shadow material (a process that may last from several months to several years), we may meet these experiences with fear, resistance, disbelief, or denial. Often, if we find the right kind of therapeutic support and cooperate with the process, we may emerge from these extraordinary states of mind with an increased sense of well-being, a higher level of functioning in daily life, and a renewed spiritual orientation. More than any other factor, a positive attitude can facilitate and often shorten the journey.

"The most important task is to give the people in crisis a positive context for their experiences and sufficient information about the process they are going through," the Grofs write in *Spiritual Emergency: When Personal Transformation Becomes a Crisis.* "It is essential that they move away from the concept of disease and recognize the healing nature of their crisis . . . pathological labels and the insensitive use of various repressive measures, including the control of symptoms by medication, can interfere with the positive potential of the process."

Spiritual crises can be triggered by the physical stress of athletics, childbirth, or medical emergencies, or by ecstatic sexual experiences, according to psychologist Emma Bragdon, author of *The Call of Spiritual Emergency.* Emotional distress, such as that caused by the death of a child or spouse, the end of a love affair, divorce, or the loss of a job, may precipitate a crisis. Of all the catalysts, however, deep involvement in spiritual practices plays the most significant role. Various forms of Eastern meditation, kundalini yoga, and Christian monastic contemplation, for example, specifically facilitate the mystical states associated with transformational crises.

Spiritual emergency may take the form of a shamanic crisis, Bragdon explains, involving journeys to the underworld and encounters with demons, followed by death and rebirth into celestial realms. It may involve the awakening of kundalini, the psychophysiological energy located at the base of the spine that, when activated by spiritual practice, rids the body of chronic muscular and emotional tension. This purification process can cause bizarre sensations of heat or cold in the body, violent shaking, spontaneous yoga postures called mudras, ecstatic visions, and emotional problems, such as depression, anorexia, insomnia, and even amnesia. Other forms of spiritual emergency include paranormal phenomena, past-life experiences, possession, and near-death experiences.

To keep people undergoing spiritual crisis from being labeled psychotic, drugged, and hospitalized in mental wards, Christina Grof founded the Spiritual Emergence Network (SEN). Located at the Institute of Transpersonal Psychology in Menlo Park, California, SEN informs people about alternative ways of viewing their crises, then directs them to volunteers sympathetic to this viewpoint. Through its information-and-referral service, the worldwide organization makes available a network of psychotherapists, medical doctors, bodyworkers, spiritual leaders, and community members who provide supportive, nurturing care to people in crisis.

In general, people in crisis may seek help from therapists with a transpersonal orientation, support groups, spiritual teachers, their families, and friends. But according to John Weir Perry, a psychiatrist and Jungian analyst, their paramount need is to form trusting relationships with those familiar with the terrain of inner space.

What people need "is not 'treatment' but rather a coming into close and deep relationship with another individual who empathizes and encourages but does not interfere," Perry writes in an essay in *Spiritual Emergency*. "A therapeutic environment is far more effective than medication. It offers the opportunity for the individual to concentrate on the inner work, to sustain the effort, and to move forward in the process."

Slowly, over time, as people in crisis purge their inner demons through dreamwork, meditation, bodywork, and transpersonal therapy, the world of consensus reality and the archetypal world enter into a rapprochement that many experience as a homecoming. When the transformative crisis fades, they enter into a more trusting relationship with life, based on increased self-acceptance and a dependable, continuous sense of spiritual connection.

Commenting on how spiritual emergency evolves into spiritual emergence, Roberto Assaigioli, founder of Psychosynthesis, writes in "Self-Realization and Psychological Disturbances":

> These crises are positive, natural and often necessary preparations for the progress of the individual. They bring to the surface elements of the personality that need to be looked at and changed in the interest of the person's further growth. . . . The physical, emotional and mental problems arising on the way of Self-realization, however serious they may appear, are merely temporary reactions, by-products, so to speak, of an organic process of inner growth and regeneration. Therefore they either disappear spontaneously when the crisis which has produced them is over, or they yield easily to proper treatment.

I went down into my inmost self, to the deepest abyss where I feel dimly that my power of action emanates. But as I moved further and further away from the conventional certainties by which social life is superficially illuminated, I became aware that I was losing contact with myself. At each step of the descent a new person was disclosed within me of whose name I was no longer sure, and who no longer obeyed me. And when I had to stop my exploration because the path faded from beneath my steps, I found a bottomless abyss at my feet, and out of it comes—arising I know not from where—the current which I dare to call MY life.

PIERRE TEILHARD
DE CHARDIN

Spiritual Emergence and the Global Crisis

Why is the incidence of spiritual emergency on the rise in our time? Some might conclude that the increase in mystical and visionary experience presages a mental breakdown occurring on a global level. Rather than viewing it as a breakdown, however, we can choose to see it as an evolutionary breakthrough, seeding our civilization with transpersonal energies needed to heal the global crisis.

"Though the problems in the world have many different forms, they are nothing but symptoms of one underlying condition: the emotional, moral, and spiritual state of modern humanity," write Christina and Stanislav Grof in *The Stormy Search for the Self.* "In the last analysis, they are the collective result of the present level of consciousness of individual human beings. The only effective and lasting solution to these problems, therefore, would be a radical inner transformation of humanity on a large scale and its consequent rise to a higher level of awareness and maturity."

While a shift on such a scale appears unrealistic, they say, the renaissance of interest in the world's ancient spiritual traditions and the mystical quest may herald the beginnings of a shift of consciousness to help reverse our current self-destructive course. Those tested in the crucible of inner transformation develop both a world view and value system that foster individual and collective survival.

"[They] tend to develop a new appreciation and reverence for all forms of life and a new understanding of the unity of all things, which often results in strong ecological concerns and greater tolerance toward other human beings," the Grofs write. "Consideration of all humanity, compassion for all of life, and thinking in terms of the entire planet take priority over the narrow interests of individuals, families, political parties, classes, nations, and creeds."

The transformational journey from the little self to what philosopher Jean Houston calls the "planetary person" requires a prolonged, often painful encounter with the shadow. "The ascent to the bright peaks of true being is always preceded by a direct descent into the dark depths," writes Karlfried Graf von Dürckheim in *Daily Life as Spiritual Exercise.* "Only if we venture repeatedly through zones of annihilation can our contact with Divine Being, which is beyond annihilation, become firm and stable."

When, after our descent to Hades, the realm of shadows, we return to the sun-drenched light of a new day, we have sacrificed our naïveté and illusions, which limited our effectiveness in building a healthier world.

Few people can be happy unless they hate some other person, nation, or creed.

Bertrand Russell

Come, come, whoever you are—wanderer, worshipper, lover of leaving—it doesn't matter. Ours is not a caravan of despair. Come, even if you have broken your vow a thousand times. Come, come yet again, come.

On Rumi's Tomb

Having reconciled the opposites within ourselves, we embrace our totality and live with a renewed sense of purpose, capable of adding our small increment of light to a world in need of healing.

Resources

Recommended Reading

A Little Book on the Human Shadow, Robert Bly (Harper & Row, 1988). A brief but insightful study by the renowned poet on how the shadow is created and how its energies can be re-owned.

Evil: The Shadow Side of Reality, John A. Sanford (Crossroad Publishing, 1981). An in-depth exploration of evil and the shadow by a respected Jungian analyst.

Meeting the Shadow: The Hidden Power of the Dark Side of Human Nature, Connie Zweig and Jeremiah Abrams, editors (Jeremy P. Tarcher, 1991). A comprehensive collection of essays by psychologists, social commentators, and spiritual teachers on the human shadow.

Avalanche: Heretical Reflection on the Dark and the Light, W. Brugh Joy (Ballantine, 1990). An honest, revealing look at a spiritual teacher's encounter with the dark side.

Embracing Heaven & Earth, Hal Stone (DeVorss and Company, 1985). Explains how disowned selves are created and how they can be integrated to form a more effective personality.

Spiritual Emergency: When Personal Transformation Becomes a Crisis, Stanislav and Christina Grof, editors (Jeremy P. Tarcher, 1989). A collection of essays by well-known spiritual teachers, psychiatrists, and psychologists on the transformational crises that can lead to healing and rebirth.

The Stormy Search for the Self, Stanislav and Christina Grof (Jeremy P. Tarcher, 1990). Maps the various stages of spiritual emergency and gives guidelines for those undergoing transformational crises and for their families and friends.

The Call of Spiritual Emergency, Emma Bragdon (Harper & Row, 1990). Discusses the causes, dynamics, and potential benefits of spiritual emergency.

Workshops and Tapes

The Dark Side: Death, Demons, and Difficult Dreams, a twelve-day residential conference led by W. Brugh Joy at various times throughout the year at Moonfire Lodge, P.O. Box 730, Paulden, AZ 86334-0730; 800-525-7718. This workshop uses films, dreamwork, psychological techniques, ancient psychic and spiritual teachings, poetry, movement, and heightened states of consciousness to help people develop a balanced and ethical way to engage the darker, more difficult mysteries of life.

The Human Shadow, two ninety-minute audiotapes by poet Robert Bly, explores the darkest realms of the soul that contain the anger, pain, fierceness, and unchecked emotions normally repressed by society. Available for $18.95 (plus $4 shipping) from Sounds True Catalog, 1825 Pearl Street, Boulder, CO 80302; 800-333-9185.

About the Author

Ronald S. Miller is an award-winning journalist and former college English instructor. He has written extensively about senior health issues, conducted a popular interview series with spiritual teachers for *Science of Mind* magazine, and developed and taught courses in human development, transpersonal psychology, and stress management. He lives in San Diego with his wife and son.

About *New Age Journal*

For close to two decades *New Age Journal* has been exploring the frontiers of human potential. This is the magazine that examines the people, places, and issues that are reshaping modern society.

New Age Journal is an international special interest magazine committed to communicating visionary ideas and practical information to modern society. Since its first issue the magazine has been instrumental in both creating as well as introducing holistic values and ideals to a society searching for balance and sanity. It has provided readers with uncommon wisdom from the great thinkers, healers, teachers, activists, and leaders of our time.

At the heart of *New Age Journal* is the principle that we all have the power to effect substantial changes in our personal lives and in society as a whole. The journal is published bimonthly with an additional special issue in December. Cost is $24 per year in the United States. Contact *New Age Journal*, 342 Western Avenue, Brighton, Mass. 02135; (617) 787-2005.